Between the fields and the city

In the period following the emancipation of the serfs in 1861, Russia began to industrialize, and peasants, especially peasants of the Central Industrial Region around Moscow, increasingly began to interact with a market economy. In response to a growing need for cash and declining opportunities to earn it at home, thousands of peasant men and women left their villages to earn wages elsewhere, many in the cities of Moscow or St. Petersburg.

The significance and consequences of peasant women's migration is the subject of this book. Drawing on a wealth of new archival data, which contains first person-accounts of peasant women's experiences, the book provides the reader with a detailed account of the move from the village to the city. Unlike previous studies this one looks at the impact of migration on the peasantry, and at the experience of peasant workers in nearby factories, as well as in distant cities. Case studies explore the effects of industrialization and urbanization on the relationship of the migrant to the peasant household, and on family life and personal relations. They demonstrate the ambiguous consequences of change for women: While some found new and better opportunities, many more experienced increased hardship and risk. By illuminating the personal dimensions of economic and social change, this book provides a fresh perspective on the social history of late Imperial Russia.

# Between the fields and the city

## the city

### Women, work, and family in Russia, 1861–1914

BARBARA ALPERN ENGEL
*University of Colorado*

CAMBRIDGE
UNIVERSITY PRESS

Published by the Press Syndicate of the University of Cambridge
The Pitt Building, Trumpington Street, Cambridge CB2 1RP
40 West 20th Street, New York, NY 10011–4211, USA
10 Stamford Road, Oakleigh, Melbourne 3166, Australia

First published 1994

Printed in the United States of America

*Library of Congress Cataloging-in-Publication Data*

Engel, Barbara Alpern.
Between the fields and the city : women, work, and family in
Russia, 1861–1914 / Barbara Alpern Engel.
p.   cm.
Includes bibliographical references and index.
ISBN 0–521–44236–2 (hardback)
1. Women – Russia – History – 19th century.  2. Women – Russia –
History – 20th century.  3. Women – Employment – Russia – History – 19th
century.  4. Women – Employment – Russia – History – 20th century.
5. Women – Russia – Social conditions.  I. Title.
HQ1662.E54    1994                                              93–31191
305.4'0947 – dc20                                                  CIP


A catalog record for this book is available from the British Library

ISBN  0–521–44236–2 hardback

# Contents

# Figures, maps, and tables

### Figures

### Maps

### Tables

vii

viii       Figures, maps, and tables

# Acknowledgments

For their contribution to the research and writing of this book, I am grateful to many institutions and individuals.

I would like to thank the W. Averell Harriman Institute for the Advanced Study of the Soviet Union, Columbia University, for a senior fellowship that supported my work in its early stages. A grant-in-aid from the Kennan Institute allowed me to explore the relationship between peasant parents and their children. Grants-in-aid from the Committee on Research and Creative Work of the University of Colorado facilitated research in Finland. Research in Russian archives and libraries was supported by grants from the International Research and Exchanges Board (IREX), with funds provided by the National Endowment for the Humanities and the United States Information Agency, as well as a grant from the Committee on Fulbright-Hays Fellowships. A fellowship from the Woodrow Wilson Center enabled me to complete the manuscript of this book. I owe a special thanks to the Wilson Center staff for doing everything they could to make my residence at the Center pleasant as well as productive.

Librarians at the following institutions facilitated my research: Butler Library of Columbia University; the Library of Congress; the National Institute of Health Library; the library of the University of Illinois at Urbana-Champagne; the Lenin Library and the Institute for Scientific Information in the Social Sciences under the Academy of Sciences (INION) in Moscow; the Saltykov-Shchedrin Public Library and the Library of the Academy of Sciences in St. Petersburg. I am particularly indebted to the staff of the Slavic Library in Helsinki, who cheerfully helped me to track down even the most elusive of references. My archival research in the former Soviet Union was assisted by the staffs of the following archives: the Central State Historical Archive of the City of Moscow (TsGIAgM); the Central State Archive of the October Revolution (TsGAOR SSSR); the Central State Historical Archive of Leningrad (TsGIAL); the Central State Historical Archive (TsGIA SSSR); and the Tenishev Archive of the State Museum of Ethnography of the Peoples of the USSR. I owe special thanks to Evdokiia L. Timofeeva for facilitating my research in the Tenishev Archive and making it so enjoyable; to Galina A. Ippolitova for her willingness to provide the endless piles of *dela* that work on this project demanded; to Gita M. Lipson for sharing with me her knowledge of archival resources; and to Valerii M. Shishkin for providing access to materials I needed for the final stage of my research.

In the course of a decade researching and writing this book, I have benefited from the encouragement and assistance of many friends and colleagues. Joseph Bradley, Daniel Brower, Gregory Freeze, Heather Hogan, Robert Johnson, Adele Lindenmeyr, Jonathan Sanders, William Wagner, Reginald Zelnik, and, especially, Timothy Mixter helped me to find my way when I was still new to the field. V.A. Fedorov provided guidance when I was a *stazher* in Moscow in 1985; and Grigorii A. Tishkin did everything in his power to make my research visit to Leningrad in 1991 both productive and pleasant. Ellen Ross and Wendy Goldman provided stimulating conversation and challenging questions. The book has benefited immeasurably from critical readings by Joseph Bradley, Laura Engelstein, Karen Fields, Wendy Goldman, Heather Hogan, David Ransel, William Wagner, Elizabeth Waters, and Christine Worobec. They have helped me to hone my arguments and to correct errors of fact and interpretation; and they have stimulated me to rethink, although not always to revise, my analyses. The shortcomings that remain are entirely my responsibility.

I would also like to express my appreciation to Pat Murphy of the history department of the University of Colorado, for resolving my computer problems more often than I like to remember and assisting in the production of the tables; and to Gladys Bloedow for negotiating bureaucracies with inventiveness and good will. Caroline Hinkley prepared several of the photographs for publication. Sarah Despres, my research assistant at the Woodrow Wilson Center, greatly facilitated my writing and made my tenure at the Center a lot more fun.

Finally, for sustaining me during the long years I worked on this book, I am more grateful than words can say to my families: in Moscow, S. and E.C., and Zh., in St. Petersburg, S.B. and I.R., E.T.; and S.M.L.; and here at home, Minette and William Alpern; and most of all, LeRoy Moore.

Parts of this book have appeared in print elsewhere in a somewhat different form. Chapter 2 appeared as "The Woman's Side: Male Out-Migration and the Family Economy in Kostroma Province," *Slavic Review* 45, n. 2 (Summer 1986): 257–71; Chapter 4 appeared as "Between Field and Factory: Women,

Work and Family in the Factories of Rural Russia in the Late Nineteenth Century," *Russian History* 16, n. 2–4 (1989): 223–37; and Chapter 6 as "St. Petersburg Prostitutes in the Late Nineteenth Century: A Personal and Social Profile," *Russian Review* 48, n. 1 (1989): 21–44. My thanks to the editors for their cooperation in the republication of these materials.

All dates in this book are given according to the Julian Calendar, unless otherwise indicated. The Julian Calendar was twelve days behind the Gregorian in the nineteenth century, and thirteen days behind in the twentieth. I have transliterated the Russian according to the Library of Congress system, with a few exceptions. When giving the first names of individuals, I have omitted diacritical signs (Avdotiia instead of Avdot'iia) and I have transliterated "e" as "yo" (Fyodor instead of Fedor). I have anglicized the plurals of Russian measurements and of well-known terms like *artel*; I have also used the anglicized versions of well-known names and places.

# Introduction

In the half century between the emancipation of the serfs in 1861 and the outbreak of World War I, it remained a very long way from the village to the city. Footpaths or unpaved, rutted roads connected peasant villages scattered over Russia's vast expanses. Following decades of rapid expansion, railroads still linked only the most substantial provincial towns to major urban centers in the early years of the twentieth century. The estate in Tver' province where Nina Berberova (born 1901) spent her childhood was seventy miles from the nearest railroad station. "These were grim, wretched wild places," she remembered. "Wolves and bears roamed the forests; fields stretched on for a hundred miles. The horizon was straight and hard, and paths, often only log paths, led into the limitless distance, where only skylarks sang their song."[1] From such remote places the peasant migrant would have to travel for days on foot or, if fortunate, by horse-drawn cart before she could reach a railroad station. And a migrant had to traverse other and no less formidable distances to live in a major urban center. The city offered another sort of life than she had known in her village. Urban dwellers looked different: The men's hair was cut city-fashion, instead of under a bowl, and their shirts were worn inside instead of outside their pants. Almost everyone wore factory-made fabrics even when they went to work, whereas villagers continued to wear homespun except on special occasions. In the city, people timed their work by the clock, rather than by the sun and the seasons as they did in the village. The pace of urban life was much faster and the noise level higher. Villagers spent their days amidst familiar faces, engaging in activities that had engaged their mothers and grandmothers before them, while in the city they encountered strangers whose ways appeared equally strange.

In the decades after the emancipation of the serfs, increasing numbers of peasant women and men traversed these distances. The terms of the emancipation of the serfs combined with other changes to intensify greatly the

---

1 Nina Berberova, *The Italics Are Mine* (New York, 1969), 10.

1

peasants' need for cash. The emancipation granted many peasants less land than they had tilled in the days of serfdom and required all but the recipients of paupers' allotments to redeem the land over a period of forty-nine years, and at a rate that often exceeded its market value. In addition to redemption payments, peasants owed taxes to the state and dues to support the work of the local elective self-government, the *zemstvo*. Explosive population growth between 1861 and 1905 forced peasants to support these fiscal obligations on a declining amount of land per capita: By 1900, the average peasant's allotment had shrunk by over a third.

The emancipation also signaled the start of Russia's industrial revolution. Industrialization proceeded slowly in the 1860s and 1870s, grew rapidly in the 1890s and then again in the years prior to World War I. Although it took place at the initiative of an autocratic state, rather than an entrepreneurial class, in many respects, Russia's industrialization resembled the process that England had experienced beginning in the late eighteenth century and Western Europe several decades later. Machinery took over the production of goods that people had formerly made by hand, destroying many of the cottage industries that had enabled peasants to supplement agricultural income in their villages. As a result, increasing numbers of people left the place of their birth to earn their living laboring in factories and mills. Russia's industrialization was also distinctive, however. The process began much later than it had in the West, and it proceeded far more rapidly and unevenly and against the background of a peasant way of life that had remained little changed for centuries. To be sure, recent scholarly work has demonstrated the significance of proto-industrialization even under serfdom. In the late eighteenth and early nineteenth centuries, thousands of peasants in hundreds of villages wove silk, linen, or cotton, while thousands more tanned hides and worked metal for sale on the market.[2] Nevertheless, on the eve of emancipation, proto-industrial production constituted only a tiny share of the national economy.[3] Most proto-industrial workers continued to shift between agriculture and domestic production and to remain within the relatively insular world of the Russian village. This was especially true for women, who were far less likely than men to travel elsewhere to market goods or search for work. For the vast majority of peasants, Russia's industrialization would bring dramatic, sometimes wrenching change.

2 Edgar Melton has surveyed this scholarship and produced his own contribution to it in "Proto-Industrialization, Serf Agriculture, and Agrarian Social Structure: Two Estates in Nineteenth-Century Russia," *Past and Present*, no. 115 (May 1987): 69–106.
3 Ibid., 80.

Labor force statistics give a sense of pace and numbers. Between 1887 and 1900, over a million people entered the industrial labor force more than doubling the number of workers. Millions more found work in artisanal trades, in service, in construction, and in other sectors of the expanding economy. In 1897, when Russia's first national census was conducted, there were 6.4 million hired workers.[4] Most of these workers derived from peasant villages. In the Central Industrial Region, where outmigration for wages was at its most intense, one of every four or five villagers was off working elsewhere by the early twentieth century. In Western Europe, too, peasants had supplied a large proportion of the workforce in the early stages of industrialization. However, in the West the path from village to city or factory was usually a one-way street, whereas in Russia, all but a few migrants went back as well as forth. Maintaining their village ties, sending a portion of their wages back to their families, migrants remained away from home for a few months or years; then they returned for good to their villages. The Stolypin reforms of 1906–7 changed this situation to some extent. The reforms were aimed at creating a strong, independent capitalist peasantry that would serve as a source of stability in the countryside. They enabled peasants more easily to sever their ties with their villages and, in some cases, deprived young peasant men of their claims to family allotments and, consequently, of their incentive to return home. While historians differ concerning the overall impact, there can be no question that the reforms increased the flow of peasants from the village and made it more likely that migration would be a one-way trip.

Industrialization and urbanization profoundly affected the peasant way of life. In Russia, the peasant household was also a family economy in the sense that every able-bodied member, including children, worked to ensure that the family household survived. Both family household and village were patriarchal in organization: Elders held power over the young and men held power over women. In the family household, males as well as females remained subject to the father's will so long as the father lived, and he deployed their labor and disposed of their earnings according to household need. The proliferation of capitalist wage relations and the expansion of industrial employment challenged these well-established power relations. Even as wage migration to distant places provided the cash that helped to sustain the peasant family economy, it loosened patriarchal control of the

4 Victoria Bonnell, ed. *The Russian Worker: Life and Labor under the Tsarist Regime* (Berkeley, Calif., 1983), 1–2.

wage earner. Moreover, urban experiences that broadened horizons and heightened expectations sometimes put the migrant at odds with the family collective, sometimes made it more difficult to merge that individual's "I" into the "we" of family or village life. As I hope to demonstrate in the following pages, changes that slackened the hold of the patriarchal family provided new opportunities for peasant women, but they also rendered women more economically and personally vulnerable.

The significance and consequences of peasant women's migration is the subject of this book. It will follow migrants as they moved between the fields and the factories and cities, looking at the peasantry from which they derived as well as at the urban lower class that they joined. The first part of the book offers an examination of the peasant way of life in villages of the Central Industrial Region, Russia's most "modern" region and the region that the greatest number of peasants left in search of wages.[5] The second part explores migrant women's experiences in the city and belongs to a growing body of literature that treats the formation of the Russian working class, although unlike the bulk of this literature, it concentrates on the experience of women. Historians of Russia have long debated the extent to which peasant migration from village to city constituted a break with the past. I want to address this question too and to ask what such a break might mean to women. But I will also look in the other direction, examining the ways that the migration of women and men affected the villages they left behind. Like its title, this study will straddle two worlds.

So did many of the women and men who populate its pages. Peasant practices helped migrants to adapt to urban life: They traveled along well-trodden paths to the city, initially received help from or resided with kinfolk or people from their locale (*zemliaki*); and they perceived the world they encountered through the prism of their peasant past. Yet, at least in the eyes of fellow villagers, the time they spent in the city changed many migrants. The city figured ambiguously in the mental landscape of Russia's peasants: It offered cash and goods the village needed, but in an unhealthy environment of freedom and license. Young people, young women in particular, risked becoming "spoiled" there. Such fears reflected the contradictory character of wage migration to a major urban center.

The effect of wage migration on the peasant world has received comparatively little attention from historians writing in English. Instead, studies of

---

5 The provinces of the Central Industrial Region were Tver', Iaroslavl', Moscow, Vladimir, Kostroma, and Nizhnii Novgorod.

peasant life emphasize the tenacity of custom and tradition and stress continuity over change. This study aims to adjust rather than to challenge this overall picture by drawing attention to some of the ways that migration affected the village and gender mediated change. In order to identify constituencies for change in the village, in the first four chapters that treat the peasantry I have heeded peasant women's discordant voices far more closely than their fellow villagers usually did. Documentation of women's discontent is available from both published and archival sources. Peasant women could bring their grievances to cantonal (*volost'*) courts, administered by the peasants themselves; if they failed to find satisfaction, they had the right to appeal to civil authorities in the district or provincial committees that administered peasant affairs, or even to petition the tsar, although relatively few women availed themselves of these possibilities. Some married women simply took matters into their own hands and fled households where they felt unhappy. If a husband attempted to bring a wife home again or, much more rarely, brought suit for separation or divorce, the woman had a chance to tell her own side of the story. In my quest for women's voices, I will draw extensively on *volost'* court cases, on petitions to the authorities, and on transcripts of divorce testimonies. The voices that emerge are those of a small minority of peasant women, who nevertheless offer an important perspective on village life. Unwilling or unable to put up with situations or treatment that others managed to accept, they expose the fault lines of peasant society, the places where it might crack under pressure.

Such women were also the most likely to respond as individuals to the siren song of the city and to seek the alternative life that it offered. They were not, however, the majority of women migrants, who were themselves a small minority of peasant women. As late as 1910, only a fraction of peasant women left the village for the city. And most of those who did were women on the margins, widows and spinsters, or women from impoverished households who left for family, not individual, reasons: to relieve the family of an unnecessary pair of hands and a mouth it could not feed; to gain additional resources for the family economy; to accompany a husband who worked elsewhere. Unskilled, usually illiterate, most of them found semidependent positions as servants, cooks, or nursemaids, or they held jobs in industries where they earned about half of what men did, wages that put them at or below subsistence level. Often, the greater a woman's independence from village and kin, the more economically vulnerable she became. I will explore the effect of economic and social circumstances on single women's efforts to shape lives for themselves in the city, by examining illegitimacy (Chapter 5) and prostitution (Chapter 6). Chapter 7 looks at a relative rarity, the co-habiting working-class family in the city.

Like the women and men they study, the following chapters will some-times weave back and forth between the village and the city. The organ-ization of this book is more thematic than chronological. The examination of village life begins in 1861, with the emancipation of the serfs, but the chapters on the city focus on a somewhat later period, from 1880 to 1914, when migration from village to city had become quite substantial. The story stops at the outbreak of World War I, which changed the picture dramatically by sending millions of men off to war and bringing unprecedented numbers of their wives, sisters, and daughters to the city. I have chosen to present my material in the form of case studies and to focus on particular regions, problems, and aspects of women's lives, rather than to attempt a comprehen-sive history of peasant women as they moved between the village and the city. Among other important topics, the role of religion in peasant women's lives remains unexplored. The primary sources I read had almost nothing to say about it, and I found few secondary works that treated the subject to my satisfaction. Nevertheless, certain themes will recur: One is the flexibility with which patriarchal village structures adapted to economic and social change; another is the ambiguous effect of such change on women them-selves. Some women experienced it as opportunity, others as loss. Their story has not been told before; it puts the history we thought we knew into a different perspective.

# 1. Patriarchy and its discontents

The world of the Russian peasant was harsh, and peasant life both precarious and extraordinarily demanding. Intense, virtually endless toil was necessary although not always sufficient to ensure survival. Family members had to cooperate: Pooling their labor as family groups enabled peasants to subsist in an environment where the weather was unreliable and the land increasingly inadequate to feed the humans who depended upon it for their livelihood. The debate continues over the extent of peasant poverty in the decades following the emancipation.[1] However, no one seriously doubts that peasants had to struggle, sometimes desperately, for survival or that the family provided a key to their success. This chapter will consider what these circumstances meant to women. It will present an overview of peasant women's lives, focusing on the commonalities in women's position across rural Russia and the patriarchal structures that continued to dominate peasant life at least until 1905.

At the center of virtually every woman's life, as of every man's, was the family, the "most significant and indispensable condition of life for every peasant," in the words of the Russian ethnographer M.M. Gromyko.[2] Family households consisted of related (and occasionally unrelated) individuals. Their size and composition varied cyclically as well as according to region; however, economically "strong" households tended to be complex in structure, consisting of blood relatives spanning two or three generations. Family households belonged to a larger peasant community, whose members shared ownership of the land and responsibility for paying the dues and obligations

---

1 For two recent and opposing perspectives on this longstanding debate, see Elvira Wilbur, "Peasant Poverty in Theory and Practice: A View from Russia's 'Impoverished Center' at the End of the Nineteenth Century," and Stephen G. Wheatcroft, "Crises and the Condition of the Peasantry in Late Imperial Russia," both in *Peasant Economy, Culture, and Politics of European Russia, 1800–1921*, ed. Esther Kingston-Mann and Timothy Mixter (Princeton, N.J., 1991), 101–27, 128–72.
2 M.M. Gromyko, *Traditsionnye normy povedeniia i formy obshcheniia russkikh krest'ian xix v.* (Moscow, 1986), 261.

exacted by state and local officials. The terms of the emancipation granted these communities substantial authority over their members, supplementing the customary controls the community had long exercised. Peasant communities had a variety of means at their disposal to enforce strict adherence to shared norms and values. Some were informal, such as ritual shaming practices resembling the charivari, gossip, and the politics of reputation. Others had a more formal character. The peasant assembly (*skhod*) and, especially, cantonal (*volost'*) courts adjudicated disputes and disciplined community members according to unwritten, customary law. The community had the right to eject utterly unregenerate people from its midst.

Both household and community were patriarchal in character in the modern, feminist sense of men's power over women but, more importantly, in a much older sense. In rural Russia fathers controlled families and families "were the units of social and economic power," to borrow Linda Gordon's language.[3] Men dominated family life and enjoyed sole access to formal power in the *skhod* and the *volost'* courts. Men controlled access to the most important resource of peasant life, the land, which was held communally, not individually, in most of rural Russia. As members of the *skhod*, male household heads regulated the periodic redistribution of land among the constituent households. Ordinarily, women could not claim a land allotment. Access to land devolved patrilineally, from father to sons or to collateral male relatives. Although every adult male potentially held the right to use land, only in exceptional cases might a daughter or a widow without sons lay independent claim to it.[4] When a son was born the household might receive an additional allotment; it gained no additional resources at the birth of a daughter.

Sexual mores favored men as well. Premarital intercourse was strictly forbidden in much of rural Russia, and peasant morality operated according to a strict double standard. While chastity for both sexes was the ideal, in reality women's sexuality was the more strictly controlled. Parents instilled habits of sexual self-control far more intensively in their daughters than in their sons. Even courtship practices that acknowledged adolescent sexuality sought to contain it. In some villages courtship was modest and restrained and took place exclusively in a community setting; in others, considerable sexual freedom was permitted. In public gatherings, a young man might sit

---

3 Linda Gordon, *Heroes of Their Own Lives: The Politics and History of Family Violence* (New York, 1988), vi.
4 See the discussion in Christine Worobec, *Peasant Russia: Family and Community in the Post-Emancipation Period* (Princeton, N.J., 1991), 42–70.

on a woman's knees, kiss her during games, and playfully grab at her breasts. In the many places where nightcourting occurred, peasant couples tested the boundary that separated sexual expression from sexual restraint. However, if it became known that a woman had transgressed the unwritten law forbidding sexual intercourse before marriage, she risked public humiliation and the loss of her chance for a decent match. Villagers kept a sharp eye out for women's deviant sexual behavior. The gates of the offending girl might be tarred, or a window in her parents' house broken. A publicly dishonored girl (and sometimes her sisters or even other unmarried maidens in her village) had enormous difficulty finding a desirable mate. Usually, only the woman bore the burden of responsibility for premarital sexual activity. Condemning an unmarried woman who had conceived a child, one peasant put it this way: "If *she* hadn't consented, nothing would have happened, and since she didn't preserve herself until marriage, there is no reason to trust her" (emphasis in the original).[5] A girl could not always count on her seducer to marry her, even if he had promised to do so. The double standard served to make single women careful and kept rates of rural illegitimacy low – under 2 percent of live births in European Russia as a whole at the end of the nineteenth century.[6]

The issue of premarital sexual relations points to one of the ways that the power of the father not only constrained a woman's actions but also protected her and secured her social position. A woman who had lost her father had a more difficult time finding a husband. "Don't buy a horse from the priest, or marry the daughter of a widow," as one peasant saying went.[7] Especially when there were no adult sons to lay claim to an allotment of land for the household, the death of a father often sent his family into destitution, thus severely reducing the daughter's chance of contracting a marriage and, perhaps, leaving her more vulnerable to seduction. Historians of Western European women have noted that a woman in a weak negotiating position in courtship was more likely to engage in premarital sex; this was likely to have

5 Tenishev archive, Gos. Muzei etnografii narodov SSSR (hereafter referred to as Tenishev archive), fond 7, opis 1, delo 1850, 19, Rostov district, Iaroslavl' province. All subsequent references in the Tenishev archive are to fond 7.
6 Ansley Coale, Barbara Anderson, and Erna Harm, *Human Fertility in Russia since the Nineteenth Century* (Princeton, N.J., 1979), 252–3. Even if we allow that the rates may have been somewhat reduced by underreporting, abortion, or the marriage of pregnant brides, they nevertheless attest to the success of village controls in preventing premarital intercourse, especially when compared to rates in Russia's major cities. This point will be discussed at length in Chapter 5.
7 V.I. Dal', ed., *Poslovitsy russkogo naroda*, 2 vols. (Moscow, 1984) 1: 274.

been the case in Russia as well.[8] Certainly, when she did engage in premarital sex, such a woman had more difficulty enforcing a suitor's promise
of marriage. Take the case of Marfa Gorbunova, for example. Gorbunova,
who lived with her widowed mother in the village of Obrudovo in Moscow
province, had allowed herself to be seduced by a youth from a neighboring
village. Soon after she became pregnant, the youth abandoned her and got
engaged to another woman. Evidently, she or a member of her family tried
unsuccessfully to stop the marriage and force the youth to marry Marfa.
Appeals to the youth, his parents, and even the village priest failed. In 1905,
Marfa's uncle took the highly unusual step of petitioning the Holy Synod for
assistance in stopping the seducer's marriage to the other woman and restor-
ing his niece's honor. Like the previous efforts, this one proved fruitless.[9]
Peasant custom occasionally recognized the particular vulnerability of girls
without fathers: In at least one region, if a boy seduced an orphan, the
community forced him to wed her.[10]

Marriage, like courtship, favored men. In Russia, marriage was nearly
universal and patrilocal, benefiting the groom's family by adding the labor of
the bride. Peasants regarded marriage as holy and necessary for every respectable woman and man. Women who did not marry were called derogatory
names and treated as pariahs, except for wisewomen, healers, and women
who claimed religious vocations.[11] Without the access to land that marriage

8  George Alter, *Family and the Female Life Course: The Women of Verviers, Belgium, 1849–*
   *1880* (Madison, Wis., 1988), 116, 127; Rachel G. Fuchs and Leslie Page Moch, "Pregnant,
   Single, and Far from Home: Migrant Women in Nineteenth-Century Paris," *American
   Historical Review* 95, no. 4 (Oct. 1990): 1021.
9  After extracting from the uncle a stamp worth ninety kopeks, without which the Synod
   refused to consider his petition, it informed him that his case must be brought before a civil
   court. Tsentral'nyi Gosudarstvennyi Istoricheskii Arkhiv gorod Moskvy (hereafter TsGIAgM)
   fond 203, op. 412, delo 39, 1–3.
10 Tenishev archive, delo 1470, 16 (Novoladoga, St. Petersburg). The community's expectations of the erring male varied considerably according to region. The complex Russian
   situation is described in Barbara Alpern Engel, "Peasant Morality and Pre-marital Relations
   in Late Nineteenth-Century Russia," *Journal of Social History* 23, no. 4 (Summer 1990):
   695–714.
11 Most spinsters became either beggars or religious wanderers or labored for a pittance in the
   households or fields of others. Galina Nosova, "Bytovoe pravoslavie," Ph.D. diss., Academy
   of Sciences, USSR, Moscow, 1969, 140, 146; Tatiana Bernshtam, *Molodezh' v obriadovoi
   zhizni Russkoi obshchiny xix-nachala xx v.* (Leningrad, 1988), 74–6; Rose Glickman, "The
   Peasant Woman as Healer," in *Russia's Women: Accommodation, Resistance, Transformation,*
   ed. Barbara Clements, Barbara Engel, and Christine Worobec (Berkeley, Calif., 1991), 148–
   62; Brenda Meehan-Waters, "To Save Oneself: Russian Peasant Women and the Development of Women's Religious Communities in Prerevolutionary Russia," in *Russian Peasant
   Women*, ed. Beatrice Farnsworth and Lynn Viola (New York, 1992), 122–3.

provided, most single women had to eke out a living working for others. But because marriage was nearly universal, relatively few women experienced lifelong spinsterhood. According to the census of 1897, in peasant villages, only 4 percent of women aged 45 to 49 had never been married, by contrast with Western Europe, where from 12 percent (France) to 15 percent (England) of women in the same age group remained single.[12] Russians also married earlier than Western European women, who married, on the average, at the age of 24 to 25 or older. How early Russian peasants wed depended upon local custom and economic circumstances. Christine Worobec has calculated that the average age at which peasants married in the 1880s ranged from a low of 23 for men and 19.4 for women in the Central Agricultural Region to a high of 24.6 for men and 21.8 for women in the Central Industrial Region, the most heavily industrialized region of Russia. In the provinces of the Central Industrial Region, supplementary income had become essential to the maintenance of most family economies, so that often a youth was permitted to marry only after he had demonstrated that he could contribute cash to the family coffers. Even so, in the Central Industrial Region, as in the Central Agricultural Region, peasants tended to marry young. Average ages of marriage include widows who were remarrying (about 16 percent of brides in 1883) and widowers (about 20 percent of grooms), in addition to people marrying for the first time. This means that age at first marriage was below these averages. In some cases, it was so low that the bride had not yet menstruated. In the province of Iaroslavl', where the average age at marriage was 23.4, the highest for women anywhere in rural Russia in the 1880s, one physician found that 4 percent of peasant women married before the onset of menstruation. In Tula province, where the average age of marriage for women was 18.7, the lowest in Russia, over 20 percent of peasant women married before they menstruated, according to another study.[13]

Even as it privileged males by granting them access to land, formal authority, and the labor of women, peasant patriarchy subordinated sons to fathers almost as thoroughly as it subordinated women to men. If his father was alive, a man's marriage did not customarily make him the head of his

12 A.G. Vishnevskii, "Rannie etapy stanovleniia novogo tipa rozhdaemosti v Rossii," in *Brachnost', rozhdaemost' i smertnost' v Rossii i v SSSR*, ed. A.G. Vishnevskii (Moscow, 1977), 105, 117. For Europe, see J. Hajnal, "European Marriage Patterns in Perspective," in *Population in History*, ed. D.V. Glass and D.E.C. Eversley (London, 1965), 102.

13 Worobec, *Peasant Russia*, 125; I. Grigoriev, "O polovoi deiatel'nosti zhenshchin Myshkinskogo uezda Iaroslavkoi gubernii," *Vrachebnye vedomosti*, 22 (1883): 4085; V. Smidovich, "Nabliudeniia nad fiziologicheskimi proiavleniiami zhenskoi polovoi deiatel'nosti," *Sbornik sochinenii po sudebnoi meditsine*, 2 (1877): 79.

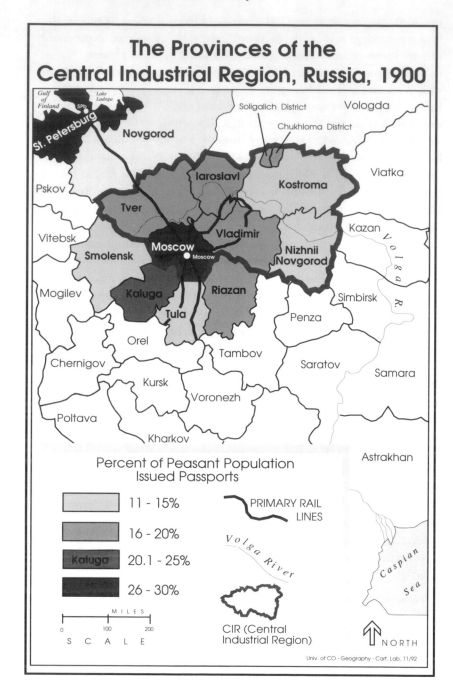

# The Provinces of the
# Central Industrial Region, Russia, 1900

Gulf of Finland

Lake Ladoga

SPb

St. Petersburg

Soligalich District

Chukhloma District

Vologda

Novgorod

Viatka

Pskov

Iaroslavl

Kostroma

Tver

Vladimir

Kazan

Vitebsk

Moscow

Moscow

Nizhnii Novgorod

Volga R.

Smolensk

Mogilev

Kaluga

Riazan

Simbirsk

Tula

Penza

Orel

Tambov

Saratov

Samara

Chernigov

Kursk

Voronezh

Poltava

Kharkov

Astrakhan

## Percent of Peasant Population
## Issued Passports

11 - 15%

16 - 20%

Kaluga   20.1 - 25%

26 - 30%

PRIMARY RAIL LINES

Volga River

CIR (Central Industrial Region)

MILES

0      100      200

S  C  A  L  E

Caspian Sea

NORTH

Univ. of CO - Geography - Cart. Lab, 11/92

own household; instead, his bride would come to live with him in the household of his parents, adding a worker (*rabotnitsa*) whose labors in the cottage, the kitchen garden, the dairy, and the fields served to enhance the household's resources. The eldest male in the family, most commonly the father, headed the peasant household. Called the *bol'shak*, he held authority over all other members of the multigenerational household, and his decisions concerning whom they would marry and the disposition of their labor were absolute according to law and custom. So long as he remained a member of his father's household, even a married son remained subject to the father's will. This arrangement might last for many years, until the married son requested permission to establish an independent household and the *bol'shak* and/or the community agreed to it, or until the *bol'shak*'s death.[14]

The teachings of the Russian Orthodox Church reinforced the patriarchal character of peasant households by emphasizing the need for unconditional obedience of children to parents and women to men. The laws of the tsarist state reinforced it too. Family law defined marriage as based on patriarchal authority and the unquestioning obedience of wife to husband.[15] An internal passport system upheld the power of fathers over sons and daughters and that of men over women by requiring a peasant to obtain the permission of the head of his household before he could live or work elsewhere. Until 1906, the head of the household could have one of its members "arrested, sent back to his village under escort, or flogged by simple application to the peasant court."[16]

Women's power was informal, by contrast with the formal, institutionalized power of men. Within this male domain, adult women carved out spaces of control for themselves. Adult women maintained and perpetuated

14  Teodor Shanin, *The Awkward Class: Political Sociology of Peasantry in a Developing Society: Russia 1910–1925* (Oxford, 1972), 260. It is a measure of the continuing importance of the daughter-in-law's labor that as late as the end of the nineteenth century, parents sometimes married their sons off to brides who were several years their elder. On household division, see Cathy Frierson, "Razdel: The Peasant Family Divided," *Russian Review* 46, no. 1 (January 1987): 35–51.

15  William Wagner, "The Trojan Mare: Women's Rights and Civil Rights in Late Imperial Russia," in *Civil Rights in Imperial Russia*, ed. Olga Crisp and Linda Edmondson (Oxford, 1989), 66.

16  Teodor Shanin, "A Russian Peasant Household at the Turn of the Century," in *Peasants and Peasant Societies*, ed. Teodor Shanin (Harmondsworth, England, 1971), 35. For the workings of the passport system, see the discussion in Jeffrey Burds, "The Social Control of Peasant Labor in Russia: The Response of Village Communities to Labor Migration in the Central Industrial Region," in *Peasant Economy*, esp. 71–2.

many of the rituals that ensured the community's cohesion; they arranged marriages and presided at childbirth and christening, central events in village life.[17] Women's talk affected the status of fellow villagers. Their evaluation of others' behavior, expressed as gossip, served to uphold community standards and norms. "A woman's word sticks like glue," as one peasant saying went.[18] Moreover, women had their own networks in the family and the community, which they could mobilize to defend their interests. Female kin might join together to resist attempts to encroach upon their sphere, as they did, for example, when physicians attempted to modernize peasant child care practices toward the end of the nineteenth century. Networks of village women sometimes engaged in acts of collective resistance to outside authorities who threatened the subsistence of the household or the community.[19]

Women's ability to work also enhanced their standing in the family and the community. Married women's work was essential to the survival of the family household and complemented men's. Women fetched water and cleaned and maintained the cottage; they ground the grain, baked the bread, and prepared and preserved the food; they made butter and cheese. Women looked after the kitchen garden and tended the livestock. Summers, the women labored in the fields as well. A man typically ploughed and sowed, while the woman fertilized and weeded, but during the harvesttime men and women worked together harvesting hay and grain, she with her sickle and he with his scythe. Winters, the woman took up her spindle and distaff and began the process of transforming raw hemp or wool into the cloth that would clothe her husband, her children, and herself. If the household needed money, a woman might bring eggs, feathers, milk, or cheese to market, or take in foundlings to rear, or do piecework for a nearby factory. Women generally put in a longer workday than men did, rising earlier and going to sleep later. In the words of one peasant proverb, "The wife grinds grain while the husband sleeps."[20] Women who performed their tasks well gained authority in the family and community.

And time itself increased women's power. A woman's standing in her household rose as she bore and raised children, sons especially. At the end

17 See Worobec, *Peasant Russia*, for a fuller discussion.
18 Dal', *Poslovitsy*, 1: 275.
19 On resistance to physicians, see Nancy Frieden, "Child Care: Medical Reform in a Traditionalist Culture," in *The Family in Imperial Russia*, ed. David Ransel (Urbana, Ill., 1978), 251. On resistance to other outsiders, Barbara Alpern Engel, "Men, Women, and the Language of Russian Peasant Resistance," in Stephen Frank and Mark Steinberg, eds., *Popular Culture in Late Nineteenth-Century Russia* (Princeton, N.J., forthcoming).
20 Dal', *Poslovitsy*, 1: 368.

Fig. 1. Peasant women selling milk by the railroad tracks, circa 1910. (Courtesy of Lanier Rowan.)

of the nineteenth century, the level of fertility in Russia was higher than anywhere else in Europe, including Ireland. During the normal twenty to twenty-two years of childbearing, married peasant women bore on the average between eight and ten babies. Less than half of their infants survived into adulthood. Grown sons at home were key to a prosperous family economy, and grown children provided insurance for old age. By ensuring the family's future, a mother gained status. When her husband became head of a household, and she became the *bol'shukha*, a woman achieved her greatest authority. She took charge of the other women in her sphere, her daughters and daughters-in-law, a position that older women not infrequently abused, judging by the complaints of daughters-in-law to peasant authorities and their testimony in divorce cases. In extreme cases – the death of the *bol'shak*, his lengthy absence, or his utter incompetence, she might even replace him as head of the household. Although women's authority remained less formalized and less visible than men's, it was nonetheless real.

How women experienced these circumstances has been the subject of some dispute, as has the character of peasant life in general. Many observers of peasant life have stressed the element of cooperation and cohesion, the organic merger of the peasant's "I" with the collective "we."[21] Although recent accounts of intergenerational and intervillage conflicts qualify this picture of untroubled harmony, most historians continue to emphasize the collective's ability to resist corrosive forces, because of the vitality of peasant culture and its flexible adaptation to change.[22] Village cohesion also helps to explain why so many peasants fiercely resisted onslaughts on their way of life during the Stolypin reforms and in the decade following the Bolshevik revolution. But village cohesion is not the entire story. Tales of harmony and collectivity omit the voices of individuals dissatisfied with village life, and they fail to account for the fact that some peasant women and men sought opportunities to escape the village. The story of this discontent provides a counterpoint to the predominant narrative, pointing toward the future and, at the same time, inward at the internal dynamics of peasant families. If unhappy families are unhappy each in its own fashion, there are nevertheless patterns in their misery and disputes that recur. Records of intravillage and intrafamily disputes and appeals to administrative institutions, to the tsar, and to the Russian Orthodox church suggest another version of women's and men's lives. Mostly, documents record the voices of victims or rebels – individuals whom the system abused so badly that they complained about it, women and men who resisted patriarchal and/or community norms. Appealing for redress, they may have exaggerated their grievances or tailored them to suit the expectations of their audience. Nevertheless, their voices remind us that some dissented from the collective version of peasant life, while their stories vividly illustrate the fault lines along which peasant life might buckle under pressure. Told from their perspective, peasant life becomes a story less of

21 Boris Mironov, "The Russian Peasant Commune after the Reforms of the 1860s," *Slavic Review* 44, no. 3 (Fall 1985): 450. The accounts of Russian ethnographers T.A. Bernshtam and M.M. Gromyko also emphasize the harmonious aspects of village life.
22 Such a view is advanced by Stephen Frank, " 'Simple Folk, Savage Customs?' Youth, Sociability, and the Dynamics of Culture in Rural Russia, 1856–1914," *Journal of Social History* 25, no. 4 (Summer 1992): 711–35. On the debates on the character and circumstances of peasant life, see Ben Eklof, "Ways of Seeing: Recent Anglo-American Studies of the Russian Peasant (1861–1914)," *Jahrbücher für Geschichte Osteuropas* 36, no. 1 (1988): 57–79.

harmony and cohesiveness than of patriarchy and its discontents. Tensions between individual needs and aspirations and community norms could serve as a motor for change in the relatively stable peasant way of life.

Often, those tensions were at their most explosive in the realm of sexuality. Sexuality is an important component in the grid of social relations, and all societies develop means of defining and then channeling and controlling it. Russian peasant culture was far from prudish. Bawdy songs, jokes, and sayings often referred to sexuality quite explicitly. Marriage rituals were saturated with erotic symbolism.[23] Russian peasants recognized women's sexuality as well as men's. However, the precariousness of most peasant family economies required that this erotic power be subordinated to household needs and contained within marriage. Peasants demanded chastity of single and married women. (Widows were regarded more leniently.) They usually excluded illegitimate children from the community, denying them access to communal lands.[24] In order to ensure that the woman did not stray, marriage was intended to satisfy wife as well as husband. A husband was supposed to sleep with his wife, "so she would not need to look at other men," as peasants sometimes put it. In turn, she was obliged to accept his sexual overtures, "to respond with a caress to the caresses of her husband."[25] A husband's failure to have intercourse with his wife generated discord in the household and might eventually prompt his wife to leave him.[26] A spouse's physical inability to have intercourse was one of the few grounds for divorce. Marriage thus turned erotic energy to the social good, creating a complete work unit (*tiaglo*) of husband and wife. Marriage rituals involved the entire community, ceremonially integrating into it bride and groom.

In marriage as in other matters, household and community needs customarily took precedence over individual preferences. Marriage was fundamentally an economic affair, so economic considerations came first. Although by

23 See the decription in Bernshtam, *Molodezh'*, 60–5.

24 S. Borogaevskii, "Nezakonnorozhdennye v krest'ianskoi srede," *Russkoe bogatstvo* (October 1898), no. 10, 238–9.

25 Tenishev archive, op. 1, delo 1470, 30 (Novoladoga, St. Petersburg). See also delo 719, 16–17 (Novgorod, Novgorod). In general, Russians were more accepting of women's sexuality than Western Europeans, according to Julie Brown, "Female Sexuality and Madness in Russian Culture: Traditional Values and Psychiatric Theory," *Social Research* 53, no. 2 (Summer 1986): 369–85.

26 A case presented in *Trudy komissii po preobrazovaniiu volostnykh sudov*, 7 vols. (St. Petersburg, 1874), 2: 568, provides an example of discord due to lack of sexual relations; on flight, see Tenishev archive, op. 1, delo 1439, 12 (Egor'ev, Riazan). See also TsGIA SSSR, fond 1412, op. 212, delo 6, 6. A substantial minority of peasant women's petitions to the tsar complain about a husband's inability to fulfill his conjugal obligations.

law the marriage partners had to consent, parents, considered to be wiser than children and more knowledgeable about the needs of the peasant economy, usually made the final choice of a spouse. Without parental permission, marriage was illegal. Parents sought in a maiden physical strength and a capacity for hard work. Almost as important in their eyes were obedience and submissiveness (*smirnost', poslushlivost'*), as well as decency, modesty, and good family background.[27] A woman's character was especially important because she usually came to live in the complex family household of her in-laws, and would have to make a lot of adjustments quickly to other people's ways. A youth's parents often considered the potential value and content of the woman's dowry, especially in areas where cash played a substantial role in peasant life.

The weight that parents assigned to the opinions and affections of the young varied considerably from family to family and from place to place. Martine Segalen's observations on the diversity of courtship patterns in rural France could apply equally well to Russia: "Marriage for love or marriage for reason? Freedom or control of the young by the parents? Let us acknowledge the possible variety of models which appear to depend on [the] economic system."[28] In the cases that follow the father prevailed completely over the son, and control obliterated freedom. Although these cases represent only one extreme along a range of possibilities, they demonstrate the magnitude of power available to fathers and why sons, as well as daughters, might come to regard it as oppressive.

In the first case, a father arranged his son's marriage solely to satisfy the labor requirements of his household; in the second, a son tried in vain to marry against his father's wishes; while in the third, the father essentially blocked the reconciliation of his son and daughter-in-law. In the first instance, Semyon Chemisov, a peasant from Orel province, submitted a petition in 1897 to the Holy Synod, the ruling body of the Russian Orthodox church. Chemisov wanted the church to grant permission for his son to marry five months before he reached the legal age of eighteen, because the Chemisov household required another woman. Such requests were not uncommon. This family household, typically, was a complex one. "My wife is

---

27 On the qualities of the ideal bride, see A.P. Zvonkov, "Sovremennyi brak i svad'ba sredi krest'ian Tambovskoi gubernii," *Sbornik svedenii dlia izucheniia byta sel'skago naseleniia Rossii* (Moscow, 1889), 76–7; Tenishev archive, op. 1, delo 23, 16 (Melenki, Vladimir); delo 1724, 21–2 (Zubtsov, Tver'); delo 1805, 10 (Rostov, Iaroslavl'). Peasant witnesses use identical referents to describe the virtues and failings of parties in divorce and separation suits.
28 Martine Segalen, *Love and Power in the Peasant Family* (Chicago, 1983), 24.

an old woman who can no longer work and the wife of my eldest son is burdened with small children," Chemisov wrote. "I am in a very difficult situation because there is no one to work in the fields and in the house, and to look after the family farm (*khoziaistvo*). My other son's wife hasn't the strength by herself to do all the washing and the sewing, and to prepare food for the entire family." So in order to gain the labor of an additional woman, he wanted to marry off his underage son.[29] Nowhere in the letter is there any reference to the feelings or inclinations of Chemisov's son. They are clearly beside the point. The church granted the requested dispensation.

In the second case, the son had chosen one woman (an orphan), and his parents another. In Russia, marriage was a religious matter and the church forbade marriage without the father's approval. When his parents refused to approve Aleksei Ryseev's choice, he petitioned the bishop of his province (Viatka) in 1896, requesting that the requirement of parental permission be waived. "My parents want me to marry a different girl," he wrote in his own hand, "but I don't want to marry her, I want to marry the girl I've chosen, Aleksandra Sheshukova, whom I know well." Invoking the qualities of the good peasant wife, he stressed in his petition that Sheshukova "is a good worker and a submissive (*smirnaia*) maiden." But despite Ryseev's attempt to couch his request in acceptable terms, the bishop reacted unequivocally to this challenge to the patriarchal family order. He instructed Aleksei to stop wasting his money on "illegal requests," and informed him that it was a sin to complain about one's father. "A sin! (*Grekh*!)" repeated the bishop of Viatka in his written response. "Remind the petitioner that in matters as important as marriage, children must solicit the counsel and blessings of their parents." No matter how old the son, "the father's authority [over him] ends only with death by natural causes."[30]

The third case involved the church's attempt to reconcile a couple after the husband had applied for divorce. The Russian Orthodox Church insisted on the sacramental nature of marriage, and made it difficult to divorce and remarry (see below). Accordingly, it strongly promoted the reconciliation of spouses. This was a lengthy and complex process, "plainly intended to defer, if not derail the divorce application," in the words of Gregory Freeze.[31] The

29  Tsentral'nyi gosudarstvennyi istoricheskii arkhiv SSSR (hereafter TsGIA SSSR), fond 796, op. 178, II stol IV otd., ed. kh. 3914, 1.

30  Ibid., op. 177, II stol, IV otd., ed. kh. 3798, 1–5, 6. For the increasingly conservative stance of the Russian Orthodox Church, see Gregory Freeze, "Bringing Order to the Russian Family: Marriage and Divorce in Imperial Russia, 1760–1860, *The Journal of Modern History* 62, no. 4 (Dec. 1990): 709–46.

31  Ibid., 738–9.

record of one such attempt is worth recounting in some detail, because it so richly illustrates the power that the head of a household might continue to wield over even a grown-up, married son. The case involved Iakov and Tatiana Nechaev, from Ves'egonsk district, Tver', who had married in 1882, he at twenty and she at twenty-three. She lived with him only briefly, then left without any documents and went off to live elsewhere. During her absence, she bore two illegitimate children, one of whom was still alive when Iakov sued for divorce in 1890. The parish priest narrates the story of the attempted reconciliation. He began, he said, by approaching Iakov, who expressed his willingness to live with his wife, despite her misconduct. Then, "in light of the fact that his [the 28-year-old Iakov's] will depended on the will of his father . . . in whose house he lived, I [the priest] considered it necessary to invite the father, too." So the father became a party in the effort to reconcile the couple. The father also said he was willing to accept the wayward daughter-in-law into his house, and the priest brought the three parties together. Tatiana agreed to come back. But she also insisted that she be able to raise her small daughter, whom the two men considered illegitimate. When she brought up the issue of the daughter, the father-in-law dug in his heels. He would accept the wayward woman, but under no circumstances would he allow into his household an illegitimate child. According to the priest, the husband felt differently, but his father's will prevailed. "Evidently, he [Iakov] would have been happy to take her even with the child, but in the face of his father's will, which was expressed stubbornly and decisively, he refused as well," although not so decisively as the father. Tatiana refused to abandon her child in order to return to her husband's household.[32] She may have had reservations for other reasons as well: The community condoned even the brutal beating of faithless wives (see below). Eventually, Iakov obtained a divorce.

The reasoning of Chemisov in the first case, the fruitless resistance of Ryseev in the second, and the submission of the son in the third illustrate an important aspect of patriarchal authority – its power to subordinate the sexuality of sons as well as daughters to the will of the father. The most extreme form of this was *snokhachestvo*, the sexual relation of father-in-law and daughter-in-law in the complex family household. Needless to say, *snokhachestvo* represented an abuse of the woman, too. It was condemned as incest by both the peasants and the Russian Orthodox Church. There is no

---

32 According to her account, she "went wrong" when she learned that her husband had lived with another woman while he was off earning money elsewhere. TsGIA SSSR, fond 796, op. 178, I stol, IV otd., ed. kh. 3080.

way of knowing how frequently it occurred, but the fact that the Russian language contains words that pertain only to that particular relationship suggests that it was by no means uncommon. Households such as the Chemisov's, where the wife was old and sickly and the son was underage were especially at risk; so were households where young husbands worked elsewhere for wages for much of the year. If peasant custom or the church offered remedies for the victims, it is hard to find evidence that they were ever applied. Male elders were inclined to take the side of the father, not the son or his wife.[33] In the Synodal archives that I explored, I found only one case involving *snokhachestvo*. After learning of his father's behavior, the son had hesitated for over a year before he brought his case to light, and when he did, it was to charge his wife with adultery. "I didn't want to disgrace my father," is how the son explained his delay.[34] A son might be so subject to his father's will that he became his father's "blind instrument," or so one peasant woman complained, as she tried to explain why her husband was unable to protect her from his father's sexual advances.[35] Even in the extreme case of *snokhachestvo*, both the customary and psychological power of the father made it difficult for a son to lodge a complaint. Men were even less likely to resist the ordinary pressures of peasant life. It was Vanka Korovin's father who decided to marry off his son, a factory worker in Moscow, "come what may." Accompanied by his friend Semyon Kanatchikov, Vanka returned to the village to attend the showing of the bride the matchmaker had chosen. Collective wisdom prevailed: "We . . . selected a bride for him," Kanatchikov later remembered. Ivan Stepanov, a textile worker at the Gan'shin factory in Moscow had lived there with a woman whom he planned to marry. But in 1899, at his parents' insistence he married someone else, a woman from his village.[36]

The prescribed role of the daughter was even more passive. Although the church forbade forced marriage, women married against their will, or alleged they had married against their will, with some frequency. In 1874, the extreme case of the forced marriage of Marfa Kravtsova came to the attention of the Synod. The case is worth exploring in detail, not because it was typical, which it was not, but because it exemplifies the forms of pressure

33  See one metalworker's complaint in A.S. Shapovalov, *V bor'be za sotsializm* (Moscow, 1934), 66–7, and the incident described in Worobec, *Peasant Russia*, 191.
34  TsGIA SSSR, fond 796, op. 163, I stol, IV otd., ed. kh. 1819, 10.
35  TsGIA SSSR, fond 1412, op. 223, delo 124, 6.
36  Reginald Zelnik, ed., *A Radical Worker in Tsarist Russia: The Autobiography of Semën Ivanovich Kanatchikov* (Stanford, Calif., 1986), 52; TsGIA SSSR, fond 796, op. 199, II stol, IV otd., ed. kh. 415. See also op. 197, I stol, IV otd., ed. kh. 488, 4.

that a family might bring to bear on a reluctant girl. It also demonstrates the strength of character that some peasant women could muster, despite the power of the patriarchal order and their own socialization to submission. The drama that unfolded began in 1869, about six weeks before Marfa's wedding, when her father finalized her engagement to a man he had chosen for her over her protests. Marfa attempted to oppose the unwanted match by the only means available to her: She tried to run away, but her father and aunts caught her, beat her with sticks, and threatened to cut off her hands and feet and then throw her out as a reprobate (*negodnitsa*). On the day of the wedding, she attempted to resist. In order to get her to the church her father and aunts had to beat her again. When they finally got her there, she refused to stand before the pulpit. No one took her side. After she blocked the ceremony, the parish priest left the church in irritation and returned to his house. Some of the assembled crowd demanded she be put in the workhouse; others insisted she be locked in the "cooler." The father ended up dragging his recalcitrant daughter to the priest's house, where the priest tried but failed to convince the girl to obey her father. A visit to the deacon was more effective: He threatened her with Siberian exile if she refused to marry. By this point, Marfa was no longer able to speak and could only cry. In that state, her future husband's family led her to the church, where the ceremony was performed without asking her consent, and with the matchmaker grasping her hands to prevent her from tearing off the wreath on her head. After the wedding, she was held a virtual prisoner in her husband's household for several weeks to keep her from complaining to the authorities. Eventually, she did complain to the local police. Witnesses verified her account of the affair.[37]

It is important to note that this case represented an abuse of parental power so flagrant that the Voronezh circuit court condemned the father after the investigation, and the Synod criticized the priest for dereliction of his duty. Few fathers overrode so brutally the inclinations of their daughters. Some consulted the daughter before they accepted a matchmaker's proposal and set the date of the wedding. But far rarer than coerced marriage was such concerted resistance by a daughter to her father's will. Had Marfa been less strong willed and determined, her case would never even have come to light. It is impossible to know how many women went to the altar unwillingly, but testimonies gathered by ethnographers suggest that most such

---

37 Ibid., op. 155, II stol, IV otd., ed. kh. 542. The narrative is a composite account based on the testimonies presented in the file.

women passively accepted their fate.[38] Applying for a divorce, one peasant woman explained her acquiescence to an unwanted marriage in these terms: "I thought 'I'll live with him, I'll have children and grow used to him.'"[39]

Although patriarchy subjected both sons and daughters, there was a significant difference between the sexes. If a man lived long enough, he usually became a patriarch in his own right and the head of a complex family household. A woman, too, gained power and status with age, but her power, while substantial, never equaled a man's. When a woman married, her husband's authority replaced her father's. A woman's submission was a given, understood as an essential ingredient in marriage and a successful family economy. During the wedding, a husband's authority over his wife was expressed symbolically, by the ceremonial transfer of a whip from father to husband. A man bore primary responsibility for his wife's conduct outside as well as inside the home, although members of a village community might mobilize to control a woman's deviant or unruly behavior in a husband's absence, or if he proved inadequate to the task.

All the insistence on obedience and submission resulted from a distrust of women's nature and the tendency to blame on women's behavior conflicts that were in fact endemic to the system. Peasant men regarded women as potentially unruly and subversive; left to themselves, they might damage the well-being of the household with their quarrels, their laziness, or their selfish insistence on their children's share of the household's goods to the detriment of the whole. It was not unusual for a woman to be blamed for inciting her husband to leave his father's household to set up a household of his own, forcing a household division.[40] It seems clear that peasant women were hardly passive ciphers and that some were prepared to give as good as they got. "Freedom will spoil even a good wife," as the saying went.[41] It was the husband's responsibility to keep these disruptive impulses in check by "instructing" and controlling his wife.

A primary means of "instruction" was beating. Peasant husbands were far from alone in their use of force. Corporal punishment was widely employed to discipline members of the peasant community. Tsarist officials routinely ordered peasant offenders beaten for a variety of infractions. After 1861,

---

38 Such testimony can be found in *Traditsionnye obriady i obriadovyi fol'klor russkikh Povolzh'ia* (Leningrad, 1985), 85, 88, 89, 92.

39 TsGIAgM, fond 203, op. 412, ed. kh. 58, 1–2 (1906).

40 Frierson, "Razdel," and I.N. Milogolova, "Semeinye razdely v russkoi poreformennoi derevne," *Vestnik Moskovskogo universiteta*, ser. 8, Istoriia, no. 6 (1987): 40–1.

41 Dal', *Poslovitsy*, 1: 291.

*volost'* courts did as well. The law limited beating to twenty lashes with the rod and, after 1867, forbade the corporal punishment of women. Peasant courts sometimes transgressed both laws, but they violated the former more often than the latter. Wifebeating, however, unlike court-ordered beatings, was a private matter, not a public one. Wifebeating was also more arbitrary. Courts ordered beatings only to punish misdemeanors, whereas custom also permitted peasant men to beat their wives in order to ensure that the woman behaved appropriately. Wifebeating served to demonstrate, as well as to reinforce, men's authority over every aspect of a woman's life, including the domestic sphere which by custom was her own. The legal scholar Robin West has noted that marital violence teaches a woman to deny her own subjectivity and to live for "the other" and do everything for his sake. Russian peasant proverbs put it more crudely: "If you beat the fur, it's warmer; if you beat your wife, she's sweeter," or "The more you beat your wife, the tastier the cabbage soup."[42] Although it seems clear that peasants disapproved of "excessive ill-treatment," there was enormous room for abuse and little recourse for women. This was especially the case if the beating arose from the wife's infidelity or from suspicion of her infidelity. A wife's infidelity dishonored a man and his family. It might also disrupt a fragile household economy and produce an illegitimate child. Sometimes, the community intervened and subjected an errant wife to rituals of public shaming and humiliation (*vozhdenie*), comparable to the charivari found in other peasant cultures. The adulterous wife might be beaten and then publicly humiliated, her skirt raised and tied over her head in a kind of bag. Naked to the waist, she would be led around the village. Or, tarred and feathered and attached to a cart, she would be dragged around the village as punishment for infidelity. But more often, the husband took matters into his own hands. In the eyes of the community, the husband of an adulterous wife was perfectly within his rights to punish his wife cruelly or to beat her senseless. A husband who murdered an adulterous wife was rarely prosecuted.[43]

Under most circumstances, peasants expected women to endure physical

---

42 Robin West, "The Difference in Women's Hedonic Lives: A Phenomenological Critique of Feminist Legal Theory," *Wisconsin Women's Law Journal* 3, no. 59 (1987): 98–9; Dal', *Poslovitsy*, 1: 291.

43 Olga Semenova Tian-Shanskaia, *Zhizn' 'Ivana': Ocherki iz byta krest'ian odnoi iz chernozemnykh gubernii* (St. Petersburg, 1914), 47–8; Stephen Frank, "Popular Justice, Community, and Culture among the Russian Peasantry, 1870–1900," *Russian Review* 46, no. 3 (July 1987): 251–3.

ill-treatment in silence. As a peasant proverb put it, "Cry young wife, but tell your grief to no one."[44] Fearful of undermining the patriarchal order, *volost'* courts treated women's complaints of ill-treatment with suspicion if the women could not supply compelling evidence. So did tsarist officials. For example, despite evidence to the contrary, in 1882 the Moscow Committee for Peasant Affairs dismissed Praskovia Kurygina's testimony that her husband beat her and insulted her, by saying that this was "merely her side of the case against her husband."[45] As a result, wives usually sought redress for physical abuse only in the most extreme cases, when their lives had become "completely intolerable."[46] And even when *volost'* courts found that a woman's claim was legitimate, their primary concern remained the viability of the family economy. They punished the abusive husband (often by flogging), then ordered the woman to return and "live peacefully" with him. As women were well aware, complaining to the *volost'* court was more likely to worsen than to improve their treatment.

No one knows how the majority of peasant women regarded beatings or how frequent and severe wifebeating really was, because of the silence surrounding wifebeating and the extent to which the community accepted it.[47] What we do know is that some women refused to tolerate beatings, despite women's socialization to submission and lack of economic options outside of marriage. Peasant court cases dating from the late 1860s indicate that such resistance antedated the economic changes of the latter part of the century.[48] The different nature of the sources used – peasant court cases in the earlier period, appeals to the authorities in the later one – precludes comparisons between the two periods. However, judging by the documents in Synodal and administrative archives, it seems clear that by the end of the century, unhappy women had become more likely to take matters into their own

---

44 Dal', *Poslovitsy*, 1: 290.
45 TsGIAgM, fond 66, op. 1, delo 13465, 2–3.
46 E.I. Iakushkin, *Obychnoe pravo* (Moscow, 1896), xx; A.A. Titov, *Iuridicheskie obychai sela Nikola-Perevoz, Sulostskoi volosti, Rostovskago uezda* (Iaroslavl', 1888), 48. See also the discussion in Frank, "Popular Justice, Community, and Culture," 253–4. On the need for proof in *volost'* courts, S.P. Nikonov and E.I. Iakushkin, *Grazhdanskoe pravo po resheniiam Krestobogorodskago volostnago suda* (Iaroslavl', 1902), 169.
47 Whether women really accepted their husbands' beatings has been the subject of some scholarly debate. Beatrice Farnsworth, "The Litigious Daughter-in-Law: Family Relations in Rural Russia in the Second Half of the Nineteenth Century," *Slavic Review* 45, no. 1 (Spring 1986): 49–64, argues that the daughter-in-law resisted abuse; Worobec, *Peasant Russia*, 188–94, contends that for the most part wives tolerated beatings.
48 Farnsworth discusses these cases in general in "The Litigious Daughter-in-Law"; the cases themselves are summarized in the various volumes of *Trudy komissii*.

hands or to pursue their claims in other venues when they could not find satisfaction at home.

By definition these women are not typical. The fact that most of my evidence about women's resistance to wifebeating derives either from petitions to the authorities or from divorce cases makes my sample less typical still. Most disputes between peasants were resolved at the community level, or before the *volost'* courts. Peasants rarely had the wherewithal or the inclination to subject their affairs to the scrutiny of outsiders. Moreover, until the revolutions of 1917, divorce remained in the hands of the Russian Orthodox church, and the church severely limited grounds for it. A divorce might be obtained only if the spouse had been exiled to Siberia; had willfully abandoned the partner and stayed away for five years; or was proved physically incapable of conjugal relations or guilty of adultery, with corroboration by witnesses. Moreover, the church defined even these limited grounds as narrowly as possible. Divorce was also expensive. Documents requiring stamps costing sixty kopeks, seventy-five kopeks, and sometimes a ruble apiece took a bite out of a peasant's budget. Parties to a divorce had to undertake costly travel to an urban or episcopal center in order provide testimony. The economic burden bore most heavily on the woman, who was much less likely than her husband to have the necessary cash at her disposal; many female defendants claimed that the cost kept them from testifying or contesting a husband's divorce suit. Finally, to apply for divorce, peasants had to submit documents, and since most peasants were illiterate, this meant they had to pay someone else to write the documents and probably to advise them as to the proper form and content. How was he to contest his wife's petition for divorce, a peasant from Tver' complained in 1908, when he hadn't the money to hire someone and, barely literate, lacked the knowledge to go about it himself.[49] To avoid such obstacles, many incompatible couples simply agreed to live separately, sometimes with the help of the *volost'* court. In other cases, women petitioned the authorities for a legal separation. It could be very difficult for a woman to obtain the documents she needed to live on her own – a point that will be discussed at length in Chapter 3. Parties to such separation agreements could not legally remarry, as could the plaintiff in a divorce case and (after 1904) the defendant after completing several years of penance.

In the years following the emancipation, the number of divorces was miniscule – about 1.3 for every thousand marriages. The number of divorces

49 TsGIA SSSR, fond 796, op. 189, I stol, IV otd., ed. kh. 4056, 15.

increased substantially by the early twentieth century, but it nevertheless remained small: In 1914, only 4.2 of every thousand marriages ended in divorce.[50] Although small in number, these divorces represent the tip of a larger iceberg. The above percentages represent only suits retained in the archives of the Most Holy Synod in St. Petersburg. If unsuccessful petitions for divorce and cases in which the plaintiff reconciled with the wayward spouse and withdrew the suit are added, the percentages are higher. Such cases often remained in local Synodal archives and are not included in the ratios of divorce to marriage. Over the years, applications by peasants represented a growing fraction of divorce petitions. While evidence drawn from divorce cases certainly does not show "typical" marriages, the transcripts can be valuable, because the scribes often incorporated extracts from the statements of both the plaintiff and the defendant and of the witnesses for both sides. Aiming to convince their audience of the merits of their position, husband and wife appealed to the customary norms of peasant life. In the oral testimonies of these peasant men and women can be ascertained popular attitudes toward women, marriage, and the relations between the sexes. Precisely because the situations are extreme ones, they cast into sharp relief structural tension within the peasant household. They also allow us to catch a glimpse of the individual woman within the community and to see the ways some responded to the patriarchal peasant way of life.

Some of the women who appear as plaintiffs or defendants in these divorce cases present themselves as helpless victims, women abused so badly and treated so heartlessly that they had no choice but to flee. Forced marriage sometimes, and ill-treatment often, figured prominently in women's explanations of their unorthodox, often adulterous behavior.[51] Take the case of Akulina Grigorievna, for example. Illiterate, she told her story with the aid of a scribe, who gave it literary form, complete with ellipses and underlining for emphasis, and who may well have embellished some of the details as well. Still, the account of a bride's difficulty in an alien household is typical enough, as are Akulina's efforts to adjust to her circumstances. "In January, 1858, I married Ivan Ivanov," her letter to the Synod reads. "My life was very hard from the first days that I lived in my husband's family.

50 William Wagner, *Marriage, Property, and the Struggle for Legal Order in Late Imperial Russia* (Oxford, England, forthcoming), chap. 2. Petitions on the grounds of adultery grew much more quickly than requests for divorce on other grounds.
51 Examples are too numerous to cite. But see, e.g., TsGIA SSSR, fond 796, op. 189, II stol, IV otd., ed. kh. 5980; op. 197, I stol, IV otd., ed. kh. 489, 554; op. 199, I stol, IV otd., ed. kh. 57 and 682.

Despite the fact that we married with their consent and blessing, my mother and father-in-law disliked me for some reason. Because of me, they began to oppress (*pritesniat'*) my husband. They demanded that he restrain me in all sorts of ways, and even *beat* me . . . (Life in my husband's family became unbearable to me, but nevertheless, I lived . . . My husband got along somehow with his father and mother, but it was hard for him, too" (emphasis and ellipses in the original). As time passed, her life grew increasingly difficult. Finally, three years and three months after the wedding, having attempted suicide only to be saved by her husband, she fled the household and took refuge in the city on the advice of her husband, or so the letter claimed. He promised to join her but never did.[52]

Praskovia Afanaseeva had good reason to leave her husband, according to a police report of 1885 that chronicled her sufferings. Shortly after their wedding in a Moscow village, her husband Fyodor began to scold her incessantly, to restrict her freedom of movement, and to beat her. He ignored her requests that he stop, so she turned to the local police, asking that they "reprimand him for this oppression." He ignored the police as well. The abuse worsened, and he started threatening her with a knife, so she took him to court and then went to live with her father.[53] At a hearing in 1904, Matrena Chufistova said she left her husband, Kozma, because he and his family beat her so badly that she was sick for a year.[54] Paraskeva Tishina testified in 1914 that she had left her husband's household five months after her wedding and found work as a servant because she had married against her will at her drunken father's insistence and then was beaten repeatedly by her husband and mother-in-law. "Life was hard among strangers," she told the court, but it was preferable to living with a man she did not love, when that involved violence and insults.[55]

Not surprisingly, a husband often challenged his wife's version of events: What a wife felt as unbearable violence, her husband might consider affectionate instruction. In such cases a woman's sense of her own experience was at odds with a husband's perception of his rights. Take, for example, the case of Anastasia Selivanova. Anastasia, a peasant from Riazan, testified that

52  Ibid., op. 168, II stol, IV otd., ed. kh. 1992, 1–2. Lacking the documents she needed to settle down, she spent years wandering from place to place. Similar complaints pervade women's petitions for separate residency permits, where adultery was rarely an issue. See TsGIA SSSR, fond 1412, op. 212–44 .
53  TsGIAgM, fond 66, op. 1, delo 15072, 4–5, 1885.
54  TsGIA SSSR, fond 796, op. 184, I stol, IV otd., ed. kh. 4040; see also op. 166, I stol, IV otd., ed. kh. 1644; op. 199, I stol, IV otd., ed. kh. 1289.
55  Ibid., op. 199 II stol, IV otd., ed. kh. 419, 1–3.

she had left her husband, Platon, three months after their marriage in 1889 because he was so "unbearably cruel in his treatment of her that she was often driven to despair, and was even tempted to kill herself." Platon, however, told a different story. He had treated his wife affectionately and tenderly from the first days of their marriage, he insisted. Disinclined to heed his advice and contemptuous of his guidance, she, not he, was responsible for the breakdown of their marriage.[56] Such differing perceptions of abuse were frequently at the root of marital discord. Men and women alike recognized that "excessive" abuse was wrong. But where to draw the line? In this case as in others, a woman's perception of "excessive" behavior could diverge substantially from a man's.

The cases also show how hard it could be for a woman to find a sympathetic hearing in her community. To be sure, as Beatrice Farnsworth has pointed out, abused women took their grievances to the peasant courts with some frequency. However, a close reading of the cases she cites indicates that the behavior that led wives to complain was often excessive by any definition – a husband hitching his wife to a cart along with the horses, then flogging her all the way back to his village; a husband mercilessly beating his wife with an iron implement, and the like.[57] In most cases, a wife required witnesses or evidence such as signs of brutality or rumors of ill-treatment before anyone would believe she was abused. And even when she could provide evidence of stupifying brutality, the court most commonly ordered her to return to her abusive husband. In the Selivanov case, as in most where the husband was the plaintiff, the witnesses took his side. Villagers considered a wife who left her husband without a compelling reason to be a troublemaker and a wanton woman. Peasant custom discouraged complaints about family matters, but the fact that a woman had never been heard to complain about her husband might serve the community as evidence that she was fabricating her allegations of ill-treatment. Why should villagers believe the woman, one peasant wondered, when "there were no rumors that [the husband] treated her cruelly or by other illegal means gave the wife cause to leave him, and she never complained about her husband."[58]

Occasionally, the lack of awareness of what went on between husbands and wives comes as a surprise. In rural Russia the community intruded into every aspect of family life. The wooden walls of peasant huts, strung side by

56 Ibid., op. 189, II stol, IV otd., ed. kh. 5647, 3–4.
57 Farnsworth, "The Litigious Daughter-in-Law," *Trudy komissii*, 2: 66–7; 208. See also I: 295; II: 151.
58 TsGIA SSSR, fond 796, op. 171, I stol, IV otd., ed. kh. 1797, 5.

side along muddy village streets, provided scanty protection against the scrutiny of fellow villagers, and everyone had his nose in everyone else's business. But reluctant, perhaps, to provide evidence against one another to the policeman who had come to take their testimony, peasants often insisted that they knew nothing. How could one person know for sure what was going on in another's household? Someone else's home was a dark forest, in the words of one peasant witness in a case of adultery.[59] Whether genuine or feigned, this ignorance worked in the husband's favor. Without strong evidence to the contrary, peasant women as well as men were inclined to trust the husband's account and to condemn his wife's behavior.

It is often clear why they did. A wayward woman was able to cause trouble for her husband and his household. As anthropologist Jill Dubisch observes, causing trouble is a form of power, albeit a negative one, which could subvert the customary patterns of village life. Disorderly women threatened a patriarchal order predicated on female submission; they also wreaked disaster on the peasant family economy, which was as dependent on the labor of women as of men. Thus, when they asserted control over their own lives against the overwhelming pressures toward conformity for the sake of the collective, wayward women disrupted the lives of others.[60] So the community mobilized to reassert control of them, or if that proved impossible, to rid itself of them.

Under such circumstances, defiance could require a kind of desperate courage. Consider, for example, the behavior of Avdotia Zapevalova, a peasant from Nizhnii Novgorod province. In 1867, her husband, Grigorii, submitted an appeal for divorce to the Synod because Avdotia had left him five years earlier. A year after she went, he had found her at the market and brought her home to his father's house. A sizable crowd accompanied them all along the way (no doubt marking the return of a wayward member of the community). As soon as they arrived home, she made it clear that she was unwilling to remain there. By his account, she used her hands to smash the glass in the windows of his house until blood ran down her arms. And she cursed her husband and all his household: If they tried to make her live with him against her will, she would not spare herself, but would go to Siberia and drag the entire family along with her. What could the husband do? He let her leave. She went to live with her father in the town of Sergach. When the case came before the Synod, Avdotia claimed she had reason to flee, that

---

59 *Chuzhoi dom – temnyi les.* TsGIA SSSR, fond 796, op. 197, I stol, IV otd., ed. kh. 455, 5.
60 Jill Dubisch, "Introduction," in *Gender and Power in Rural Greece*, ed. Jill Dubisch (Princeton, N.J., 1986), 17.

her husband had treated her cruelly. Grigorii, however, insisted that he had never laid a violent hand on her. The witnesses all upheld his story. Reputation, the collective opinion of an individual's character, looms large in their account. No one had a good word to say about Avdotia. Villagers agreed she was a dissolute woman, a troublemaker. When she was urged to honor her marital vows, she said in their hearing "I cannot abide my husband." The witnesses spoke with one voice about the husband, too. His family had a good reputation. He treated her well and gave her no cause to leave. As evidence, they cited the fact that she had not complained about her husband during the year she had lived with him. But Avdotia rejected this version of her story and insisted on the truth of her tale of mistreatment: It was mistreatment that drove her from her husband's household. The villagers' testimony could not disprove abuse, because his cruel treatment of her "was always within the family, and hidden from outside witnesses."[61] Such a solitary voice was unlikely to receive a sympathetic hearing from either fellow villagers or the church. No one found her argument convincing.

The town acts as a backdrop to this account. Its role in the narrative is scarcely visible: Avdotia never mentions it, and neither do her neighbors. Nevertheless, the town is significant. The town of Sergach provides a refuge for the wayward Avdotia. Her father lives there, removed from the village and from the communal punishments meted out to parents who harbored their runaway daughters. In the village, parents might be fined, imprisoned, and in the case of fathers, beaten with the lash for sheltering a daughter who fled her husband. Moreover, in a town, Avdotia could find work that would keep her from becoming an economic burden on her father.

The town and its blandishments played a far more visible and disruptive role in the lives of other women. Unlike Avdotia Zapevalova, such women raised no complaints about abusive spouses or in-laws. Rather, they found too limited the menu of choices that the village offered them and sought a different life for themselves. Agrippina Sharovatova, a peasant from Tambov, was attracted by the relative freedom of life in town. She did not like "peasant labor," she told her husband, and preferred the free life of the city (*svobodnaia gorodskaia zhizn'*). Her husband, Fyodor, eventually let her go off to the provincial town of Kirsanov, where she found work as a servant. This new life suited her so well that she refused to return to the village, where rumors soon spread she was living with another man. At the hearing in 1913, Agrippina made no effort to defend her reputation or to deny these

61 TsGIA SSSR, fond 796, op. 151, I stol, IV otd. ed. kh. 414, 1–6.

allegations. Yes, she acknowledged, she had lived with her lover for close to a decade. By now, she had lost the habit of her husband, she said, and had no desire to be reconciled with him. A woman who flouted collective norms so flagrantly and made no attempt to excuse herself earned the unqualified condemnation of the entire village. Although no one claimed that she had had sexual relations with anyone besides her husband and her lover, Sharovatova's neighbors nevertheless concurred that "she fully deserves to be called a prostitute." Sixty-one male heads of households signed a declaration (*prigovor*) that condemned Agrippina as a wanton woman who had led a "dissolute life" from the first days of her marriage to Fyodor.[62] Fyodor received his divorce.

Most of the women who figure in these and other cases were young and childless when they fled their husbands. The early years of marriage were the time when a woman was most powerless and most vulnerable to abuse. Once children, especially sons, arrived, a woman's position improved; it also became harder to leave, because leaving meant either abandoning children or supporting them on a woman's miserable wages. Women lowered their expectations of life and learned to take satisfaction where they could. If abuse did not diminish, women learned to endure it. And if they waited long enough, they would achieve a position of real power, especially over young women. Nevertheless, the voices of these wayward women have something to tell us. Women who refused to play by the rules of peasant patriarchy constituted a dissonant element in the harmony of peasant life. The collective's attempts to silence or exclude them is a measure of the negative power that such women exercised.

## Conclusion

Russian peasant life was hard, and the need to labor unrelenting. Patriarchy served to harness the energy of family and community to work for the good of the whole. Peasant culture, the family, and the community met most members' material, emotional, and spiritual needs. As we shall see in the chapters to follow, historians have good reason to emphasize the durability of the peasant way of life: The institutions of peasant life shaped the way that many migrants responded to the challenges of an urban environment.

Nevertheless, the patriarchal peasant way of life was not suited to every village member. Some people had more difficulty than others merging their

62 Ibid., op. 197, I stol, IV otd., ed. kh. 1022, 1, 3, 4–6.

"I" into the collective "we." They included individuals on whom patriarchy bore with unbearable weight, such as severely abused wives, and women whom patriarchy failed, such as wives married to feckless husbands or wives ejected without reason from the husband's household. Still others, however, refused to endure treatment that other women might have taken in stride, for reasons that surely had to do with their own individual characters. Their resistance draws attention to the seams in the web of peasant life and the sometimes problematic relationship between the individual and her community. To such women, the town or city offered encouragement by providing a visible alternative. It was a place where an outsider might find employment and anonymity. In the popular perception, urban life represented danger but also a freedom that was absent in the village. Indeed, these were two sides of the same coin. While contact with urban culture was not necessary to generate unconventional aspirations or personal discontent, contact could widen and deepen them. How to deal with this was one dilemma that villagers faced in the decades following the emancipation. The ways that peasants responded to the threats as well as the opportunities represented by a market economy and urban culture will be the focus of the following chapters.

# 2. The woman's side

It isn't the land that attaches a man to the village, it's the family (*rodnye*).
Prokopovich

In the decades following the emancipation of the serfs, peasant migration from the village steadily increased, in response to a growing need for cash and declining opportunities to earn it at home. Most of the peasants who left were male: Men migrated, while women stayed at home.[1] Comparable in many respects to the patterns of migration that historians have identified elsewhere in Europe, the Russian variant differed in at least one noteworthy way: Migrants from Russian villages remained attached to their birthplace by legal as well as emotional bonds. Both household and village kept a firm grip on migrant members, due in large part to the laws of the tsarist state. The emancipation of 1861 reinforced the powers of household and village heads and restricted peasants' mobility in order to ensure the fulfillment of fiscal and military obligations and to avoid the formation of a "rootless" (and potentially rebellious) proletariat. Peasants needed a passport to live outside their village. Issued for three months, six months, or a year, each passport required the permission of the head of the household or the village elder. The passport system guaranteed that a migrant remained tied to his village and sent a portion of his wages home.[2]

Through marriage, peasant women provided a crucial link in the urban-rural nexus. Marriage added an emotional and sexual dimension to the migrant's attachment to his village; it also brought a woman worker (*rabotnitsa*)

1 The literature on migration is enormous. Caroline Brettell, *Men Who Migrate, Women Who Wait: Population and History in a Portuguese Parish* (Princeton, N.J., 1986), is especially useful for thinking about the demographic and other effects on women of men's migration.
2 See the discussion in Jeffrey Burds, "The Social Control of Peasant Labor in Russia: The Response of Village Communities to Labor Migration in the Central Industrial Region," in *Peasant Economy, Culture, and Politics of European Russia 1800–1921*, ed. Esther Kingston-Mann and Timothy Mixter (Princeton, N.J., 1991), 52–100. The system operated much the same way in relation to women, but as we shall see in the next chapter, they were subject to a somewhat different authority structure.

into his parents' household to labor in the migrant's absence. In the vast majority of cases, the peasant woman who married a migrant remained at home, while her husband lived elsewhere for most or all of the year. This was especially the case when the migrant chose an urban destination. According to the census of 1897, while 43.7 percent of adult male workers in St. Petersburg were married, a mere 8.1 percent lived with their families as head of the household; in Moscow, married men constituted a larger proportion of workers (52.9 percent), but an even smaller proportion were heads of households residing with their families (3.8 percent).[3] The overwhelming majority had left their families in their villages.

This chapter will examine the impact of men's migration and the prolonged separation of husbands and wives on peasant family life and the position of peasant women. The focus will be on Soligalich and Chukhloma, two districts of Kostroma province that were closely studied by the *zemstvo* physician Dmitrii N. Zhbankov, a peasant by birth. However, the discussion will be broadened to encompass the sections of Iaroslavl' and Tver' provinces that were similarly located far from major cities or centers of trade. Peasants in Soligalich and Chukhloma shared with their counterparts in Iaroslavl' a long history of extensive and far-ranging outmigration. Their history of interaction with a larger world probably enabled these peasants to adapt more readily than the peasants of Tver' to the changes that industrialization wrought. Nevertheless, by the end of the nineteenth century the outmigratory regions of Kostroma, Tver', and Iaroslavl' all shared the characteristics that led writers to entitle them a "woman's kingdom": women's numerical preponderance and their relative power.[4]

The need for extraagricultural earnings had a long history in Soligalich and Chukhloma, as it did in most of the Central Industrial Region. Generally poor soil, inadequate pastureland, and cool summers and long winters made supplementary income essential throughout the region. In Soligalich and Chukhloma, the lack of local industry and indigenous raw materials (with the exception of some forestlands) and the distance from trading centers made it almost imperative that this income be sought elsewhere. Under

---

3 N.A. Troinitskii, ed. *Chislennost' i sostav rabochikh v Rossii na osnovanii dannykh pervoi vseobschei perepisi naseleniia Rossiiskoi imperii 1897 g.* (St. Petersburg, 1906), 1: 46, 66.

4 V.P. Semenov, ed. *Rossiia: Polnoe geograficheskoe opisanie nashego otechestva*, 11 vols. (St. Petersburg, 1899) 1: 110; A. Balov, "Ocherki Peshekhoniia," *Etnograficheskoe obozrenie* 35, no. 4 (1897): 57. D.N. Zhbankov chose to give his study of the two districts the title *The Woman's Place (Bab'ia storona)*. I have omitted discussion of Moscow and Vladimir provinces in this chapter because both were characterized by heavy concentrations of rural industry, leading to different patterns of interaction with the market.

serfdom, the two districts had the highest level of feudal dues (*obrok*) in the entire province of Kostroma – thirty, forty, even fifty rubles for each married couple (*tiaglo*) – and peasants sought work in the cities to pay them.[5] They remained away for all or part of the year and sent most of their wages home. These peasant migrants were almost exclusively male and constituted more than 20 percent of the adult male population at the end of the eighteenth century. Kostroma's "kingdom of women" had never been an impoverished domain, as peasant villages went. Peasants went off to learn trades early, around the age of twelve. As a result, migratory laborers from Soligalich and Chukhloma usually engaged in skilled trades, working as coppersmiths, metalworkers, joiners, carpenters, or blacksmiths, or they became petty tradesmen – butchers and tanners, for example.[6] The income they sent home created an unusually high level of material well-being. According to a survey of Kostroma province on the eve of the emancipation, the families of migrants lived "a step above the rather dirty and not particularly fastidious life of the ordinary peasantry, and their lifestyle (*obraz zhizni*) resembled that of petty merchants."[7]

The emancipation of the serfs intensified these patterns and left the peasant households of Soligalich and Chukhloma still more economically dependent on the money men sent home. Domestic crafts were very poorly developed in the two districts. Peasant women might raise flax to clothe their families, but they did not weave linen for sale or manufacture fishnets for the market, as did peasant women in Iaroslavl' and Tver' at the time of the emancipation. Peasant land allotments were reduced, and the amounts required to redeem them were set high. In Soligalich and Chukhloma, the land yielded only enough grain to last about seven and a half months of the year. After that, grain, the staple of the peasant diet, had to be purchased. The loss of meadow and pastureland caused the number of head of cattle and horses steadily to decline.[8]

In response to declining opportunities at home, even the more well-to-do peasant families resorted to the customary practice of sending their sons

5  *Materialy dlia statistiki Kostromskoi gubernii*, vyp. 3 (Kostroma, 1872), 155.
6  N.N. Vladimirskii, *Otkhozhie promysly krest'ianskogo naseleniia Kostromskoi gubernii* (Kostroma, 1926), 18–20; A. Iatsevich, *Krepostnye v Peterburge* (Leningrad, 1933), 8.
7  Ia. Krzhivoblotskii, *Materialy dlia geografii i statistiki Rossii, sobrannye ofitserami General'nogo shtaba. Kostromskaia oblast'* (St. Petersburg, 1861), 500.
8  Concerning land allotments, see E.V. Matveeva, "K voprosu o sviazi rabochikh tekstil'shchikov Kostromskoi gubernii s zemlei v 90e gody XIX veka," in *Promyshlennost' i proletariat gubernii verkhnego Povolzh'ia v kontsa XIX–nachale XX vv.* (Iaroslavl', 1976), 2; Vladimirskii, *Otkhozhie*, 14.

elsewhere for training when they reached the age of twelve, and as a result, some sort of training was the norm for young men from the districts. Of the 21,210 candidates reviewed by the Chukhloma military recruitment center between 1874 and 1916, only 525 had learned no trade (498 more were engaged in intellectual professions.)[9] Their skills enabled the painters, carpenters, joiners, and other craftsmen from Soligalich and Chukhloma to earn a decent wage, but only if they migrated elsewhere, usually to St. Petersburg. After paying for room and board and other incidental expenses of urban life, in the 1880s a painter might manage to bring home with him seventy-six rubles after a season's work; a carpenter came home with slightly less. They fared considerably better than unskilled workers from provinces such as Tver', who sent home, on the average, sixteen rubles a year in the 1890s.[10] Villagers in Soligalich and Chukhloma came to depend on the infusion of cash earned elsewhere: A study of peasant budgets conducted in 1908 found that outside earnings constituted 52.4 percent of household income in the two districts.[11]

In the Central Industrial Region in general, outmigration increased substantially in the fifty years following the emancipation, as measured by the number of passports issued (see Table 2.1). These figures do not tell the entire story, however. The number of departing migrants fluctuated considerably from year to year. Moreover, in any given year, some people left for the first time while others, seasoned migrants, returned to the village and remained there until they regained their health, recovered from an accident or from alcoholism, or otherwise recuperated. In four villages of Kostroma, only three of seventy-nine adult men had had no migratory experience whatever, according to a sampling that Zhbankov conducted in the mid 1880s.[12] If these numbers are at all typical, then it is likely that the proportion of men with outmigratory experience was far more substantial than the numbers of passports indicates.

Substantial male outmigration affected family life and demographics in the village. For one thing, it influenced both the rate and the age at the time of marriage. At the end of the nineteenth century, brides in the outmigratory districts of Kostroma tended to be younger than their counterparts elsewhere

9 N.N. Vladimirskii, *Kostromskaia oblast'* (Kostroma, 1959), 113.
10 On earnings of Kostroma workers, see *Trudy komissii po izsledovaniiu kustarnoi promyshlennosti v Rossii* (St. Petersburg, 1885), vyp, 8, 188–9; 228–31. On Tver', *Statisticheskii ezhegodnik Tverskoi gubernii za 1897 god* (Tver', 1898), 34.
11 Vladimirskii, *Otkhozhie*, 7.
12 D.N. Zhbankov, *Bab'ia storona* (Kostroma, 1891), 103–10.

Table 2.1. *Peasant labor migration as a proportion of village population (women and men)*

| | Proportion of passports issued to local peasant population | | | | |
|---|---|---|---|---|---|
| District | 1861–70 | 1871–80 | 1881–90 | 1891–1900 | 1906–10 |
| Tver' | 8.0 | 14.6 | 14.4 | 16.7 | 23.0 |
| Iaroslavl' | 9.1 | 17.0 | 16.4 | 18.9 | 23.1 |
| Moscow | 10.0 | 18.0 | 20.4 | 29.9 | 34.2 |
| Vladimir | 4.8 | 16.0 | 16.7 | 19.1 | 24.2 |
| Kostroma | 3.9 | 12.3 | 13.8 | 13.1 | 20.0 |
| Kaluga | 8.8 | 17.2 | 18.3 | 20.5 | 25.4 |
| Nizhnii Novgorod | 3.1 | 8.8 | 9.6 | 11.0 | 12.0 |

*Source*: Jeffrey Burds, "The Social Control of Peasant Labor in Russia: The Response of Village Communities to Labor Migration in the Central Industrial Region, 1861–1905," in Esther Kingston-Mann and Timothy Mixter, eds., *Peasant Economy, Culture, and Politics of European Russia, 1800–1921* (Princeton, N.J., 1991), 58.

in Kostroma, or in rural Russia as a whole (see Table 2.2). In Chukhloma district, where the proportion of men migrating was greatest, the rate of marriage was also higher than the norm for Kostroma province as a whole, although by the first five years of the twentieth century the rate had dipped slightly below the norm (see Table 2.3). This pattern appears to illustrate Robert Johnson's contention that migration for wages reinforced the peasant practice of early marriage, by enhancing the prosperity of the parental household.[13] The matter, however, is not so straightforward. In Iaroslavl', a province where male outmigration was as common as in Soligalich and Chukhloma, and peasant households among the most prosperous in rural Russia, migration for wages produced a more "urban" pattern of marriage. Far fewer men and women married before the age of twenty-one in Iaroslavl' than elsewhere in rural Russia, and the rate of marriage was unusually low: Of every thousand peasant men over forty, fifty-two had never been married in 1897, as compared to thirty-two of every thousand men in Soligalich and

13  Robert Johnson, "Family Relations and the Rural-Urban Nexus: Patterns in the Hinterland of Moscow, 1880–1900," in *The Family in Imperial Russia*, ed. David Ransel (Urbana, Ill., 1978), 268–9.

Table 2.2. *Proportion of people marrying at age twenty or earlier (in percentages)*

| Place | 1880* | | 1895 | | 1900 | |
|---|---|---|---|---|---|---|
| | Men | Women | Men | Women | Men | Women |
| All Kostroma | 41.7 | 51.8 | 32.7 | 47.9 | 35.2 | 51.1 |
| Soligalich | 42.7 | 56.6 | 34.9 | 56.5 | 32.8 | 53.8 |
| Chukhloma | 29.2 | 49.5 | 33.2 | 66.4 | 50.6 | 67.2 |
| Tver' | 36.1 | 56.8 | 35.3 | 53.7 | 39.0 | 61.8 |
| Iaroslavl' | 20.1 | 40.5 | 14.4 | 37.0 | 15.8 | 37.3 |
| All rural Russia | 34.3 | 57.2 | 33.2 | 56.4 | 34.5 | 58.1 |

* The figures for 1880 are based on all marriages; those for subsequent years, on marriages outside of urban areas.
*Source*: Statistical yearbooks of the Russian empire.

Table 2.3. *Marriage rates for each thousand adults*

| Place | 1871–1875 | 1876–1880 | 1891–1895 | 1896–1900 | 1901–1905 |
|---|---|---|---|---|---|
| Soligalich | 9.3 | 7.9 | 9.23 | 8.85 | 7.96 |
| Chukhloma | 9.4 | 8.6 | 10.55 | 9.69 | 8.39 |
| Average rural Kostroma | 8.7 | 8.3 | 9.11 | 9.31. | 8.72 |

*Sources*: For 1871–80, *Materialy dlia statistiki Kostromskoi gubernii*, vyp. 6, p. 8; for 1891–1905, Z.G. Frenkel', "Osnovnye pokazateli, kharakterizuiushchie dvizhenie naseleniia v Kostromskoi gubernii v tri poslednie piatiletiia," *Trudy IX gubernskogo s"ezda vrachei Kostromskoi gubernii*, vyp. 3 (Kostroma, 1906), 78 – 83.

Chukhloma, and forty of every thousand men in Russia as a whole.[14] This suggests that the character of migrant men's work might be as important an influence on demographic patterns as migration itself. The high proportion of tradesmen (about 30 percent) and craftsmen (about 30 percent) among

14  In that age group, 15.5 of every 1,000 peasant women from Iaroslavl' had never been wed, as compared to 9.3 in Soligalich, and 7.2 in Chukhloma. Tsentral'nyi statisticheskii komitet. *Pervaia vseobshchaia perepis' naseleniia Rossiiskoi imperii, 1897*, 89 vols. (St. Petersburg, 1897–1905), 18: 39–40; 50: 28.

Iaroslavl' migrants surely contributed to its more urban (and more middle-class) pattern of postponing marriage or refraining from it altogether. Although complex family households were also to be found in Iaroslavl', sons preferred to establish their own households after marriage, and so they waited until they had accumulated sufficient capital to live on their own.[15] By contrast, outmigratory Kostroma stayed closer to the peasant pattern, according to which a son married early and remained in his father's household for the first few years at least.

Early marriage better served the needs of the peasant household. Marriage brought the migrant's parents a worker, who lived with them and labored in place of her migratory husband. And marriage cemented a migrant's loyalty to his parents' household. "Peasants regard marriage as a way of attaching a person to the household," in the words of one observer of peasant life. A wife in the village tied a young man more firmly to it, made his "heart more inclined toward home."[16] As one historian has observed: "It is hard to say whether the obligation to marry and to leave a worker (*rabotnitsa*) in the household was always a painful one, but it was a rather typical occurrence," and he quotes a worker from Tver' province, subsequently a Bolshevik, who remembered: "After lengthy efforts and a struggle with my family, in 1896 I succeeded in . . . going to Petersburg; but to do this I had first to marry, so as to leave a worker in the household."[17] A migrant with a wife in the village was more likely to send a substantial portion of his earnings home and to maintain his village ties.[18]

For all these reasons, it was important that the bride be a peasant and preferable that she not have worked elsewhere. A city-bred wife was unlikely

15 K. Vorob'ev, *Otkhozhie promysly krest'ianskago naseleniia Iaroslavskoi gubernii* (Iaroslavl', 1903), 13–15; *Statisticheskoe opisanie Iaroslavskoi gubernii* (Iaroslavl', 1904) II, vyp. 1, 96–7. Men from Tver', who tended to marry younger, tried to save up money for separating after the wedding, according to the Russian ethnographers L. Anokhina and M. Shmeleva, *Kul'tura i byt kolkhoznikov Kalininskogo oblast'* (Moscow-Leningrad, 1964), 22. See also the discussion in Christine Worobec, *Peasant Russia: Family and Community in the Post-Emancipation Period* (Princeton, N.J., 1991), 125. Unfortunately, Worobec does not separate outmigratory from sedentary populations, as Johnson does in his sample.

16 S. Kanatchikov, *Iz istorii moego bytiia* (Moscow-Leningrad, 1929), 20, 45; Tenishev archive, op. 1, delo 1724, 19.

17 Iu. A. Shuster, *Peterburgskie rabochie v 1905–1907 gg.* (Leningrad, 1976), 31.

18 Interestingly, some observers explained the comparatively late age of marriage in Iaroslavl' in terms of similar considerations: Peasants there, it was said, were hesitant to marry off sons because they knew that soon afterward the son would want to establish a separate household, depriving the parents of his earnings. See *Otkhozhie promysly krest'ianskago naseleniia Iaroslavskoi gubernii* (Iaroslavl', 1907) (hereafter *Otkhozhie promysly*), 38–9.

to have either the experience or the inclination to do agricultural labor and, in addition, peasants believed that city people had a different morality from countryfolk and were subject to greater temptation. As a result, even a short stint of domestic service in a city could disqualify a peasant girl as a suitable match.[19] However, so long as a son chose his bride from the village, and his parents approved the match, men who went off to work in the city usually enjoyed the freedom to decide whom they would marry, in contrast to peasants of the agricultural regions, whose parents were more likely to arrange marriages for them.[20] Around the end of October, young migrants returned to the villages of Soligalich and Chukhloma bearing trinkets, yards of silk, and other presents, prepared to court the local maidens. But even the relative freedom to choose his bride served in the end to consolidate a migrant's commitment to the family economy.

The honeymoon was brief. Whether or not marriage was merely "an economic and physiological agreement," as some observers seemed to think, the struggle for survival came first everywhere in rural Russia.[21] Having married in January, a migrant from Soligalich or Chukhloma was off to St. Petersburg again by March. He had lived with his bride for about two months and left her "neither a maiden nor a widow, a real orphan," as they sang in one local folk song.[22] Only young wives without children could visit their husbands, and then only rarely, because of distance and cost (twenty-five to thirty-five rubles roundtrip, according to Zhbankov). Besides, where migration was seasonal, as in the construction trade, migrants were gone during the spring and summer, precisely the time when their wives were needed in the fields. The migrant might return to the village during the slow winter months, but in some cases he visited as rarely as every three to five years.[23]

When men did return to the village, they often lived there "like guests," doing no work around the house or yard.[24] This treatment underscores the distinguishing characteristic of the migrant's contribution to the family economy: cash and goods that could be purchased with cash. The availability

---

19 Tenishev archive, op. 1, delo 588, 3 (Galich, Kostroma). This point will be developed at length in Chapter 3.

20 Ibid., 9; Zhbankov, *Bab'ia*, 63, 80–2.

21 Tenishev archive, op. 1, delo 588, 5. Or, as Zhbankov put it: "If marriage in the agricultural zone is strongly subject to economic needs, then here its character is primarily economic" (*Bab'ia*, 82).

22 Tenishev archive, op. 1, delo 589 (Galich), 19; Zhbankov, *Bab'ia*, 134.

23 Zhbankov, *Bab'ia*, 72, 83.

24 *Materialy dlia statistiki*, vyp. 3, 103–4.

of cash transformed consumption patterns in villages with substantial male migration. To be fashionable (*modno*) became very important. For special occasions, the youths abandoned their peasant shirts and sheepskin coats, bast shoes or felt boots for short jackets (*pidzhaki*), galoshes, and a fashionable overcoat; while the women exchanged their sarafans and homespun blouses for wool or silk dresses.[25]

It was men who provided the cash to purchase these things. To acquire tea, leather for boots, cotton and factory-made clothing, and other consumer items, in addition to necessities, a woman depended on the money a man sent home. When she really needed the money to buy something, and her husband, a factory worker, had sent her too little, one village wife would go to visit him in Moscow and "rob" him, as her son put it.[26] A letter a peasant woman from Chukhloma wrote her husband in St. Petersburg in the 1880s conveys a similar combination of dependence and practicality, as well as a thorough knowledge of her household's needs: "If you're thinking of coming to the village, then bring money for expenses, but if you are going to spend the winter in St. Petersburg, send even more money and the presents that I wrote you about before, so things won't be so dull for us (*skuchno*). . . . My dear husband, bring tea with you. . . . Our harness is all tattered, so we cannot use the horse. If there were money, we could have shoes made; in fact, one of the leather boots is falling apart, and we need fur coats, so look after your money."[27]

In contrast to their husbands, the majority of peasant women contributed to the family economy almost exclusively in kind. This was especially the case in Soligalich and Chukhloma, because of the lack of local cottage industry. In Tver' and Iaroslavl', many peasant women labored at home to earn income. The greatest numbers planted flax, then engaged in the arduous processes required to transform it into linen and then cloth; they also kept dairy cows and marketed the milk. Winters, Tver' women wove nets, made lace, and knitted socks, mittens, and sashes. In the vicinity of major shoe-making towns, women sewed cheap shoes in their cottages. However, in the 1890s, the amount of money that Tver' women could earn at most women's

---

25 "K voprosu o polozhenii rabochego klassa v Kostromskoi gubernii," *Materialy dlia statistiki Kostromskoi gubernii* (Kostroma, 1881), vyp, 4, 56; Tenishev archive, op. 1, delo 587 (Galich, Kostroma), 16–20.

26 Tsentral'nyi gosudarstvennyi arkhiv Oktiabrskoi revoliutsii (hereafter TsGAOR SSSR), fond 7952, op. 3. delo 273, 53.

27 Zhbankov, *Bab'ia*, 114–15.

trades was "wretched and insignificant," in the words of one student of women's work, largely because middlemen (and much more rarely, women) took such a huge bite out of their earnings. Netmakers earned about seven to eight kopeks after subtracting the cost of light and materials; women who made shoes at home earned about fifteen to twenty kopeks a day, and so did lacemakers. By the close of the nineteenth century, low wages in domestic trades prompted all but the most desperate of Iaroslavl's women to set aside their spindles and looms and to cease to work for the market.[28]

The number of women migrants was quite small during the days of serfdom, and it increased only slowly after 1861: In the 1880s, slightly over 2 percent of the women of Soligalich and Chukhloma lived outside of their villages. Through the end of the nineteenth century, in the two districts and in Iaroslavl', the proportion of women who migrated remained lower than in other areas with high levels of male outmigration such as Novgorod and Tver' provinces. A relatively high remuneration for men's labor and the comparative well-being that it brought evidently served to limit women's migration, a point that will be explored at greater length in the following chapter. So long as there was land to be worked by the households of parents or in-laws, female hands were needed to work it. Even extra hands found employment close to home. Summers, unmarried women who wanted to buy themselves clothes, along with childless widows and soldiers' wives, hired themselves out for the season, earning between twenty and forty rubles, depending on how experienced they were and how many weeks they worked.[29]

As a result, those few women who did leave were the most marginal members of the peasant household, nonmarriageable women (those over age twenty-three) and childless widows, and they tended to remain in the city. Other women left as members of families. Between 1874 and 1883, approximately the same number of passports were issued to families in Soligalich

---

28 The student of women's work is I. Krasnoperov, "Zhenskie promysly Tverskoi gubernii," *Mir bozhii*, no. 2 (1898): 24–7. Also on Tver', see Anokhina and Shmeleva, *Kul'tura i byt*, 17–29, and *Statisticheskii ezhegodnik Tverskoi gubernii za 1897 g.* (Tver', 1898), 3–4. On Iaroslavl', see A. Balov, "O neobkhodimosti otkrytiia v Poshekhonskom uezde zhenskikh professional'nykh shkol," *Iaroslavskie gubernskie vedomosti*, no. 21 (1892): 2–3; *Obzor Iaroslavskoi gubernii. Otkhozhie promysly krest'ian Iaroslavskoi gubernii* (Iaroslavl', 1896), esp. 18, 51.

29 On women's migration, see *Materialy dlia statistiki Kostromskoi gubernii*, vyp. 3, 159; vyp. 4, 284; vyp. 6 (Kostroma, 1884), 79; vyp. 7 (Kostroma, 1887), 208. For work and wages of women who stayed at home, see Tenishev archive, op. 1, delo 622 (Chukhloma, Kostroma), 16–19.

and Chukhloma as were issued to individual women. Family members were not listed separately, making it impossible to be sure about the precise number of sisters, mothers, or, most commonly, wives who left the country-side with their menfolk, but judging by the descriptions of sixty-two households in four villages of Chukhloma district, a family passport typically included only one adult woman. In this small sample, seven women from six households (10 percent of the total number of households) lived in St. Petersburg. Only two of them, a widow and a spinster, had gone off on their own. The others were married women who accompanied their husbands to the city, leaving mothers, sisters-in-law, spinster sisters, or aunts at home to look after the household and the land. Generally, only the most successful male migrants brought the women of their households with them to the city. Only one of the wives earned wages herself; the rest contributed to the family economy by reducing men's expenses, acting as cooks and housekeepers in the apartments or workshops where the husbands, sons, or brothers plied their trades.[30] About 95 percent of adult women remained in the countryside.

For women in migratory regions, marriage to men who migrated was not only the expected but the preferred order of things. From among the candidates who presented themselves, it was the woman – and not her parents – who usually made the selection in Soligalich and Chukhloma.[31] Even in the days of serfdom, women's sewing circles would grow more lively when migrants returned from St. Petersburg, signaling the start of the courting season. Later, marriageable women who did agricultural labor for wages would stop a month earlier than widows and soldiers' wives, in order to be free to participate in the round of evening gatherings (*posidelki*) at which marriageable young men and women got to know each other.[32] Under serfdom and afterwards, women favored the migrant, who sent money home, displayed sophisticated urban ways, and dressed modishly. Men who remained in the village, even those who were financially better off, were clearly not "Petersburgers" (*Pitershchiki*). In the words of two local folk songs, "Peasant lads are nitwits" (*krestianskii syn durashen*).[33]

30 The number of family and women's passports can be found in *Materialy dlia statistiki*, vyp. 6, Table 3. Household listing can be found in Zhbankov, *Bab'ia*, 103–10.
31 Tenishev archive, op. 1, delo 588, 11; Zhbankov, *Bab'ia*, 82.
32 Tenishev archive, op. 1, delo 619, 9 (Chukhloma and Galich, Kostroma); delo 622, 19 (Chukhloma).
33 Writes the correspondent from Galich: "If some boy is home over the summer, no girl will accept his attentions, because he's not a *Pitershchik*." Tenishev archive, op. 1, delo 587, 5; Krzhivoblotskii, *Materialy dlia geografii*, 516. The songs can be found in Zhbankov, *Bab'ia*, 126, no. xxv; 127, n. xxvii.

Fig. 2. Peasant women cultivating a field, circa 1910. Note the women's covered heads. (Courtesy of Lanier Rowan.)

When a woman married a man who worked elsewhere, it tied her still more closely to the soil and increased her burden of physical labor. The Russian growing season was very short – five and a half to six months, by comparison with eight to nine months in western Europe. Especially during the harvest season or *stradnaia pora* (literally, the time of suffering), the period from mid July to the end of August, agricultural labor pushed the peasants to their limits. To get everything done "a partnership was essential."[34] Generally, a relatively strict division of labor prevailed: Men had responsibility for farming, while women took charge of the household and the garden. In the fields, men performed the most physically demanding tasks, such as plowing, harrowing, and sowing, while women fertilized and weeded. Men harvested with the scythe and women with the sickle. But in "the woman's kingdom," even heavy agricultural labor – men's work in other areas – was conducted primarily, sometimes exclusively, by women, either by themselves or with the aid of a hired hand. This may be a measure of the

34 Steven Hoch, *Serfdom and Social Control in Russia: Petrovskoe, a Village in Tambov* (Chicago, 1986), 91–2.

continuing importance of farming to peasants in these areas. In Moscow province, according to Robert Johnson, farm work was often left to the very old and the very young, while women cared for their children. On the other hand, Johnson may be mistaken in assuming that young children limited women's role as agricultural producers. In Soligalich, Chukhloma, and elsewhere in outmigratory areas, the old looked after small children, or the children were left in the care of older siblings, while their mothers labored in the fields.[35] In the areas where male outmigration was at its greatest, like Chukhloma, Kostroma, and Rybinsk, Iaroslavl', more women than men bore full responsibility for agriculture, whereas in more settled areas, men were many times more likely than women to be fully in charge of the fields. In the parts of Tver' that produced flax and dairy products for market, women often did all the harvesting in addition to coping with the flax harvest and caring for the livestock.[36] So demanding was the agricultural labor that when women engaged in it, their biological cycles were sometimes interrupted: During the thirty to sixty days of the *stradnaia pora*, "a significant minority" of women, in the words of one physician, "the great majority," according to another, who were neither pregnant nor nursing ceased to menstruate altogether.[37]

The patterns of male outmigration affected women physically in other ways as well. In Soligalich and Chukhloma, the rhythm of women's sex life was "irregular" to say the least: Restraint for seven to nine months, then "excessive indulgence," as Zhbankov put it, between November and March

---

35 Semenov, ed., *Rossiia*, 1:110; Balov, "Ocherki Peshekhoniia," 57. Krasnoperov provides a detailed description of the physical labor that the peasant women of Tver' performed in their husbands' absence in "Zhenskie promysly v Tverskoi gubernii," 22–4. Robert Johnson, *Peasant and Proletarian: The Working Class of Moscow in the Late Nineteenth Century* (New Brunswick, N.J., 1979), 61. On the delegation of child care and women's labor, see David Ransel, "Infant-Care Cultures in the Russian Empire," in *Russia's Women: Accommodation, Resistance, Transformation*, ed. Barbara Clements, Barbara Engel, and Christine Worobec (Berkeley, Calif., 1991), 113–32 and below.

36 According to the census of 1897, in the Rybinsk district, 5,647 men and 6,937 women were engaged independently in agriculture, and in the Chukhloma district, 5,872 women and 4,276 men, whereas in the Varnavin district of Kostroma, 16,296 men and 2,849 women engaged independently in agriculture; in the Vetluga, 15,426 men and 1,979 women. In the Soligalich district slightly more men than women engaged independently in agriculture, whereas in the Danilov, Romanov-Borisogleb, and Uglich districts of Iaroslavl', the numbers were roughly the same. *Pervaia vseobshchaia perepis'* 18: 160–4; 50: 140–7. On Tver', see Anokhina and Shmeleva, *Kul'tura i byt*, 25.

37 Z.G. Frenkel', "Osnovnye pokazateli, kharakterizuiushchie dvizhenie naseleniia v Kostromskoi gubernii v tri poslednie piatiletiia (1891–1905)," *Trudy IX gubernskago s"ezda vrachei Kostromskoi gubernii*, vyp. 3 (Kostroma, 1906): 65; Zhbankov, *Bab'ia*, 91. In Riazan, another province with substantial male outmigration, A.O. Afinogenov observed the same phenomenon. *Zhizn' zhenskago naseleniia Riazanskago uezda v period detorodnoi deiatel'nosti zhenshchiny i polozhenie dela akusherskoi pomoshchi etomu naseleniiu* (St. Petersburg, 1903), 44.

Table 2.4. *Births for thousand inhabitants*

| Place | 1891–1895 | 1896–1900 | 1901–1905 |
|---|---|---|---|
| Soligalich | 47.16 | 43.79 | 42.02 |
| Chukhloma | 44.52 | 45.02 | 42.72 |
| Average for rural Kostroma | 52.29 | 50.36 | 48.19 |

*Source*: Z.G. Frenkel', "Osnovnye pokazateli kharakterizuiushchie dvizhenie naseleniia v Kostromskoi gubernii v tri poslednie piatiletiia (1891–1905)," *Trudy IX gubernskago s"ezda vrachei Kostromskoi gubernii*, vyp. 3 (Kostroma, 1906), 78–83.

when the men returned from the city.[38] Women who conceived in the winter bore their babies in the summer and early fall. In one canton of Soligalich that Zhbankov studied in the early 1880s, over 62 percent of babies were born between July 1 and the end of November. The statistical yearbook for 1883 shows that Chukhloma had an even higher percentage of babies born in that five-month period – over two-thirds. By comparison, Russia as a whole showed a more normal distribution: In 1883, slightly over 45 percent of babies were born during those five months.[39] The distribution of births in Soligalich and Chukhloma meant that during the *stradnaia pora*, many women had just given birth or were in the final weeks of pregnancy. They rarely spared themselves. If their hands were needed, women worked until the onset of labor pains and returned to work within a few days of childbirth. The strain caused pregnant women to lose their infants. Wives of migrants were more likely to miscarry, or to bear infants prematurely, than women with husbands at home. The irregularity of women's sexual life and, perhaps, the comparatively large number of miscarriages reduced the number of children women bore. While the rate of marriage in Soligalich and Chukhloma was higher and the age at marriage lower than the average for rural Kostroma, the birthrate per thousand inhabitants was considerably below the norm for the province (see Table 2.4).

38  D.N. Zhbankov, "K voprosu o plodovitosti zamuzhnikh zhenshchin. Vliianie otkhozhikh zarabotkov," *Vrach* 7, no. 39 (1886): 700.

39  Fifteen years later, the distribution of births had barely changed. D.N. Zhbankov, "Vliianie otkhozhikh zarabotkov na dvizhenie narodonaseleniia," *Vestnik sudebnoi meditsiny*, no. 1 (1885): 41. *Statisticheskii vremennik Rossiiskoi imperii. Dvizhenie naseleniia v evropeiskoi Rossii za 1883 god* (St. Petersburg, 1887), 83, 100. The distribution of births was far more regular in Iaroslavl' and Tver' too, because a much smaller proportion of men were employed in construction and labored over the summer season.

Table 2.5. *Infant mortality, birth to one year\* (per hundred births)*

| Place | 1891–1895 | 1896–1900 | 1901–1905 |
|---|---|---|---|
| Soligalich | 26.32 | 27.44 | 26.47 |
| Chukhloma | 28.23 | 27.76 | 26.50 |
| Average for rural Kostroma | 32.50 | 32.13 | 31.14\*\* |
| Rybinsk, Iaroslavl' | | 26.8 | |
| Danilov, Iaroslavl' | | 27.0 | |
| Average for rural Iaroslavl' | | 29.0 | |
| Average for rural Tver' | | 32.1 | |
| Average for Orthodox population of European Russia | | 28.5 | |

\* I have not included rates for children aged one to five, but their mortality rates in Soligalich and Chukhloma were very close to the average for the province.
\*\* The author gives no average for rural areas in these years, so I have totaled the figures provided for all districts, then divided by twelve. He used a different method to arrive at his figures for 1891–5 and 1896–1900.
*Sources*: Frenkel', "Osnovnye pokazateli," 78–83; for Iaroslavl' and Tver', the figures are drawn from *Obshchestvennoe i chastnoe prizrenie v Rossii* (St. Petersburg, 1907), 294, 296. The time frame is 1895–9. This source cites slightly lower rates of infant mortality for Soligalich and Chukhloma and slightly higher rates for Kostroma as a whole (27.1, 27.4, and 32.6, respectively.)

At the same time, babies born to the wives of migrants from outmigratory Kostroma and some districts of Iaroslavl' stood a somewhat better chance of surviving infancy than infants born elsewhere in rural Russia (see Table 2.5). Infant mortality was a scourge of rural Russia: From one-fourth to one-third of infants perished before the age of one. Historians have attributed the high rates to the illiteracy and cultural backwardness that led peasants to cling to harmful health practices and to the importance of the woman's role as worker, which led women to neglect their infants.[40] However, the comparatively low infant mortality rates of Soligalich and Chukhloma, Kostroma, and much of rural Iaroslavl' suggest that additional factors should be

40 Nancy Frieden, "Child Care: Medical Reform in a Traditionalist Culture," in David Ransel, ed., *The Family in Imperial Russia*, 236–8; David Ransel, "Infant-Care Cultures," 113–32. *Obshchestvennoe i chastnoe prizrenie v Rossii* (St. Petersburg, 1907), 286–95, gives infant mortality rates at the end of the nineteenth century.

considered. In these areas, as elsewhere in rural Russia, peasant mothers did not tend carefully infants they bore in the summer months. Indeed, pressed to the limit, they were likely to be even more negligent. They either swaddled their infants and hung them on trees, or left them beneath a canopy in the fields, breastfeeding them in spare moments. More dangerously, they put them in the care of older children or the elderly who relied upon the *soska*, a pacifier made of a rag filled with chewed bread or gruel.[41] But the seasonal pattern of childbirth, so hard on the mothers physically, meant that a higher proportion of infants in Soligalich and Chukhloma than elsewhere were born after the harvest season and so avoided these practices during their tender early months.[42]

The infant mortality rates of Soligalich, Chukhloma, and parts of Iaroslavl' also suggest a connection between the well-being of mother and child. In areas where outmigration raised the standard of living, pregnant and nursing mothers ate better. Observers of peasant life were virtually unanimous in praising the positive effects of migration on life in these villages. Peasants not only used dishes made of pottery rather than wooden bowls and lighted their rooms with candles instead of burning a wooden splinter, but they consumed more meat as well.[43] The relative well-being observed in Soligalich and Chukhloma before the emancipation continued into the decades that followed. In 1880, a correspondent for the *Kostroma Provincial Gazette* wrote from Soligalich: "In the past twenty years, the level of well-being of the local population has risen to such an extent that people of earlier times simply would not recognize peasant life," and as evidence of this he pointed to houses that looked better and were kept more neatly, the widespread consumption of tea, and the women who wore wool and silk dresses on special occasions.[44] Later reports reaffirm this positive tone and for a far more extensive area. Peasant diet had become more nourishing, clothing and footwear more stylish, and houses more spacious and noticeably cleaner and neater. "Each peasant woman washes her hut once and sometimes twice a week without fail. Peasants no longer sleep on the stove or on planking between the stove and the ceiling, as the agricultural population does, but in separate beds with cotton curtains."[45] While such glowing descriptions should

41  *Obshchestvennoe i chastnoe prizrenie*, 273; Ransel, "Infant-Care Cultures," 118–19.
42  In 1895, 428 of every 1,000 babies in Soligalich and Chukhloma were born between September and December, by comparison with 343 of every 1,000 in rural Russia as a whole.
43  Zhbankov, "K voprosu," 56–7.
44  "Iz Kostromskoi volosti Soligalichskago uezda," *Kostromskie gubernskie vedomosti*, no. 37 (1880): 213.
45  Semenov, ed., *Rossiia*, 1: 103; see also *Otkhozhie promysly*, 57.

be treated with caution, the reports of better hygiene are indirectly confirmed by lowered infant mortality rates.

Women's comparatively high cultural level may also have played a role
in preserving infant life. Outmigration served to foster peasant women's
connection to a larger world. Zhbankov reported that the postal station of
Kartsov, which served five cantons of Soligalich province, processed 12,954
pieces of personal mail in 1883 alone – close to one letter per person.[46]
Literacy was important to the woman who married a migrant. She needed to
correspond with her husband about domestic matters, about money and
household needs. If she could neither read nor write, she would have to
depend on someone else to write for her, and if she did, the writer would
learn about her family's affairs.[47] Literacy also helped a woman to deal with
local authorities, to run her household, and to fulfill other responsibilities in
her husband's absence, such as renting out land and hiring workers. In areas
with substantial outmigration, parents increasingly recognized the need to
educate their daughters and were willing to send them to school. In 1867, a
higher proportion of girls attended primary school in Chukhloma and
Soligalich than anywhere else in Kostroma. In Chukhloma, there were 35
girls for every 100 boys attending primary school and 23.3 per 100 in
Soligalich, as compared to 16.7 per 100 in Kostroma as a whole.[48] And even
when parents kept girls home or took them from school to care for infants
and toddlers, literate brothers and fathers, or literate spinsters and widows,
would sometimes give them lessons. Between the emancipation and the
census of 1897, the literacy of the women of Soligalich, Chukhloma, and
Galich rose noticeably, and Iaroslavl' boasted the highest female literacy
rates of any province in European Russia. In general, women's literacy rates
in provinces with substantial male outmigration to the cities far exceeded
rates in primarily agricultural regions (see Table 2.6). Comparatively low
infant mortality rates and high literacy rates can be read as evidence of
peasant women's well-being.

Men's migration improved peasant women's position in less measurable
ways, too. Marriage to a migrant gave women greater control over their own
lives, as well as a measure of dignity that led contemporary observers to
distinguish them sharply from their sisters in more purely agricultural areas.

---

46  Zhbankov, Bab'ia, 98–9.
47  This point is made in Ia. Kuznetsov, "O prichinakh slabago poseshcheniia shkol devochkami
    vo Vladimirskoi gubernii," Vestnik Vladimirskago gubernskago zemstva, no. 23–4 (1905): 120.
48  "Statisticheskoe obozrenie Kostromskoi gubernii na osnovanii perepisi 1867 goda," in
    Statisticheskii vremennik Rossiiskoi imperii, II, vyp. 1 (St. Petersburg, 1871), 236.

Table 2.6. *Percentage of literate peasants by age group, 1897*

| Place | Men | Women | | |
|---|---|---|---|---|
| | | All | 10–19 | 20–29 |
| Kostroma Province | 36.0 | 9.3 | 20.8 | 15.2 |
| Galich | 41.7 | 12.9 | 31.2 | 22.3 |
| Soligalich | 41.0 | 12.3 | 31.2 | 22.3 |
| Chukhloma | 50.0 | 21.7 | 46.4 | 36.7 |
| Tver' | 36.7 | 8.1 | 21.8 | 11.8 |
| Iaroslavl' | 48.9 | 21.6 | 46.8 | 34.1 |
| Rural Russia | 25.2 | 9.8 | 17.1 | 14.7 |

*Source: Pervaia vseobshchaia perepis' naseleniia Rossiiskoi imperii, 1897*, 89 vols. (St. Petersburg, 1897–1905), vols. 18, 43, 50.

The wife's contribution in kind was essential, and the complementarity of roles and mutual dependence served to make marriage more of a partnership. Especially in households where all the men were absent in the summertime, men had to depend completely on women to maintain the agricultural economy. While fifty-three of the sixty-two households in the small sample from Chukhloma held land, an adult (over sixteen) male was present in only twenty-two of them year-round. Not only did the men in the remaining thirty-one households depend completely on women; husbands were not on hand to "instruct" their wives during much of the year. Especially if she was the wife of a household head, a married woman was on her own.

As a result, wives of migrant men conducted themselves more independently. By contrast with the "oppressed pariahs of the black earth regions, who are frightened of saying a word in the presence of their master," the women of areas with substantial male outmigration tended to be independent, self-reliant, and self-assured, and to know "the value of their labor and themselves."[49] In men's absence, women worked harder, but breathed more freely. Evidence from a variety of sources suggests that physical violence by

49 Zhbankov, *Bab'ia*, 68–9.

men against women was comparatively rare in the peasant marriages of
Soligalich and Chukhloma. The folk songs Zhbankov recorded serve as
one example: Although the picture they portray of the relations between the
sexes is rarely happy, it is almost never brutal. In Zhbankov's words: "In the
songs, there are no complaints about cruel treatment or beatings, while songs
from the more remote 'uncultured' locales are filled with such complaints."[50]
Elsewhere, too, migrant men were far less likely to brutalize their wives. In
neighboring Galich, all "industrious Petersburgers (*ispravnye Pitershchiki*)
spoiled their wives a lot," mistreating them only when drunk and regretting
it afterwards.[51] *Volost'* courts in Iaroslavl' judged harshly husbands who
beat their wives. At the end of the nineteenth century, observers from the
province noted that outmigration had led to a decline in the authority of
husband over wife: One could increasingly encounter wives who were "completely the equals" of their husbands.[52] In Kaliazin district, Tver', a *zemstvo*
correspondent wrote approvingly that as a result of men's migration and
women's assumption of men's responsibilities, " 'women's moans' resound
far less often than in other places; instead, women are often very important
in the family."[53] Migration shifted the balance in the relations between
the sexes, strengthening women's position in both the family and the
community.

The unusually high number of widows also increased women's voice in
community affairs. Apparently, migratory men did not benefit equally from
the comparative well-being their wages created. Like other workers in St.
Petersburg, migrants from Soligalich and Chukhloma labored long hours,
and in order to save money to send home they lived crowded together in
damp and dingy rooms and ate poorly. As a result, many died prematurely;
this was especially true of painters, whose susceptibility to tuberculosis was
unusually high because they inhaled paint fumes.[54] In 1897, the proportion
of widows between the ages of thirty and fifty in Soligalich and Chukhloma
was 14.3 percent and 18.2 percent, respectively, as compared to 9.8 percent
in the province as a whole. In Zhbankov's household sample there were 26
widows, ranging in age from twenty-two to one hundred, and only 2 widowers.[55] A participant in the Ninth Annual Congress of Kostroma Physicians in

50 Ibid., 119.     51 Tenishev archive, op. 1, delo 588, 22.
52 Ibid., delo 1781, 15; see also delo 1832, 10–11 (Iaroslavl', Iaroslavl'); C.P. Nikonov and
   E.I. Iakushkin, *Grazhdanskoe pravo po resheniiam Krestobogorodskago volostnago suda* (Iaroslavl',
   1902), 171–2.
53 *Sbornik statisticheskikh svedenii po Tverskoi gubernii*, 10 vols. (Tver', 1885–96), 5: 36–7.
54 *Trudy IX gubernskago s"ezda vrachei Kostromskoi gubernii* (Kostroma, 1905), vyp. 2, 28.
55 Zhbankov, *Bab'ia*, 103–10.

1906 reported that whereas one would expect around 120 old women for every 100 old men, in Soligalich and Chukhloma, for every 100 old men "there are 212 and even 286 old women."[56] A high proportion of migrants from Iaroslavl' engaged in comparatively well-paying and healthy work, like trading, and as a result, they lived longer than migrants from Soligalich and Chukhloma: In Iaroslavl' province, 11.5 percent of peasant women between thirty and fifty had lost their husbands. The proportion of widows was nevertheless higher than in areas where the rates of male migration remained low. Widows, especially older widows with several children, were likely to remain widows and to head their own households. Of the fifty-three households with land in Zhbankov's sample, sixteen (close to a third) were headed by widows over the age of forty-five.

Their importance in the household and numerical preponderance in the village won women in some outmigratory areas a growing voice in village self-government. In 1888, the District Committee on Peasant Affairs of Myshkin district, Iaroslavl' province, requested permission to allow women working land as heads of households to have a voice in the *skhod*, the organ of village self-government. Women's participation is necessary, the committee explained to the Iaroslavl' Provincial Committee on Peasant Affairs, because a substantial number of women in the district till the land independently, exercising the right of a head of houschold (*domokhoziaika*) to land, and paying the fiscal obligations on land in the same way male heads of households did. Moreover, the Committee argued, so many male household heads had migrated to earn money elsewhere that unless women participated, there would be no quorum for decision making in the *skhod*. The Provincial Committee rejected the request, citing as the reason its fear that the *skhod* would soon become dominated by women. This, its members claimed, would violate the law. But in 1890 the State Senate, Russia's highest judicial body, overruled the Provincial Committee. Women heads of households, the Senate resolved, have the right to an equal vote with men in the village *skhod*.[57] By the second half of the 1890s, there were reports of women exercising that right in several of the regions with sizable male outmigration. In Iaroslavl', women's voice in the *skhod* was limited to the allocation of land and fiscal obligations, but in some villages of Vladimir, Tver', and Kostroma provinces, women took part fully both as independent household heads (i.e., widows)

56  *Trudy IX gubernskago s"ezda vrachei*, vyp. 2, 28. In Chukhloma in 1897, there were 204 women to every 100 men over fifty; in Soligalich, 164 women to every 100 men.
57  I. Danilov, ed., *Sbornik reshenii pravitel'stvyuiushchago senata po krest'ianskim delam, 1890–1898* (St. Petersburg, 1898), 1–2.

and as substitutes for absent men. Women's new role in village affairs was based on their vital contribution to the village economy. As one village correspondent explained it, "women's vote is necessary, because men are absent, and it is just, because women do all the work."[58]

It was primarily older women, such as widowed heads of households or the wives of absent male household heads, who benefited from this enhanced authority. The position of younger women, especially in the complex family household, was more ambiguous. In the absence of her husband, her primary protector, the young wife became more vulnerable to abuse by her in-laws. The extremes of abuse that might occur in a husband's absence emerge in a case that came to the attention of the Holy Synod in 1882. The case involved *snokhachestvo*, the sexual relations of father-in-law and daughter-in-law. The plaintiff was a peasant from Vladimir, a man literate enough to compose his letter himself. According to his account, he had lived with his bride a mere two months after his marriage in 1869, and then his father sent him off to St. Petersburg to work as a coachman (*"Po vole roditelia,"* "by my father's will," is how he put the reason for his departure). Sometime thereafter, the father seduced the bride. The migrant learned about it from his wife, who explained her sexual submission in terms of his father's brutal treatment of her and her own desperate position. Without her husband there to protect her, she claimed, she had no other choice but to flee without a passport or to take her own life. During the proceedings, she gave every evidence of wanting to escape from her situation, pleading either that the husband come home or that she go to live with him in the city. Nevertheless, despite his wife's helpless position and the obvious culpability of his father, it was his wife, not his father, whom the migrant was more inclined to blame. She had complained to no one about her father-in-law's advances, so her submission must have been voluntary, he insisted in his plea for divorce on the grounds of his wife's adultery.[59]

In this instance, when a man's loyalty to his father conflicted with his loyalty to his wife, loyalty to the father triumphed. But that was not

---

58 *Svod zakliuchenii gubernskikh soveshchanii po voprosam otnosiashchimsia k peresmotru zakonodatel'stva o krest'ianakh* (St. Petersburg, 1897), 1:242–6, 252–3, 267, 274. See also Semenov, ed., *Rossiia*, 1:110; Zhbankov, *Bab'ia*, 69. In Peshekon'e district, Iaroslavl', women attended the district assembly as well, and without having to don a man's hat, as apparently was the custom elsewhere (Tenishev archive, op. 1, delo 1788, 27).

59 He did not get the divorce. See TsGIA SSSR, fond 796, op. 163, I stol, IV otd., ed. kh. 1819. A virtually identical account can be found in fond 1412, op. 223, delo 124, although in this case, the wife resisted her father-in-law's overtures. For another attempt at *snokhachestvo* in a son's absence, see op. 189, II stol, IV otd., ed. kh. 5507.

inevitably the outcome, especially as the years of serfdom receded and the young became increasingly self-assertive.[60] The wage that husbands earned independently put discontented wives in a stronger position to instigate household divisions, thus reducing their tolerance for abuse. The desire to keep the daughter-in-law in her place sometimes led the *bol'shak* to discourage his son from paying special attention to his wife, and even to forbid the son to correspond directly with her.[61] But if the young bride launched a struggle with her in-laws, the migrant would often take her side, sending her money secretly to store in her trunk for the future.[62] Nineteenth-century observers frequently accused young brides of taking advantage of their husbands' affection to induce a separation from the complex family household.[63] In that sense, men's migration could exacerbate tensions in the complex family household by increasing the economic independence of the young.

Migration could also create tensions between husbands and wives by corroding marital as well as family ties. Infidelity became more common, and by wives as well as husbands. Dmitrii Zhbankov, the indefatigable chronicler of Kostroma province, claimed personally to have observed twenty-two cases of illegal cohabitation in Chukhloma and Soligalich districts. Distance and the very different lives that men and women led sometimes outweighed the interdependence that linked them. "There was no intimacy" between his peasant mother and his migrant father, remembered the son of a worker at the Guzhon factory in Moscow.[64] Men's lengthy absences were especially hard on young wives: Time and children had not yet cemented ties between the couple, and young wives were the most sexually needy, according to peasant belief. They found it hard to endure long periods without a man.[65] One case of wifely infidelity from Chukhloma district wound up in civil court. The accused, Sidorova, had rarely seen her husband since their wedding

---

60 On youthful self-assertiveness, see Stephen Frank, " 'Simple Folk, Savage Customs?' Youth, Sociability, and the Dynamics of Culture in Rural Russia, 1856–1914," *Journal of Social History* 25, no. 4 (Summer 1992): 711–35.

61 Anokhina and Shmeleva, *Kul'tura i byt*, 175; Tenishev archive, op. 1, delo 618, 6 (Soligalich, Kostroma).

62 *Sbornik statisticheskikh svedenii po Tverskoi gubernii*, 5:36.

63 See, for example, the comments cited in Cathy Frierson, "Razdel: The Peasant Family Divided," *Russian Review* 46, no. 1 (Jan. 1987): 46–9.

64 TsGAOR SSSR, fond 7952, op. 3, delo 273, 57–9.

65 Tenishev archive, op. 1, delo 489, 51–2 (Zhizdra, Kaluga); delo 1767, 31 (Peshekhon'e, Iaroslavl'). I stress peasant belief here because it seems necessary to underscore the cultural construction of sexuality. In the contemporary United States, it is generally believed that women reach their sexual peak in their thirties, long past their peak period according to the Russian peasantry.

in 1861, twelve years earlier. When she bore a child by another man, terror of what her husband might do led her to murder it.[66] Sidorova's murderous terror is understandable: Villagers roundly condemned women's adulterous behavior and turned a blind eye to the brutal beatings it provoked.

A husband's lengthy absence, however, might reduce a wife's culpability. Wayward wives of migrant peasants often appealed to beliefs about women's sexuality to explain their behavior. Paraskeva Komarova, a peasant from Danilov district, Iaroslavl', claimed that her "youth" was to blame for her illicit pregnancy. Her husband had left for St. Petersburg shortly after their marriage in 1863, and during his two-year absence she had taken up with another man.[67] Anna Voronina used much the same language. A peasant from Moscow, Anna had married Mikhail Voronin, a peasant from Tver', in 1860. Shortly after the wedding, he left her in his father's house and went off to Moscow. Rumor soon reached him that she was carrying on with other men. Living apart from her husband, she had been unable to muster the strength to keep from having adulterous relations with other men, she would subsequently say, referring not only to the overwhelming nature of her sexual needs but also to her womanly weakness, which required a husband's discipline and control.[68]

Peasants in outmigratory areas sometimes found such explanations compelling. While they would never condone a woman's adulterous behavior, their beliefs about women's unruly nature and the need for male supervision often made them more understanding of it. For example, peasants were often tolerant of soldiers' wives (soldatki) who became involved with other men during their husbands' absences. A former soldier in Anton Chekhov's tale "Peasant Women" explained his wayward wife's behavior in these words: "She's a soldier's wife. Young women behave like that – they find it hard to keep to themselves. She's not the first and she won't be the last." Ethnographic reports from parts of rural Russia suggest similar, relatively tolerant attitudes to soldatki.[69] From the peasant perspective, the situation of young wives of migrants who remained away for long periods probably resembled the soldatka's. Sidorova's husband, for example, proved understanding of his adulterous and murderous wife and treated her "with great compassion."

66  Sudebnyi vestnik, no. 14 (1873): 4.
67  TsGIA SSSR fond 796, op. 152, I stol, IV otd., ed. kh. 526.
68  Ibid., op. 155, I stol, IV otd., ed. kh. 435, 1–3. See also op. 189, I stol, IV otd., ed. kh. 4477; op. 197, I stol, IV otd., ed. kh. 2111.
69  Anton Chekhov, "Peasant Women," in The Fiancee and Other Stories (Harmondsworth, England, 1986), 68. For the reports of correspondents, see Tenishev archive, op. 1, delo 59, 7 (Shuia, Vladimir); delo 1439, 13 (Egor'ev, Riazan); delo 1465, 42–3 (Skopin, Riazan).

As an observer of peasant life put it: "Men who've spent time in the cities . . . are not especially cruel. Knowing their own sins, they are more willing to forgive their wives."[70]

Fellow villagers could be forgiving too. Witnesses in divorce suits brought by migrant husbands were sometimes quite measured in their attitudes toward adulterous wives. When Vasilii Komarov sued his wife, Praskovia, for adultery in 1871, peasant witnesses found him to be at least as culpable as she. During his prolonged absence following their marriage in 1863, his wife conceived and bore a child. Nevertheless, fellow villagers testified that they had noticed nothing wrong with Praskovia's behavior apart from the fact that she bore the illegitimate child. No one denied the illegitimate birth. He, on the other hand, had frequently beaten his wife during his visits to the village. Betraying the most intimate knowledge of the couple's relationship, witnesses pointed out that he had ceased to have "marital relations" with her altogether.[71] Although the witnesses never said so explicitly, their testimony clearly implied that by treating her with unnecessary brutality and refusing to sleep with her, he was responsible for her behavior.

Witnesses in the divorce suit of Ivan Lukianov were likewise more sympathetic to the wife. Ivan and Ekaterina, peasants from Tula, had been married in 1890. She lived in the village, running the household and farm that he had inherited from his parents, while he held a steady job in St. Petersburg. He accused her of carrying on in his absence and of bearing an illegitimate child. Without disputing Ekaterina's adultery, one witness noted that in every other respect, her behavior conformed to peasant ideals: Her conduct was always "good and modest" and she had a "mild and compliant" character. Ivan, by contrast, violated community norms in many respects. He was impudent, passionate, and vicious, and neither sober nor moral. In a tone of condemnation that survives even the style of the Synod's scribe, the witness noted that Ivan had left the village soon after his marriage and remained away for two years without sending any money home to maintain his household. Evidently, Ivan's failure to behave properly and to pay his taxes and Ekaterina's otherwise exemplary conduct and success in running her household outweighed patriarchal attitudes toward female chastity.[72]

In both these cases, witnesses manifest a kind of ambivalence toward

---

70  *Sudebnyi vestnik*, no. 14 (1873): 4. A similar case, from Belev district, Tula, was reported in *Sudebnyi vestnik*, no. 167 (1868). For the quote on men's tolerance, see A.A. Titov, *Iuridicheskie obychai sela Nikola-Perevoz, Sulostskoi volosti, Rostovskago uezda* (Iaroslavl', 1888), 43.

71  TsGIA SSSR, fond 796, op. 152, I stol, IV otd., ed. kh. 526, 4.

72  Ibid., op. 189, I stol, IV otd., ed. kh. 4333, 2–3.

urban life. Living in the city changed men and might undermine their loyalty to the village, the testimony implies. These feelings emerge far more explicitly in a divorce case from Tver'. Even more than the preceeding one, this case indicates the extent to which respect for a good and hardworking *khoziaika* could outweigh concerns about her morality in outmigratory areas where so much depended on the woman. The plaintiff in this case was Nikolai Pavlov, a peasant from a village in Zubtsov district. Shortly after his marriage in 1886 to Anna, a peasant from the neighboring district of Starits, his domestic circumstances forced him to leave to seek work in St. Petersburg. During his unbroken absence of several years, Anna began to spend time with other men and, eventually, she bore an illegitimate child. No one who testified in the divorce suit denied these basic facts, not even Anna herself. Nevertheless, every witness whom Nikolai summoned on his own behalf was reluctant to accuse Anna of wrongdoing. Lavrentii Vasiliev, the village elder, refused to say anything either good or bad about her behavior. Maria Ivanova, another villager, testified that although Anna had borne a child by someone other than her husband, she was a hardworking woman and her behavior was good. Anna lives at home and labors, testified another witness. Anna works more than most men, reported a third. Although Nikolai apparently sent money home regularly, if the villagers condemned anyone, they condemned him. Their statements reveal an element of resentment against his neglect not only of his wife but also of his village. Pavlov returned to the village very rarely, observed the elder, and once he did not return for three years. Although he had come home twice in the preceeding year, he did not remain for long. "Nikolai Pavlov lives in the city of St. Petersburg and if he comes home, it is only to bring a suit against his wife," noted another witness, in an even more pointed reference to Nikolai's negligent ways. Yet another drew explicitly the connection between Anna's "fall" and her husband's behavior that was implicit in others' testimony: "Anna Pavlova once behaved honorably (*chestno*), but because of her husband's extended absence, she fell into sin."[73] Oblivious to the extenuating circumstances that preoccupied these villagers, the church granted Nikolai a divorce in 1905.

It would be mistaken to conclude from this that villagers found it "completely normal and not at all reprehensible for a peasant woman to take a lover in a husband's absence." More flexible attitudes demonstrate neither acceptance of women's adultery nor frequency of adulterous behavior. The double standard continued to prevail in migrant peasant villages, if in rather less harsh a form. Fear of her husband's reaction to her adultery led the

73 Ibid., ed. kh. 4477, 1–7.

terrified Sidorova to infanticide; fear restrained other women, too. So did their lack of opportunity, their physical exhaustion, and perhaps a greater degree of loyalty and a more romantic attitude toward marriage. Whatever the reasons, most wives remained faithful to migrant husbands. In the words of Sergei Derunov, a peasant from Iaroslavl', "Despite the long absence of their husbands, wives rarely became 'spoiled.' "[74]

All commentators agree that while women strayed, they strayed less frequently than their absent husbands.[75] It was far easier for a husband to keep tabs on his wife's behavior in the village than for a wife to know how her husband behaved in the relative anonymity of the city. If the husband continued to send money home regularly, she might be inclined to overlook a fleeting liaison, that is, if she had even learned of it.[76] But if a man developed a more enduring attachment to another woman, it was a serious matter, especially if it led the husband to abandon his village wife. The link marriage forged between village and city was especially fragile when sons had been married by the will of their parents. Ivan Stepanov's story provides a case in point. Ivan, a peasant from Volokolamsk, Moscow, was a textile worker at the Ganshin factory in Moscow, where he lived with Evfrosiniia Andreeva, whom he hoped to marry. But his parents refused to permit it. Instead, they married him to Daria, a village woman, in 1899. Ivan soon left her, refused to have anything to do with her, and resumed his cohabitation with Evfrosiniia.[77]

Life became hard for the abandoned wife. Her in-laws were likely to find her at fault for their son's defection and to abuse her. They might load her with extra work, or even eject her from their household altogether. If she had no children, she could either return to her parents or hire herself out as an agricultural laborer. A woman with children was in the most difficult position.[78] Ivan's abandoned wife, Daria, eventually sued for divorce on the grounds of abandonment. But it was rare for a peasant woman to have the

74 Quote on acceptance of women's infidelity is from Praskov'ia Tarnovskaia, *Zhenshchiny-ubiitsy* (St. Petersburg, 1902), 207; Sergei Ia. Derunov, "Poshekhonskie portnye," *Vestnik Iaroslavskago zemstva*, no. 95–6 (May–June 1880): 20.

75 Even wives accused of adultery in their husbands' absence often brought countersuits for adultery. For example, see TsGIA SSSR, fond 796, op. 199, I stol, IV otd., ed. kh. 803; 853; II stol, IV otd., ed. kh. 140, 3–4; 737, 5.

76 Not every woman did. For example, two and a half years after her marriage, the twenty-one-year-old Liubov Ukhova, a peasant from Uglich, Iaroslavl', sued her husband for adultery with a prostitute (TsGIA SSSR, fond 796, op. 199, I stol, IV otd., ed. kh. 1144).

77 Ibid., II stol, IV otd., ed. kh. 415, 1. See also ed. kh. 140 and TsGIAgM, fond 203, op. 412, 1 (1905).

78 Zhbankov, *Bab'ia*, 91–2; Tenishev archive, op. 1, delo 5, 21 (Vladimir Vladimir); delo 589, 20 (Galich, Kostroma).

resolve or the means for such an action. More commonly, the wife would turn for help to the *volost'* court or *volost'* administration. The *volost'* administration, like the head of a household, retained the right to revoke or withhold a migrant's passport and to command his return to the village. Officials were prepared to use their authority on behalf of a wife, but only if she could prove that her husband had neglected his fiscal obligations.

One such case came before a *volost'* court in Vladimir province in 1871. Although it occurred relatively early in the period under study, the circumstances it reflects – the hardships faced by an abandoned wife, the limited authority she could exercise over her husband – did not change much during the decades that followed. The husband had long worked in St. Petersburg and had grown estranged from his wife and slow to pay his fiscal obligations. As a result of these tardy payments, every year the community inventoried the wife's belongings and prepared to sell her cow. The woman's suffering was emotional as much as economic. The husband stayed with someone else during his periodic visits to the village to renew his passport. Not once had he come to see her in the past six years, the wife complained. Moreover, he had alienated the affections of their children, a twenty-two-year-old son and twelve-year-old daughter who lived with him in the city. They shared his contempt for rural ways and, evidently, for their mother too. The children no longer regarded her as their mother, she said, and this caused her great sorrow and pain. Although she suffered from the husband's neglect, so long as he paid his taxes she was powerless to command his presence in the village. Instead, she requested that the court make him pay his obligations on time. She also asked that the son send her thirty-two rubles a year to help support her and to hire someone to work the land. But what she really wanted was to undo the process of urbanization that her husband had initiated and to force the son to return to the village and to take up peasant work. In her words: "It is necessary for a young man to grow accustomed to peasant labor and to care for his parent." But she lacked the authority to overrule her husband's will.[79]

Tensions between migratory husbands and village wives were rooted in the different worlds that men and women inhabited. By contrast with their

---

79 *Trudy komissii po preobrazovaniiu volostnykh sudov*, 7 vols. (St. Petersburg, 1874), 2: 268–9. See also II: 575, 618; III: 95. Widows sometimes had more power over their sons. For example, the widowed mother of a factory worker in the industrial town of Ivanovo succeeded in getting her unwilling son to leave his job and return to the village by threatening to get his passport revoked and have him beaten. Nikifor Makhov, *Zhizn' minuvshaia* (Ivanovo, 1939), 34.

migrant husbands, fathers, and brothers, who lived in the city and worked for wages, the women who remained in the village lived like peasants and depended on the land. While some might labor at home for the market, few had extended experience of urban life. Women who migrated were usually spinsters or childless widows who left the land for good. And while the proportion of women migrants would grow, they remained a small minority of the female population in areas such as Soligalich and Chukhloma, and much of Iaroslavl'. Most women followed in the footsteps of their mothers, marrying migrants, remaining in the village, and maintaining the family economy.

Despite the occasional tensions between town and country and the breakdown of relationships between particular husbands and wives, the urban-rural connection proved tenacious. There were many reasons for this tenacity. Some, such as traditions and a feeling for the land, are hard to measure. Others, for example the economic advantages of continuing outmigration, are much easier to determine. Men's wage levels meant that a wife and children in the village were the only family most men could afford. Unless he worked as a tradesman or contractor, in the 1880s the maximum a migrant from Soligalich and Chukhloma could hope to earn was between 100 and 300 rubles a year, and the higher amount could be attained only if a migrant became a highly qualified metalworker or blacksmith. A painter, working from March to November, earned between 80 and 180 rubles a year; a carpenter, working from April to November, earned between 75 and 240 rubles. In Zhbankov's time, the average wage of a migrant from Soligalich was around 125 rubles, from Chukhloma, around 175 rubles.[80] These wages had increased by the eve of World War I, reaching 241 rubles for a painter and 222 for a carpenter.[81] This was enough to rent a cot in a damp basement or a corner in a shared apartment, to buy a few presents for the folks at home, to contribute to the peasant economy, to visit the village occasionally, and to have a few drinks and a good time once in a while. But it was insufficient to raise a family decently in St. Petersburg.

According to a study conducted by S.N. Prokopovich in 1909, in order for a worker in St. Petersburg to marry and keep his wife with him, he had to earn between four hundred and six hundred rubles a year; only when his

---

80 I have taken these figures from *Trudy komissii po izsledovaniiu kustarnoi promyshlennosti*, vyp. 8 (1888–9), 228–31. Zhbankov's figures are considerably lower. D.N. Zhbankov, "O gorodskikh otkhozhikh zarabotkakh v Soligalichskom uezde, Kostromskoi gubernii," *Iuridicheskii vestnik* 22, no. 9 (Sept. 1890): 136–7.

81 Vladimirskii, *Otkhozhie*, 38–40.

wage exceeded six hundred rubles could he afford to educate his children. Prokopovich's calculations assume that only male heads of households contributed to the family income. According to him, men who earned less could marry only because they had an allotment in the village and a wife who would stay there, cultivate it, and raise the children. As will be shown in Chapter 7, it was rare for urban working-class families to depend entirely on the husband's wage. Nevertheless, he is correct that the expense of urban life kept many fully urbanized workers from marrying at all; it sent others who did marry into utter destitution. Men who maintained their village ties were in a far better position to have a family and to provide decently for their children than fully urbanized workers who earned a comparable wage or their peasant brothers who stayed at home.[82] This was especially true for seasonal workers such as those who derived from Soligalich and Chukhloma, but it was also the case with relatively poorly paid men from provinces such as Tver'. Even the Stolypin land reforms of 1906–7, aimed at breaking up the mir and creating a strong, independent capitalist peasantry, affected the provinces of the Central Industrial Region less than others.[83] To be sure, as subsequent chapters will show, in the years before World War I, enormous numbers of women and men flocked from these provinces to the cities, where some of them met and married; and some village couples pulled up stakes and settled in the city. But the Stolypin reforms did not really alter the migratory patterns discussed in this chapter. Until economic circumstances changed dramatically, outmigration and the bifurcated family would remain the most effective way for the majority of households in the Central Industrial Region to allocate their human resources. In fact, not even the Bolshevik revolution of 1917 altered the rhythm of outmigration. It ended only with the industrialization drive and the collectivization of agriculture in the 1930s, which finally broke the urban–rural connection.

As a family strategy, outmigration had a significant impact on others besides the migrant. It removed adult men from households for months and even years and left households made up of nuclear families and widows without a *bol'shak* altogether. In such cases, outmigration altered the patriarchal family and community patterns usually regarded as typical for the peasantry and provided some women with an unusual opportunity to be

82 S.N. Prokopovich, *Biudzhety Peterburgskikh rabochikh* (St. Petersburg, 1909), 26–9.
83 S.M. Dubrovskii, *Stolypinskaia zemel'naia reforma* (Moscow, 1963), 574–6; 582–4. Dorothy Atkinson, "The Statistics on the Russian Land Commune, 1905–1917," *Slavic Review* 32, no. 4 (Dec. 1973): 733–88, argues that even the relatively low figures that Dubrovskii cites are inflated.

their own mistresses, even as it added enormously to their labors. Outmigration reduced married women's fertility and the rate of infant mortality. It also raised the standard of living and women's level of literacy, and it altered consumption patterns in the direction of more urban ways. Whatever the disadvantages of marriage to a migrant in terms of women's additional burdens, in Soligalich and Chukhloma at least, women preferred a migrant to a man who stayed at home.

Still, in Soligalich and Chukhloma, and probably in other areas with comparable patterns, outmigration offered fundamentally different experiences to women and men. While men might return in winter months, they took no part in the agricultural labors of their wives; women, in turn, might visit the city, consume manufactured goods, and learn to read and write, but women's connection to a cash economy and the wider world mostly depended on men. Their disparate experiences made it likely that women's consciousness would be the more "conservative," that is, the more bound up with the familiar, the more resistant to rapid change. This, of course, is conventional wisdom. What the evidence in this chapter suggests, however, is that in areas with high levels of male migration, married women's conservatism was the result of their perfectly understandable efforts to hold on to a world that was not only familiar and secure but also, comparatively speaking, substantially under their control. It was not only the traditionalism of family and community and the requirements of the rural economy that kept women from leaving the village; to some extent, the constraints on women's migration would derive from women themselves.

# 3. Out to work

Russian peasant women were the most stable element in the village, nineteenth-century observers agreed. By contrast with the rural women of France, for example, who were more likely than their brothers to leave the village, Russian peasant women stayed at home. In the words of D.N. Zhbankov, "They cling to the family and to the land and need particularly unfavorable circumstances to compel them to move somewhere else."[1] Historians Leslie Page Moch and Louise Tilly have argued that it was the urban demand for labor that shaped patterns of migration and household labor allocation in France.[2] In the case of Russia, however, as in Portugal and parts of Africa and Asia, the village also shaped patterns of migration by constraining women's mobility.[3] Russian women were not free to leave the village whenever they chose. According to the law, if peasants wanted to leave their native districts, they had to have passports (*vid na zhitel'stvo*). To obtain one for herself, a single woman or widow required the permission of the *bol'shak* and/or the *volost'* elder; a married woman required the permission of her husband.

Although peasant women were denied direct access to the land, patriarchal attitudes and Russia's system of partible inheritance attached marriageable and married women to the village at least as firmly as men. Landholding

1 D.N. Zhbankov, "Otkhozhie promysly v Smolenskoi gubernii," *Smolenskii vestnik*, no. 81 (July 11, 1893): 2. For France, see Leslie Page Moch, *Paths to the City* (Beverly Hills, Calif., 1983), 142–3. Women also predominate in rural–urban migration in much of Latin America. See James Fawcett, Siew-Ean Khoo, and Peter Smith, "Urbanization, Migration, and the Status of Women," and Peter Smith, Siew-Ean Khoo, and Stella Go, "The Migration of Women to Cities: A Comparative Perspective," both in *Women in the Cities of Asia*, ed. James Fawcett, Siew-Ean Khoo, and Peter Smith (Boulder, Colo., 1984), 3–11; 15–32.
2 Leslie Page Moch and Louise Tilly, "Joining the Urban World: Occupation, Family, and Migration in Three French Cities," *Comparative Studies in Society and History* 27, no. 1 (Jan. 1985): 35; also, Moch, *Paths to the City*, 142–3.
3 Caroline Brettell, *Men Who Migrate, Women Who Wait: Population and History in a Portugese Parish* (Princeton, N.J., 1986), 136–7; Fawcett, Khoo, and Smith, eds., *Women in the Cities of Asia*, 49.

patterns assured that almost all peasant women married, and at a relatively early age. Families that needed extraagricultural income also required someone to stay at home to till their allotment and to look after the household and the children. It made economic sense that the woman remain close to home, because whatever work a woman engaged in (with the exception of prostitution, of which more in Chapter 6), she would earn less money than a man. But patriarchal attitudes reinforced (and occasionally replaced) economic calculations. Fathers, sons, and brothers considered it a "dishonor" to send their wives, daughters, or sisters to work alone and unsupervised in unfamiliar and far-off places.[4]

These concerns were particularly pressing in the case of marriageable women. Portuguese villagers' conviction that "young women who left their father's household would be led astray, and become 'used goods,' " was equally widespread in rural Russia.[5] Russian peasants feared the demoralizing effects of life outside the village (*na storone*) on the young of both sexes. Without parents and community to protect and restrain them, young people in cities or factory settlements might succumb to the many temptations. But migrant women on their own were in the greater danger, because peasants believed them to be less rational than men and more susceptible to their feelings. A woman, a young woman in particular, required the guiding hand of a man. Unlike the threats confronting men, the threats confronting migrant women bore an explicitly sexual character. As one Russian peasant put it: "Out in the world, a girl often falls despite herself. . . . A man finds a way to seduce her. He uses money, or presents, or various other things. But what means does a boy have to seduce a girl at home?"[6] A Russian peasant maiden who hoped to marry thought twice about migration. Thus, maintaining marriageable and married women in the village not only ensured the family economy, it also preserved the patriarchal peasant order by containing women's sexuality. As a result, the women who were most likely to leave were spinsters and widows, the most marginal members of the household and village.

Nevertheless, by the last decades of the nineteenth century, these longstanding patterns had slowly begun to break down in parts of rural

4  Quoted in M.I. Tugan-Baranovskii, *The Russian Factory in the Nineteenth Century* (Homewood, Ill., 1970), 408.
5  Brettell, *Men who Migrate*, 136; see also Fawcett, Khoo, and Smith, eds., *Women in the Cities of Asia*, 49.
6  Tenishev archive, op. 7, delo 719, 5 (Novgorod, Novgorod). For concerns about women's chastity, see also delo 1465, 42–3 (Skopin, Riazan); delo 1438, 15 (Egorev, Riazan); delo 1822, 33 (Borisogleb, Iaroslavl').

Fig. 3. Waiting for the train at a provincial railroad station, circa 1910. Note the homespun, village-style clothing of both women and men and the hair of the men, trimmed under a bowl. Cups and pots on the trunk, lower right, indicate that the women have just had their tea. (Courtesy of Lanier Rowan.)

Russia. The demographic and economic changes that prompted increasing numbers of peasant men to leave the village led more and more of their wives and, especially, daughters to depart as well. The growth of factory production in particular deprived women of the chance to earn money while remaining in the village. Factory or machine production either replaced many traditional crafts or reduced drastically the wages that people could earn by engaging in them. Household industries became subordinated to the rhythms and needs of factory production and household laborers became dependent on middlemen (more rarely, women) who claimed their share of the laborers' earnings.[7] Women never ceased to labor, but what they could earn by remaining on the land and working only within their households declined both absolutely and as a proportion of the household income.

7  This process is described in Rose Glickman, *Russian Factory Women: Workplace and Society, 1880–1914* (Berkeley, Calif., 1984), 31–52.

Table 3.1. *Ratio of women to men among peasants and peasant immigrants in Moscow and St. Petersburg*

| Moscow | | | St. Petersburg | | | |
|---|---|---|---|---|---|---|
| Year | Men | Women | Year | Men | Peasant Women | Immigrant Peasant Women |
| 1871 | 1000 | 394 | 1869 | 1000 | 310 | 300 |
| 1882 | 1000 | 483 | 1881 | 1000 | 385 | |
| 1902 | 1000 | 650 | 1890 | 1000 | 646 | 362 |
| | | | 1900 | 1000 | 667 | 368 |
| | | | 1910 | 1000 | 807 | 480 |

*Source*: Joseph Bradley, *Muzhik and Muscovite* (Berkeley, Calif., 1985), 34; *Perepis' Moskvy 1882 g.* (Moscow, 1885), 2: 11; Reginald Zelnik, *Labor and Society in Tsarist Russia* (Stanford, Calif., 1971), 224; *S.-Peterburg po perepisi 15 Dekabria 1881 g.* (St. Petersburg, 1883), 1, chast' 1, 245; *S.-Peterburg po perepisi 15 Dekabria 1890 g.* (St. Petersburg, 1891), chast' 1, vyp. 1, 84; *S.-Peterburg po perepisi 15 Dekabria 1900 g.* (Petrograd, 1903), chast' 1, vyp. 1, 168; *Petrograd po perepisi 15 Dekabria 1910 g.* (St. Petersburg, no year), chast' 1, 290.

Increasingly, the extra hands in a household were female as well as male. In the decades following the emancipation of the serfs, the number of women migrating from village to city increased even more rapidly than the number of men, although women's migration remained a fraction of men's right up to the outbreak of World War I (see Table 3.1). A decreasing proportion of these migrant women were spinsters and widows. By 1900, one-third of the peasant women in St. Petersburg were married; another 17.6 percent were marriageable women aged sixteen to twenty-five.[8]

This chapter will explore the causes and consequences of women's migration at the end of the nineteenth century and in the early twentieth, distinguishing where possible among marriageable women, married women, and spinsters and widows, the last category being comprised of women who often migrated for different reasons. Information on the number and proportion of women migrants is very difficult to obtain: *Zemstvo* statisticians who

8 *S.-Peterburg po perepisi 15 Dekabria 1900 goda*, fasc. 1 (St. Petersburg, 1903), 137–9. See also Judith Pallot, "Women's Domestic Industries in Moscow Province, 1880–1900," in *Russia's Women: Accommodation, Resistance, Transformation*, ed. Barbara Clements, Barbara Engel, and Christine Worobec (Berkeley, Calif., 1991), 171–7, 180.

meticulously counted the number of passports issued to peasant men often ignored almost entirely the comings and goings of peasant women,[9] rendering it all but impossible to draw a composite picture of women's migration from villages of the Central Industrial Region. The data we do have suggests it was highly uneven: Some provinces – Kaluga, for example – sent almost none of their women out to work, while considerable numbers left Moscow and Tver' by the early twentieth century (see Table 3.2). This chapter draws on statistical materials from Iaroslavl' and Tver', whose migration patterns were unusually well documented.[10] The two provinces contributed the greatest number of peasant migrants to the city of St. Petersburg and a smaller but still sizable number of the migrants to Moscow.

The economic profiles of the two provinces were sufficiently dissimilar to affect the character of women's migration. Of the two, Tver' was the poorer: Its soil was the less fertile, and it was by far the more heavily populated, with a population density that in the 1880s was twice the average for European Russia.[11] Local trades were lacking in some parts of the province (Zubtsov and Staritsa districts, in particular) and in others were insufficient to absorb all the extra hands. Moreover, work in the village often paid too little to make staying home worthwhile for able-bodied men and, increasingly, women as well. As a result, migration from Tver' increased rapidly in the decades following the emancipation. The number of peasants who went off to St. Petersburg almost doubled between 1869 and 1881, and it almost tripled between 1881 and 1900, growing from 66,000 to 172,300. By the turn of the century, close to a third of all the men in the province were migrants, as were almost 9 percent of the women (see Table 3.2).

Even working in St. Petersburg, migrant men usually contributed only marginally to the well-being of their villages, because the majority of them were unskilled laborers. No more than a third engaged in carpentry, stonemasonry, or boot and shoemaking, that is, in work that required some training; about 4 percent more were tradesmen. On the other hand, 15 percent of male migrants from Tver' were unskilled laborers (*chernorabochie*);

---

9  The figures cited in Svavitskaia's study of *zemstvo* census materials illustrate the relative inattention to women's migration: Z.M. Svavitskaia, *Zemskie podvornye perepisi 1880–1913, pouezdnye itogi* (Moscow, 1926).

10  Moscow and Vladimir are not as useful to study because of the high concentration of rural factories in the two provinces. Rural industry was relatively insignificant in Tver' and, outside of the cities of Rybinsk and Iaroslavl', in Iaroslavl' as well.

11  V.I. Pokrovskii, *Istoriko-statisticheskoe opisanie Tverskoi gubernii*, 3 vols. (Tver', 1879–82), 2: 109.

9.2 percent more worked in textile factories; and 9 percent were employed as servants. The rest engaged in a variety of other labor-intensive, poorly paid trades. In the words of a *zemstvo* correspondent, "In St. Petersburg, peasants from Tver' work as yardmen (*dvorniki*), coachmen, floorwashers, servants, ragpickers, garbagemen, and so forth. . . . They drive cockroaches from kitchens."[12] Much of this work paid poorly. In 1895, male migrants from Tver' province sent home, on the average, seventeen rubles ninety kopeks; in 1896, fourteen rubles, twenty-nine kopeks.[13]

In addition to the decline of cottage industry, men's meager earnings provided reason for growing numbers of women to leave the villages of Tver'. Unable to pay their fiscal obligations, still less to satisfy the need for cash to purchase consumer items, men were in a poor position to keep their women home. The proportion of women who migrated from Tver' province grew even more rapidly than the proportion of men who migrated. In 1890, there were 408 peasant women from Tver' for every 1,000 peasant men in the city of St. Petersburg. In 1900, there were 410 for every 1,000, and by 1910 there were 825 (see also Table 3.2).

On the whole, peasants in Iaroslavl' were considerably better off, and the relatively low rate of natural population increase helped to maintain their comparative well-being. In addition, the cities of Rybinsk and Iaroslavl' were major trade and industrial centers and provided employment for peasants in surrounding villages, as well as for migrants from other provinces, Tver' among them. The majority of the men who left Iaroslavl' chose the capital as their destination and pursued "the sort of trades that don't demand a lot of physical labor, but at the same time, pay well," in the words of an investigator for the Iaroslavl' *zemstvo*.[14] In the early twentieth century, close to one-third (31.9 percent) of male migrants were tradesmen. Another 17.4 percent engaged in some sort of artisanal labor requiring an apprenticeship, and 11.4 percent more worked in construction. Only about 3.8 percent of male migrants worked in factories, and most of these were employed within Iaroslavl' district, the most heavily industrialized in the province.[15] Altogether, over 60 percent of the men who migrated from Iaroslavl' engaged in trades that entailed training and/or a skill. They were more likely than migrants

12 *Sel'sko-khoziaistvennyi obzor Tverskoi gubernii za 1894* (Tver', 1895), 15–16.
13 *Statisticheskii ezhegodnik Tverskoi gubernii za 1897* (Tver', 1898), 34.
14 *Obzor Iaroslavskoi gubernii za 1891* (Iaroslavl', 1892), 6.
15 K. Vorob'ev, *Otkhozhie promysly krest'ianskago naseleniia Iaroslavskoi gubernii* (Iaroslavl', 1903), 13–15.

Table 3.2. *Outmigration of men and women*

Tver' men

| Outmigration from | 1880's* | | 1896 | | 1910 | | 1913 | |
|---|---|---|---|---|---|---|---|---|
| | Number | Percent | Number | Percent | Number | Percent | Number | Percent |
| Bezhets (1889) | 14,750 | 13.7 | 33,336 | 27.8 | 44,927 | 36.3 | 42,196 | 34.6 |
| Zubtsov (1887) | 10,916 | 22.6 | 17,911 | 34.4 | 21,012 | 39.6 | 21,073 | 38.9 |
| Staritsa (1886) | 17,630 | 26.7 | 30,456 | 40.7 | 37,501 | 49.2 | 35,828 | 46.8 |
| Tver Province | 108,877 | 14.6 | 258,221 | 30.4 | 272,703 | 33.7 | | |

## Tver' women

| Outmigration from | 1880 s* | | 1896 | | 1910 | | 1913 | |
|---|---|---|---|---|---|---|---|---|
| | Number | Percent | Number | Percent | Number | Percent | Number | Percent |
| Bezhets (1889) | 2,271 | 1.9 | 8,104 | 6.2 | 16,258 | 12.4 | 16,141 | 12.3 |
| Zubtsov (1887) | 1,652 | 3.2 | 7,268 | 11.2 | 6,933 | 12.4 | 6,743 | 11.4 |
| Staritsa (1886) | 2,381 | 3.3 | 9,487 | 11.7 | 9,551 | 11.3 | 10,883 | 12.8 |
| Tver Province | 27,528 | 3.3 | 82,521 | 8.9 | 101,191 | 11.1 | | |

* Bezhets, 1889; Zubtsov, 1887; Staritsa, 1886; Tver' as a whole, 1379.
Sources: Z.M. Svavitskaia, Zemskie podvornye perepisi 1880–1913, pouezdnye itogi (Moscow, 1926); Sel'sko–khoziaistvennyi obzor Tverskoi gubernii za 1896 g. (Tver', 1897); Statisticheskii ezhegodnik Tverskoi gubernii za 1910–11 (Tver', 1913).

from Tver' to become established, year-round workers, and a higher proportion of them took passports that allowed them to stay away a year or more.[16]
Their wages often added to the well-being of their households and contributed
to "repeasantization." Instead of whetting their taste for urban life, the
money enabled many to expand their holdings in the countryside. Proportionally more peasants in Iaroslavl' purchased land individually than anywhere
else in the Central Industrial Region. In 1905, 23 percent of peasants' holdings
in Iaroslavl' had been purchased by individuals, as compared to 15 percent
in Tver' and 14 percent in the Central Industrial Region as a whole.[17]

The economic differences between the two provinces influenced the character of women's migration. Judging by the St. Petersburg census, women's
migration from Iaroslavl' remained less substantial than it was from Tver':
In 1890, there were 291 peasant women for every 1,000 men from Iaroslavl'
province: in 1900 there were 319, and in 1910 there were 603. This was far
below the overall ratio of 807 peasant women for every 1,000 peasant men in
the city of St. Petersburg in 1910. At the turn of the century, about 7.5
percent of Iaroslavl' women left their villages on their own passports. The
professional and demographic profiles of the women from the two provinces
also differed. To be sure, only a tiny minority of the women from either
province plied trades that required skill or training, and those who did
learned the skills of their menfolk. Almost 6 percent of migrant Tver' women
worked as shoe or bootmakers. Most of them came from villages in Kaliazin
and Korcheva districts close to the footwear-producing town of Kimry, and
most had acquired their skills in their parents' households. Girls who trained
at home as well as girls who apprenticed formally acquired fewer skills than
boys. Girls began their apprenticeship between the ages of ten and twelve,
two years later than boys, and the training lasted a shorter period of time.[18]
As a result, most village women knew only how to prepare the leather or
assemble the materials, subsidiary work which earned them two rubles fifty
kopeks a week, while a master might earn up to five rubles. Wages were
better in St. Petersburg, where the demand for a woman's shoemaking skills
was sufficient to prompt employers to pay the cost of her travel to the city.[19]
About the same proportion (5.3 percent) of women migrants from Iaroslavl'

16  Dan Field, "The Province at the End of the Alphabet," unpublished paper presented at the
    AAASS convention, 1989, 13.
17  Ibid., 9.
18  Pokrovskii, *Istoriko-statisticheskoe opisanie*, 3: 157.
19  Lev Krylov, *Selo Troitskoe, chto v Viaznikakh Kaliazinskago uezda Tverskoi gubernii* (Tver',
    1905), 19.

were craftswomen. They worked in the tailoring trade and were employed by the fashionable shops of St. Petersburg. The numbers were growing. At the turn of the century, about a fifth of Iaroslavl' migrants in the tailoring trade were young apprentices, an increase over previous years.[20]

Skilled women remained a tiny minority, however. Most women migrants from Tver' and Iaroslavl' had nothing to sell but their labor, and they plied the unskilled trades that were typical for their sex. Still, the ways that women from the two provinces earned their livings differed. Almost 20 percent of migrant women from Tver' worked in factories, as compared to a tiny minority of women from Iaroslavl'. The largest proportion of migrant women from Iaroslavl' (58.5 percent) engaged in domestic service, almost double the proportion from Tver'. Tver' women were far more likely than women from Iaroslavl' to hire out as a group (artel), rather than individually, and to engage in backbreaking, dirty, poorly paid labor in other people's fields or in the peat bogs near Moscow. The differences remind us that compared to other positions available to unskilled women, domestic service might seem attractive. Whatever its disadvantages, it provided a roof over one's head, regular meals, and a steady income so long as the job lasted.[21] Most migrant women from Iaroslavl' stayed away year-round, whereas in the 1890s, almost a quarter of women migrants from Tver' left their villages only temporarily to labor for a season. Every spring, about two thousand women left the province on foot, in some cases walking over a hundred versts (about seventy-five miles) and then catching the train to St. Petersburg, where they hired out as artels to toil in gardens at the edges of the city. In the summer, their workday began at 3:30 or 4:00 A.M. and continued until 10:00 or 11:00 at night, with short breaks for meals and tea. In addition to their room (usually an unheated barn or shed) and board (watery gruel, potatoes, and cabbage), the women earned twenty rubles for the season in the 1890s. Many had already taken a portion of this money in advance, in order to pay their households' taxes. More than five hundred women left Zubtsov and Rzhev districts of Tver' to hire out in artels as peat cutters in the peat bogs near Moscow. For long days of working knee-deep in the bogs, the women earned four rubles a month with room and board, five rubles without it. Hundreds of women worked at brickmaking plants, recruited by forewomen who traveled to Tver' villages, many with money to bring workers to the city for the summer season. Women from Tver' tilled and harvested

---

20  *Otkhozhie promysly krest'ianskago naseleniia Iaroslavskoi gubernii* (Iaroslavl', 1907), 65–8 [hereafter *Otkhozhie promysly*].

21  The risks and rewards of domestic service will be discussed in Chapter 5.

the fields of peasant migrants from Iaroslavl'. And they traveled in artels southward, spreading out across Samara province to reap grain during the harvest season, or to repair peasant huts and to turn manure into briquettes for heating.[22]

These dissimilar employment profiles reflect the economic contrasts between the two provinces and the different trades plied by migrant men; they are also connected to differences in women's ages, marital status, and the duration of their migrant experience. Iaroslavl' peasants were in a better position to protect vulnerable women from the vagaries of the marketplace and from threats to their chastity. Young, marriageable women were less likely to leave Iaroslavl' than Tver' even after the 1890s, when the competition of factory production led most Iaroslavl' women to stop spinning and weaving flax for the market. In the early twentieth century, the average age of women migrants from Iaroslavl' was thirty-five. In St. Petersburg in 1900, only 19 percent of the Iaroslavl' women migrants were under twenty-one, as compared to 36.4 percent of all peasant women migrants; and 46 percent were aged between thirty and sixty, compared to 35.7 percent of all peasant women in the city. Women migrants from Iaroslavl' were older than the men: Thirty percent of the men were under twenty-one, and only 38.6 percent of them were between thirty and sixty. Almost a quarter of the women who left Iaroslavl' were widows. Another 36.4 percent were single, but at least a third of these were over twenty-five, old enough to be considered spinsters in peasant society. The rest were married. Close to three quarters of women migrants from Iaroslavl' chose an urban destination and they remained away over nine years on the average. In fact, a significant number of Iaroslavl's women migrants would never go back to their village. Among them were spinsters and widows who were unlikely to find a welcome back home, but their numbers also included women who chose to continue living and working in the city, such as tailors. Overwhelmingly young and single, the majority of women tailors from Iaroslavl' (86.6 percent) became fully urbanized craftswomen.[23]

Information on the age and marital status of women migrants from Tver' is more impressionistic. The St. Petersburg census of 1881, the only one to

22  For the trades of Iaroslavl' women, see Vorob'ev, *Otkhozhie*, pp. 28–33. On Tver', *Statisticheskii ezhegodnik Tverskoi gubernii za 1897*, 16–17; 31; *Statisticheskii ezhegodnik Tverskoi gubernii za 1901* (Tver', 1902), 10–11; I. Krasnoperov, "Zhenskie promysly Tverskoi gubernii," *Mir bozhii*, no. 2 (1898): 28–9; A. Katelin, "Brodiachaia Rus'," *Severnyi vestnik*, no. 4 (1894): 4–5. Description of the lives of garden workers derives from *Peterburgskii listok*, no. 85 (Mar. 1894): 3.
23  *Otkhozhie promysly*, 62–70.

list the age of peasants by their province of origin, indicates that at least for this early period, migrant women from Tver' were more likely than migrants from Iaroslavl' to be young and vulnerable: Of the women migrants from Tver', 11.3 percent were aged sixteen to twenty, but only 8.2 percent of the women from Iaroslavl' fell into the same category; 14.9 percent of the women from Tver' and 10.8 percent of those from Iaroslavl' were aged twenty-one to twenty-five. One *zemstvo* correspondent suggested that the proportion of the young among women migrants from Tver' was still greater and that peasants who left the family to earn money "were primarily the unmarried young, who sought to buy clothing and save money for their wedding and dowry."[24] In Tver' more than in Iaroslavl', the migration of marriageable women was related to changes in consumption patterns, as well as to the growing number of extra hands in the village and the reduction of opportunities to earn money there.

Women's clothing had long played a significant role in courtship. When a woman made with her own hands everything that she wore, her attire advertised her skill and ability to work, thereby demonstrating her attractiveness as a wife.[25] But in the decades following the emancipation, marriageable peasant women in outmigratory regions became enthusiastic consumers of urban-made goods, and the significance of their clothing changed. As early as the 1870s, peasant women in the villages of Tver' had taken to wearing colorful wool and silk dresses, expensive shawls, earrings, rings, belts, shoes, even hats on special occasions. Urban attire was becoming popular elsewhere as well. If indifference to fashion demonstrates an absence of individualistic striving to differentiate oneself, as Boris Mironov has argued, then these new consumption patterns suggest a shift in peasant self-perception in the direction of greater individualism, as well as a new desire in women as well as men to "move up in the world."[26] Manufactured clothing and urban-style fashion had become a mark of prestige in many villages of the Central Industrial Region.

Where men's trades paid well enough, as they did in Soligalich and Chukhloma and in much of Iaroslavl', a woman's father or brothers bought things for her. The fashionable young peasant women who appear in Figure

24 *Statisticheskii ezhegodnik Tverskoi gubernii za 1897*, 31.
25 M.M. Gromyko, *Traditsionnye normy povedeniia i formy obshcheniia Russkikh krest'ian xix v.* (Moscow, 1986), 108–9.
26 Boris Mironov, "The Russian Peasant Commune after the Reforms of the 1860s," *Slavic Review* 44, no. 3 (Fall 1985): 451; Eugen Weber, *Peasants into Frenchmen* (London, 1979), 230.

Fig. 4. Maria, Praskovia, and Liuba Vorob'eva, peasants of Romanovo-Borisogleb district, Iaroslavl' province, dressed up to have their photograph taken, 1916. Note their urban-style dress, leather shoes, and bared heads. (Courtesy of Iurii Bogorodskii.)

4 were the daughters of a peasant worker. Their father, Khariton Vorob'ev, had worked since the age of twelve at the Mendeleev oil refinery in Romanovo-Borisogleb, Iaroslavl', where he earned wages sufficient to dress his daughters Maria, Praskovia, and Liuba in urban style and to keep them on the land. But where men's wages barely paid the taxes, a woman who fancied urban-style clothing would have to earn the money herself. Although the women had to work hard for every kopek, marriageable women in Tver'

villages were prepared to spend as much as thirty to forty rubles over a three-year period, an enormous sum in the 1870s, in order to acquire the dresses and goods they fancied.[27] Even when she came from a relatively poor household, a marriageable woman might spend just about everything she earned to clothe herself; only in times of desperate need would the men in the household draw on the savings that a young woman had set aside.[28] If there were no opportunities to earn money close to home, poor households in particular let women go elsewhere to earn it.

Often, urban-made clothing constituted part of the dowry. Dowries were to be found in most, although by no means all of rural Russia. They typically consisted of clothing and linens, the trunk to store them, and perhaps cash, grain, and a few animals as well, depending on a family's economic status. These items would remain the woman's property even after marriage. As cash became more important in the village, and luxury items replaced homemade goods, it grew more costly to dower a daughter. In the 1890s, correspondents to the Tver' *zemstvo* complained that in addition to higher taxes, economic decline, and a rising cost of living, the need to provide a dowry was driving peasants into debt. "People borrow money to provide a dowry for their daughters, because here all fiancés demand a dowry that starts at ten rubles but can go as high as a hundred rubles or more, depending on the fiancé, the wealth of his family, and her means" (from Novotorzhok district). "Ten years ago you could dress a girl decently for fifty rubles; now it costs no less than a hundred" (Kashin district). "It's become customary to provide a dowry for your daughter. Not one youth will marry a girl who lacks one. A girl needs a silk dress, a fur . . . and a large silk kerchief" (Rzhev district).[29] Faced with demands for cash that they could not provide, men became more willing to allow marriageable women to go off to earn wages elsewhere, so that they could lay aside a dowry for themselves.[30]

The village retained its authority over women who went off to work.

27  *Sbornik materialov dlia statistiki Tverskoi gubernii*, vyp. 2 (Tver', 1874), 106–7; *Statisticheskoe opisanie Rzhevskago uezda, Tverskoi gubernii. Mestnoe izsledovanie* (Tver', 1885), 133–4.

28  *Materialy po statistike narodnago khoziaistvo v S.-Peterburgskoi gubernii*, vyp. 5, ch. 2 (St. Petersburg, 1887), 159; TsGAOR SSSR, fond 7952, op. 3, delo 96, 136. See also the discussion in Chapter 4.

29  *Statisticheskii ezhegodnik Tverskoi gubernii za 1897*, 56.

30  This process was not confined to Tver'. See *Sbornik statisticheskikh svedenii po Moskovskoi gubernii. Otdel khoziaistvennoi statistiki*, t. 7, vyp. 4 (Moscow, 1882), 149; Z.A. Ogrizko and V.T. Shmakova, "Krest'iane otkhodniki Riazanskoi gubernii v kontse xix i v nachale xx veka," in *Istoriko-bytovye ekspeditsii, 1951–1953*, ed. A.M. Pankratova (Moscow, 1955), 145, 149; TsGAOR SSSR, fond 7952, op. 3, delo 96, 136.

Parents, husbands, or village or *volost'* elders held the power to revoke or to renew the passport a woman required to live and work outside her native district. The village community sometimes demanded emotional as well as financial allegiance, not just the sending of money to fulfill fiscal obligations but also periodic visits to the village to ensure the migrant's continuing ties. Villagers expected this allegiance of women as well as men. A *volost'* elder actually withheld the passport of a peasant spinster working as a servant in Moscow, because she failed to visit her village. In 1883, she complained to the Moscow Provincial Committee on Peasant Affairs about it. Her fellow villagers wanted her to come home for a visit before they granted her passport, she wrote, despite her timely payment of all her fees. Membership in the community, not money, was the issue. Villagers wanted to see her because "They hardly know her any more and have no idea what she is doing."[31] In the eyes of others, peasants who left the village still belonged to the community.

Women migrants themselves often shared this perception. Most marriageable women surely conceived of their path from the village as a two-way street. Much of the work an unmarried woman did was seasonal and temporary and paid only enough for the woman "to feed herself and manage to buy a little clothing (*koe-kak spravit'sia s nariadom*)," as a *zemstvo* correspondent put it.[32] Especially if she lacked skills, as the majority did, leaving permanently meant working forever for someone else; whereas if she married in the village, she would eventually become mistress (*khoziaika*) of her own household.[33] A *khoziaika* had a higher status than a servant or unskilled laborer and, unlike them, she worked for herself. If her family had a house and an allotment of land, a marriageable woman was likely to keep her eyes fixed firmly on the village and to regard migration as a temporary expedient, much as women did elsewhere in Europe and continue to do in the developing world. Robert Johnson has confirmed this pattern. On the basis of urban censuses, he has proposed that younger women were more likely to settle in the city for short periods, while older ones made a more permanent move.[34]

---

31  TsGIAgM, fond 66, op. 1, delo 14380. In this case, the authorities intervened to assure the woman her documents.

32  *Statisticheskoe opisanie Rzhevskago uezda*, 133–4.

33  Vadim Aleksandrov made this important point to me in 1985.

34  Robert Johnson, "Mothers and Daughters in Urban Russia: A Research Note," *Canadian Slavonic Papers* 30, no. 3 (Sept. 1988): 368.

Did their stay away from home change the way young women viewed life in the village? It did, but not by much. Kin and village-based institutions often mediated women's experiences outside the village as they mediated men's. When they left home, the women followed well-trodden paths; they worked in factories and lived in urban neighborhoods inhabited by others from their family, village, or locale. People they knew helped them find a job and a place to live. On the pages of *Peterburgskii listok*, a popular newspaper, we can read about peasant fathers or mothers who found positions for their daughters, of older brothers who helped their sisters, of female kin who helped each other.[35] Workers' memoirs tell us much the same story about the importance of kin and *zemliak* ties. For example, at the age of sixteen, P. Sleptsova first left her village in Mozhaisk district, Moscow, in the company of a cousin who already had a job at the Prokhorov factory in Moscow. The cousin assisted Sleptsova in obtaining employment there too. Evgeniia Toptygina left her village at seventeen and headed for the Sharygin factory in Moscow because her mother knew people already employed there. Anna Boldyreva, who took a job at the Pal' textile mill in St. Petersburg, followed in the footsteps of her neighbors. "By tradition, our factories were filled by people from Novotorzhok and Kashin [districts of Tver']," she later recalled.[36] Workers hired in the village would travel to the factory together. Sergei Prokhorov himself once visited the village of Dolgynikha, where A.S. Mozzhenkova had been working at a textile mill since the age of thirteen. Offering false promises of better wages, he convinced her and six other girls to go to Moscow and work for him. It is unlikely that the unmarried factory woman "lived a singularly isolated existence."[37]

Kin and *zemliak* relations structured the lives of women living at 14/2 Nizhegorodskaia Street in 1908–9 as well. The building, located at the northern end of the first quarter of the Vyborg district of St. Petersburg, housed people from a variety of estates and occupations. In eighty-one apartments, physicians, pensioners, military personnel, students, craftsmen and women, skilled and unskilled workers, servants and laundresses lived

35 On the importance of *zemliak* ties, see Robert Johnson, *Peasant and Proletarian: The Working Class of Moscow in the Late Nineteenth Century* (New Brunswick, N.J., 1979), 69–75. Examples can be found in *Peterburgskii listok*, no. 270 (2 Oct. 1892): 3; no. 283 (15 Oct. 1893): 3; no. 292 (24 Oct. 1893): 3; no. 193 (17 July 1894): 4; no. 219 (12 Aug. 1894): 3.
36 I. Kor, ed., *Kak my zhili pri tsare i kak zhivem teper'* (Moscow, 1934), 29; TsGAOR SSSR, fond 7952, op. 3, ed. kh. 167, 27; Anna Boldyreva, in *Tekstilshchik*, no. 1–2 (1923): 120.
37 Kor, ed., *Kak my zhili*, 47. The quote is from Glickman, *Russian Factory Women*, 120.

crowded together.[38] Of the forty-two resident Russian migrant peasant women under age twenty-five, only five had no evident ties to kin or *zemliaki*. Eight of these women under twenty-five lived in the same apartment as family members, although not with their parents. The sisters Evdokiia and Maria Kudriavtseva, migrants from Tver' aged twenty-four and fifteen, worked as servants in apartment number twenty-four; while Irina and Maria Danilova, migrants from Vologda aged twenty-two and nineteen, served in apartment eighteen. In apartment fifty-eight, the entire Kulikov family, migrants from Tver', lived together: twenty-three-year-old Anna worked as a tailor, Pavel, thirty-four, as an unskilled laborer, and Elena, twenty-nine, as a servant. Together, they supported their fifteen-year-old sister, Zinaida. Twenty-one-year-old Khristina Kozlova, a servant, lived with her brother Vasilii, a tailor, in apartment sixty-one. Finally forty-four-year-old Aleksandra Ivanova and fifteen-year-old Klavdiia Ivanova, evidently her niece, moved simultaneously from apartment sixty-three to apartment six, where both continued to work as servants. Fellow villagers of four more women resided in the same building; two more women lived near others from their *volost'*. Finally, twenty-four women under age twenty-five lived at the same address as people from their district (*uezd*); in several cases, in the very same apartment.

Such ties provided continuity with their village past and mediated contact with the new urban surroundings. They might also perpetuate traditional patterns of female submission and constrain a woman's choices. The story of Anna Galiutina suggests how much even a relatively self-assertive, wage-earning woman might sometimes remain subject to family needs. Galiutina was born to a poor peasant household in the province of Riazan. Withdrawn from school at the age of eleven to tend her younger siblings, she soon tired of working at home for free. She wanted to earn wages as her girlfriends did and, like them, to buy nice clothing. Despite her father's resistance, Galiutina began working at a local factory at the age of thirteen, her mother having bribed the village elder to add a few years to her age. In 1914, when she was seventeen, Galiutina moved to Moscow and started work at a textile mill. She first lived with an aunt who rented out rooms and needed help in caring

38 Tsentral'nyi gosudarstvennyi istoricheskii arkhiv Leningrada (hereafter TsGIAL), fond 1026, op. 1, ed. kh. 347. This untapped source for Russian social history contains the books kept by the house administrations of over five hundred apartment buildings in the city. For everyone in residence (sometimes including short-term visitors) the books record province, district, canton, and village of origin (for peasants); occupation, age, marital status, name, number and age of dependents; as well as date of arrival and departure, and sometimes the former address and/or the address to which the person moved.

for boarders; in 1916 she went to live with an uncle whose wife needed a companion; and then Galiutina returned to the aunt. Despite the taste for attractive clothing that had initially led Galiutina to seek work, she sent virtually her entire salary to her parents in the village. When her desires conflicted with their needs, the parents' needs prevailed: "I remember when father was still alive, I saved up ninety rubles to buy a velvet overcoat, but father took the money from me to make repairs, although I cried and got angry. And after father's death, I gave all my money to mother so that she could improve the family farm." Galiutina did not even decide whom she would marry. Three years after she began living in Moscow, she went home for the Easter holidays and for the betrothal her mother had arranged in her absence. She quit her job after the wedding and returned to live with her husband in the village.[39] This pattern was more typical for women than men. In villages of Tver', parents also determined whom the daughter would wed. The youths had some freedom of choice, but not their sisters. Although the daughter's consent had become essential, a father retained sufficient authority to pressure or threaten the daughter if she failed to agree to a match.[40]

Even so, the time outside the village left its mark. This posed a dilemma for physicians attempting to train peasant women for midwifery work in rural areas in the latter decades of the nineteenth century. Despite efforts to shelter peasant women students from outside influences, and the women's relatively brief sojourn (a year) at midwifery school, the vast majority of those who took the course moved permanently to the city. "Graduates no longer like to live in the countryside and don't remove their city clothes," one report read.[41]

Migration reinforced women's tastes for urban products and other tangible artifacts of urban culture. Women came home with fashionable clothing, singing the latest songs and dancing city dances. In the villages of Iaroslavl' that young unmarried women left to earn money in St. Petersburg, young people's clothing, especially women's, followed the latest fashion "to the

39 O.N. Chaadaeva, ed., *Rabotnitsa na sotsialisticheskoi stroike: Sbornik avtobiografii* (Moscow, 1932), 68–9.
40 L.A. Anokhina and M.N. Shmeleva, *Kul'tura i byt kolkhoznikov Kalininskogo oblasti* (Moscow–Leningrad, 1964), 174; Tenishev archive, op. 1, delo 1724, 28–9 (Zubtsov, Tver'). See also the testimony in *Traditsionnye obriady i obriadovyi fol'klor Russkikh Povolzh'ia* (Leningrad, 1985), 82–8.
41 Samuel Ramer, "Childbirth and Culture: Midwifery in the Nineteenth-Century Russian Countryside," in *The Family in Imperial Russia*, ed. David Ransel (Urbana, Ill., 1978), 223–6.

smallest detail."[42] Migration could affect a woman's personality, too. Peasant midwives who had trained in the city had trouble getting along with the local peasantry. People noticed that women who had worked for a time elsewhere, especially in cities, tended to be more developed intellectually and personally than those who remained at home: "They were distinguished by a livelier speech, greater independence, and a more obstinate character."[43] They might flout customary divisions of labor by gender, as did one peasant woman from Novgorod, a former chambermaid in St. Petersburg. At the close of the nineteenth century, she outraged fellow villagers by teaching her sons to keep house and even to bake bread and wash dishes. Wives who had spent some time out in the world (*v liudiakh*) before they were married were the most likely to engage in such unconventional behavior, a village correspondent noted. Such a bride might have difficulty adapting to the subordinate role of daughter-in-law.[44]

A divorce case brought before the Synod in 1913 illustrates the frictions that might arise when women migrated instead of staying at home. The suit was brought by Andrei Kiselev, a peasant from Novotorzhok district, Tver', who complained that six months after their marriage in 1903, his wife Olga left his house without any cause. Olga had worked before the marriage, and Andrei had difficulty accepting this aspect of her past. After their marriage he would reproach her, saying "You're a factory woman, not a peasant." When she left him, she went to live and work at a textile mill in their district. "She fell in love with the dissipated factory life," he complained in his suit. Eventually, she conceived a child by another man. Olga told a different tale, however, in which she figured as victim. "I lived with my husband around twenty days, and then he left for Moscow. I remained alone in an alien household, in a family that consisted of his brother and his wife," her narrative began. It is not clear whether she was treated more harshly or more unjustly than most new brides, but she certainly felt she had been mistreated. Her testimony is worth quoting at length because of the aggrieved sensibility it reveals and the unwillingness to accept punishment as part of the natural order.

> From the first days of my marriage, I had to endure mockery from my sister-in-law and later, unbearable attacks. They also did not feed me enough, for no reason at all. I began to suffer from anemia as a result of

42   F.S., "Vliianie otkhozhikh promyslov na ekonomicheskoe sostoianie i na vneshnii i vnutrennyi byt kraia," *Iaroslavskie gubernskie vedomosti*, no. 24 (1892): 2.
43   Tenishev archive, op. 1, delo 719, 5 (Novgorod, Novgorod).
44   Ibid., 25. See also Anokhina and Shmeleva, *Kul'tura i byt*, 174.

malnourishment and my difficult life. I got really sick. But instead of helping me in my sufferings, my sister-in-law scolded me and would not let me go to the hospital six versts [about four miles] away. When my husband returned after a six-month absence, I noticed that he was more disposed to my sister-in-law than to me; then he began to persecute me and beat me. On July 8, in broad daylight in front of a crowd of people on the street he beat me painfully, although I had done nothing to deserve it. As a result of these inhuman torments, in exhaustion, almost senseless and unable to work, far from my family, I crawled to the hospital six versts away, and they brought me to my mother.

Andrei returned to Moscow. When Olga felt better, she attempted to return to her husband's household, but according to her, her brother and sister-in-law refused to accept her. As a result, she was forced to seek sustenance elsewhere. In her opinion, if anyone was at fault for the break-down of her marriage, it was her husband, Andrei. None of the villagers summoned as witnesses agreed with her version of events, but one of them was also reluctant to blame her. According to Ignatii Karpov, Andrei and Olga's problems were due to their different personalities and the different lives they had led – Andrei in the village, Olga at the factory. Andrei was a practical and prudent man, whereas Olga had a free and lively character and "was not particularly bashful in her replies," as a result of the time she had spent elsewhere, he implied.[45] The growth of women's self-assertiveness was exactly what peasants feared would happen if women migrated.

The belief that migration deprived women of their modesty and submis-siveness caused many fathers and brothers to be reluctant to let young and marriageable women go off to work elsewhere; it also made parents unwilling to allow their sons to wed a woman with migrant experience. Although the inability of the village to feed itself, pay its taxes, and clothe its daughters had led the parents of Tver', especially the poorer peasants of Tver' and other regions, to adjust their expectations and send their daughters out to work by the end of the century, prejudice against the migrant woman lin-gered on. Women migrants appear to have had great difficulty finding a spouse in the village. In 1899, the only year such statistics were compiled, of the 17,065 peasant women who got married in Tver' province, only 54 (.3 percent) had worked elsewhere, as compared to 22 percent of the men who married.[46] To be sure, these figures reflect economic circumstances as well as prejudice: Households that sent their women elsewhere were the most

45 TsGIA SSSR, fond 796, op. 197, I stol, IV otd., ed. kh. 201, 1–5.
46 *Statisticheskii ezhegodnik Tverskoi gubernii za 1901* (Tver', 1902), 142–3. About 30 percent of men and about 7.7 percent of women took passports that year.

impoverished. Women from impoverished households who did not choose to remain in the city may have had difficulty finding husbands in the village even when they had money in their pockets. Economics probably complemented cultural biases against the migrant woman: In some cases, spinsterhood became a consequence as well as a cause of women's migration.

### Spinsters and widows

Men's migration also contributed to the number of "superfluous" women in the village. A minority of migrant men chose to marry women they met in the city, and some did not marry at all, adding to the number of spinsters back home. In the villages of Iaroslavl', in particular, the proportion of unmarried peasant women over thirty was unusually large: Of every 1,000 women, 151 remained single, by comparison with Tver', where only 58 of every 1,000 had not wed, about the same number of spinsters as in rural Russia as a whole. Spinsters comprised approximately 15 to 20 percent of the women migrants from Iaroslavl' province.[47]

The records do not tell us why spinsters left the village. No doubt many migrated for strictly economic reasons. They came from households that had no use for their labor and insufficient resources to maintain them; they had no way to support themselves if they stayed at home. But some surely made a personal choice to leave the village. Like one unmarried woman weaver, aged thirty-two, from Kineshma, Kostroma, who turned her back on employment opportunities near home to live and work in St. Petersburg, they were attracted by the higher pay they could earn in the city.[48] Perhaps, too, they wanted a life of their own, however modest, and sought their fortune, as Zhbankov put it, away from the perpetual surveillance of family members and fellow villagers.[49] Whatever the combination of necessity and volition, spinsters who left retained few ties to their native village. They stayed away for extended periods, often for good. Many found work as domestics. About 40 percent of women migrants from Iaroslavl' who worked

47 Statistics on spinsterhood are drawn from the relevant volumes of the census of 1897. The proportion of spinsters among Iaroslavl's migrants is calculated from Vorob'ev, *Otkhozhie*, 10–12. There is no information on the number of spinsters leaving Tver'.
48 *Krest'ianskie biudzhety po Kostromskoi gubernii*, vyp. 1: Fabrichnyi raion. Sost. N.I. Vorob'ev, N.P. Makarov (Kostroma, 1924), household no. 70.
49 D.N. Zhbankov, *Bab'ia storona* (Kostroma, 1891), 72. A similar point is made by Andrei Simic, *The Peasant Urbanites: A Study of Rural-Urban Mobility in Serbia* (New York, 1973), 76–8.

as chambermaids, nurses, laundresses, and maids-of-all-work were over twenty-one and had never been married.

Widows comprised another 25 percent of women migrants from Iaroslavl' around the turn of the century. The widow was at one and the same time the most vulnerable and the most independent of village women, under no man's authority and no man's protection. If she had no children, the widow rarely had access to land, and she was often unwelcome in her in-laws' household. With children, the widow gained the right to remain in her in-laws' household, but she was vulnerable to abuse without a husband to intercede for her. The widow within her own household was freer and might obtain an allotment of land if she had children. But she had to farm the allotment by herself or with hired help. If her children were too small to assist her, the odds against her succeeding were high. A widow retained access to land only if she was able to fulfill the fiscal obligations attached to it.[50] Widows who migrated were sometimes relatively young. Either they had no children, or they had children who were too young to assist around the house and in the fields. The odds of a widow finding another husband in the village were small. In rural Iaroslavl' seventy-three of every thousand women aged thirty to thirty-nine were widows, and they outnumbered widowers in their age group eight to one. The rate of widowhood was lower in rural Tver', where sixty-five of every thousand women between thirty and thirty-nine were widows, but even so, there were seven widows for every widower in that age group.

Like spinsters, widows usually left the countryside for strictly economic reasons. Superfluous and economically defenseless, these women became a kind of "widowed proletariat," tossed out of the village and onto the city streets.[51] But there is evidence that at least some of these migrant widows were enterprising after their fashion and ambitious for their children as well. E. Dobrynkina, who chronicled peasant life for the Vladimir *zemstvo*, described this sort of energetic peasant widow, who left her children with family members, or paid a fee to a neighbor to care for them, then went off

---

50 F.L. Barykov, A.V. Polovtsov, and P.A. Sokolovskii, eds., *Sbornik materialov dlia izucheniia sel'skoi pozemel'noi obshchiny* (St. Petersburg, 1880), 135–6, 172, 376; N. Brzhevskii, *Ocherki iuridicheskogo byta krest'ian* (St. Petersburg, 1902), 62–3; Christine Worobec, *Peasant Russia: Family and Community in the Post-Emancipation Period* (Princeton, N.J., 1991), 65–7. Rodney Bohac, "Widows and the Russian Serf Community," in *Russia's Women*, ed. Clements, Engel, and Worobec, 95–112, discusses the situation of the widow under serfdom.

51 Vorob'ev, *Otkhozhie*, 11. The real proportion of widows in both Iaroslavl' and Tver' may have been even higher than the census indicates, because those who left permanently were not included in it.

to the town or city to work during the winter, returning with her wages in the summer to clothe herself and her children and to set aside some money in order to "fulfill her dream of building her own hut and living independently with her children."[52]

Other widows who went to the city remained there for good. For example, the mother of K.S. Ovsianikova was widowed when her daughter was a mere six months old. The mother left her village in Riazan for Moscow, where she found a position as a domestic servant, while the daughter remained in the village in the care of her aunts. When she reached the age of nine, Ovsianikova joined her mother in Moscow, where the mother had apprenticed her to a seamstress.[53] When the mother of Aleksei Andreev was widowed in 1892, she sent her two small sons to distant relatives in Kaluga, agreeing to pay the relatives three rubles a year, then went off to Moscow. No longer young, without skills, she took whatever job she could find to keep a roof over her head, food on her table, and her children cared for in the countryside. Her employment history reads like an inventory of the limited opportunities available to a person of her age, sex, and background. At one time or another she worked in a shop that made scarves, cooked for an artel of workers, took in laundry and washed floors, and peddled small items like apples and candy. All the while, she never ceased to think of her son and the need for his education. When Aleksei became seven, he joined his mother in the corner she rented in a basement in the Presnia district of Moscow and began to attend school.[54] Another woman, widowed in 1898, earned seven rubles a month cooking for thirty people in a sewing workshop in Moscow; she left her three daughters in the village until they became ten, when the mother brought each of them to the city and apprenticed them in the needle trades.[55]

When kin, godparent, or friendship networks failed to provide for their children, widows fell back on charity. Among the orphans who crowded overburdened children's shelters in Moscow province were children whose widowed mothers had left them to earn a living elsewhere. When she took up work at a rural factory in 1891, a mother placed her seven-year-old son,

---

52  E. Dobrynkina, "Starye devy v Muromskom uezde," *Ezhegodnik Vladimirskago gubernskago statisticheskago komiteta* 1, vyp. 2 (1876): 89–92.

53  Kor, ed., *Kak my zhili*, 39.

54  TsGAOR SSSR, fond 7952, op. 3, delo 389, 34–6. Here, as elsewhere, I have omitted women's names because the source does not provide them.

55  Ibid., delo 96, 121–2.

Ivan Chizhov, in a children's shelter; nine years later, having become sixteen and old enough to work, he joined her at the factory. The mother of Ekaterina Ivanova left the five-year-old at the same shelter. Four years later in 1894, Ekaterina went to join her mother in Moscow and began attending school. In 1892, two years after her widowed mother had left her in the children's shelter, Evdokiia Aleksandrova, now seven, went to join her widowed mother, who was living in Moscow and wanted "to teach her."[56] Such women maneuvered within their limited options to provide for their children as well as themselves.

In addition to a way to earn a living, migration presented younger spinsters and widows with the opportunities and risks of courtship, if the women were so inclined. It is mistaken to assume that all migrant widows, or spinsters, were inexorably "destined for a solitary life in the city."[57] Village women generally married early. Around the turn of the century, about 57 percent married at the age of twenty or earlier. Early marriage in the village meant that a spinster by village standards might well be a sexually desirable woman by urban ones, especially given the numerical preponderance of men in Russia's cities. One kind of evidence for this is the age of women bearing illegitimate children. As historians have argued, illegitimacy often represents a courtship that failed. (See the discussion in Chapter 5.) Between 1885 and 1900 more than half of the women who bore illegitimate children in the city of St. Petersburg were over twenty-five, that is, old enough to be considered a spinster in the village; about a quarter of them were over thirty.[58] Migrant peasant women made up the vast majority of women who bore illegitimate children in both Moscow and St. Petersburg.

By contrast with illegitimacy, marriage rates provide evidence of successful courtship. In about 10 percent of the marriages that were celebrated in Moscow and St. Petersburg in the late nineteenth and early twentieth centuries, the bride was a widow. Only a painstaking search through parish

---

56 TsGIAgM, fond 184, op. 2, delo 873, 69–74.

57 Johnson, *Peasant and Proletarian*, 66.

58 *Statisticheskii ezhegodnik S.-Peterburga* for the years 1886–99. During these years, the proportion of single mothers over twenty-five slowly declined, but they remained over half the total. Many of these women were not giving birth for the first time, which means the age at first birth was actually lower. I have surveyed the peasant women who gave birth at the St. Petersburg Maternity Home in the first months of 1890 and found that of the 138 whose age at first birth could be ascertained, 16.6 percent gave birth before age twenty; 59 percent bore their first children between the ages of twenty and twenty-four; another 16.6 percent between twenty-five and twenty-nine. Another 4.5 percent were over thirty. TsGIAL, fond 145, op. 1, ed. 112.

records would reveal what proportion of these widows were peasants and the ages at which they wed. But more impressionistic evidence suggests that while the odds were certainly against her, well into her thirties a widow could still hope to find a husband in the city. For example, in 1902, one thirty-two-year-old peasant widow living in the city of Moscow married a thirty-eight-year-old migrant with a house and allotment in his village.[59] Marfa Ivanova, a thirty-six-year-old widow from Tver', who had been supporting herself as an unskilled laborer in St. Petersburg for at least five years, married an urban resident (*meshchanin*) in 1913.[60] The experience of Tatiana Erofeeva is an unusual one, but it illustrates the possibilities for an attractive and energetic widow, especially if she had no children. A migrant to St. Petersburg from Tver', Erofeeva, at thirty, had already been widowed twice, but in the city, she nevertheless found a third husband, a widower with children who came from a neighboring village.[61] In St. Petersburg at the turn of the century, almost 10 percent of peasant widows were thirty years old or younger, and another 13.6 percent were under thirty-six. These women were eligible for marriage or for a consensual relationship. Marriage could even cause a widow to return to the countryside. This was the experience of E.S. Safronova, a peasant woman from Riazan province. Born to a poor family, Safronova left for Moscow to work after she was widowed at the age of nineteen. She worked as a servant for thirteen years, then at the age of thirty-two married Afanasii Safronov, also a peasant from Riazan, and they returned together to his village.[62] In his short story "Briukhany," the writer S.T. Semenov presents a "manly" widow of forty, who worked as a cook and set her cap for a handsome yardman's heart.[63] He reminds us that widows, like other unattached women, could forge a life for themselves in the city.

## Married women

Of all the categories of migrant peasant women, married women were probably the most diverse. They represented a substantial minority of women

---

59  TsGIAgM, fond 203, op. 412, ed. kh. 16, 4–5.
60  TsGIAL, fond 1648, op. 1, delo 156, 2056.
61  *Peterburgskii listok*, no. 102 (14 Apr. 1894): 2; for another case of a widowed servant remarrying, see *Peterburgskii listok*, no. 348 (Dec. 19, 1892): 3.
62  Ogrizko and Shmakova, "Krest'iane otkhodniki Riazanskoi," 150.
63  S.T. Semenov, *V rodnoi derevne* (Moscow, 1962), 375.

migrants, including 38.7 percent of those who left Iaroslavl' on their own passports at the turn of the century.[64] Like their sisters who left the village on a family passport, some became the "dependents" of men. More women migrated as dependents from Iaroslavl' than from Tver', because Iaroslavl' men were more likely to be in a position to support them. According to the census of 1897, about 60 percent of all female migrants from Tver' to St. Petersburg were dependents, as compared to 71 percent of women migrants from Iaroslavl'.[65] A high proportion of these dependents were children, who left on family passports. Even so, at the turn of the century close to a third of all migrant peasant women from Iaroslavl' who left on their own passports did not work for wages.[66]

When married women went off to work, it was almost invariably because their families desperately needed the money. Marriageable women contributed their wages to the family economy, by contrast with widows and spinsters, whose earnings remained largely their own. A married woman worked for the family even when she went off separately from her husband and to a different destination.[67] Family life in the city and at the factory and the ramifications of married women's separate earnings will be examined in Chapter 7.

In the remaining pages of this chapter, I want to look at the small but significant minority of married peasant women who found new opportunities and the chance to live a different kind of life in the city or the factory. Such women encountered difficulties that shed another light on the bonds that linked peasant women to the village. The fact that some women struggled hard to break those bonds indicates that at least a minority of women left the village not because need drove them, or the village rejected them, but because they sought a life elsewhere that would suit them better.

According to Russian law, a wife was required to live with her husband, and the law strictly forbade any action that encouraged husbands and wives to live separately. If a woman wanted to leave her husband's household for

---

64 Vorob'ev, *Otkhozhie*, 5, 11.
65 Computed from B.V. Tikhonov, *Pereseleniia v Rossii vo vtoroi polovine xix v.* (Moscow, 1978), tables 1 and 8.
66 Vorob'ev, *Otkhozhie*, 28–33. We have no comparable figure for Tver'. My contention about dependent children is based upon *Perepis' Moskvy 1902 goda*, vol. 1 (Moscow, 1904), vyp. 1, 35, 37.
67 *Obzor Iaroslavskoi gubernii. Otkhozhie promysly krest'ian Iaroslavskoi gubernii* (Iaroslavl', 1896), 18, 41, 51.

some reason, before 1888 the law required that she receive her husband's permission. No matter how viciously he abused her, or whether or not he supported her financially, without his permission village authorities had no right to grant her the passport (*vid*) she needed to work outside her district.[68]

*Volost'* courts and peasant officials were sometimes prepared to bypass the laws and to allow wives of particularly feckless or abusive husbands to take passports of their own and go elsewhere to earn their living. For example, in 1887 a *volost'* court in Kaliazin district, Tver', granted a passport to a peasant wife who wanted to work as a cook in Moscow, despite her husband's disapproval. The husband was known as an immoral man, and so long as he continued his dissolute behavior, the court stated its willingness to allow her a passport. In another decision by the same court, a wife gained permission to live apart from her drunken and abusive husband, to reclaim the property she had brought to his household – including pillows, a blanket, and icons – and to harvest the flax she had sown on his land. Similarly, in cases of truly egregious ill-treatment by a husband, petitioning the tsar might win a woman some redress.[69]

But for the most part, peasant and other officials refrained from interfering with the husband's absolute authority to refuse or revoke a wife's passport. In addition to ensuring the viability of the peasant economy, men's power over women's mobility reinforced their authority in the household. A peasant from Smolensk put it this way: "Now, if worse comes to worst, at least I can refuse to grant her a passport. If women could come and go as they pleased, they might get completely out of hand."[70] To be sure, evidence of men relinquishing their authority amicably occasionally shows up in the records. Such men were likely to be migrants, who were less dependent than villagers on women's labor. One exemplary peasant husband parted peacefully from his servant wife in the early 1870s, but occasionally took coffee with her in St. Petersburg. When asked how they decided to separate, the husband responded: "We never talked about it at all. Afterwards, she left

---

68  S. Kozhukhov, "O praktike Pravitel'stvennago Senata po voprosu o vydache krest'ianskim zhenam otdel'nykh vidov na zhitel'stvo," *Zhurnal Ministerstva Iustitsii*, kn. 3 (1901): 158–67.

69  *Sbornik statisticheskikh svedenii po Tverskoi gubernii*, 10 vols. (Tver', 1885–96), 5: 37. For petitions to the tsar, TsGIA SSSR, fond 1412, op. 221, delo 183 (1884–7); op. 223, delo 43 (1886–7); delo 124 (1882) and delo 224 (1882). See also *Trudy komissii po preobrazovaniiu volostnykh sudov*, 7 vols. (St. Petersburg, 1874), 2: 126–7; 3: 169–303; N. Lazovskii, "Lichnye otnosheniia suprugov po russkomu obychnomu pravu," *Iuridicheskii vestnik*, 6–7 (1883): 358–414.

70  *Pis'ma iz derevni. Ocherki o krest'ianstve v Rossii vtoroi poloviny xix veka* (Moscow, 1987), 182.

and we never said anything further about it." In 1908, the thirty-five-year-old Ivan Gorbachev, a peasant from Tver' and an unskilled worker in an armaments plant, wrote the police that he had nothing against a separate passport being issued to his wife.[71] But judging by the documents, refusals were far the more common response to a wife's request to live on her own. Most husbands strenuously resisted the loss of control over the wife's labor power and even more so over her person. Letters in local archives attest to a wife's lack of legal recourse in such situations. For example, in 1869, a peasant woman from Zarai district, Riazan, wrote her *volost'* administration requesting a separate passport. Already working in St. Petersburg and raising her eight-year-old son there, she wanted to stay in the city, while her husband wanted her back in the village. Formerly, they had lived together in St. Petersburg, but the two had gotten along badly. He drank constantly and could not hold a steady job, and he sold their household goods and spent the money on drink. Her complaints about his dissolute behavior and cruel treatment had led the city police to send the husband back to the village with a police escort, leaving her on her own. But no sooner did he reach home than he began to demand that she join him. Her efforts to remain in the city proved fruitless, and in 1870 he succeeded in having her returned to their village.[72]

Failing to find satisfaction at the village or district level, women sometimes appealed to their district, or even to their Provincial Committee on Peasant Affairs (1861–89). These committees assisted the governor in supervising peasant self-administration.[73] Appeals to them represent extreme cases and were surely the tip of a much larger iceberg: Most quarrels were resolved closer to home, although rarely in favor of granting a woman her passport, judging by complaints to the Moscow Provincial Committee.[74] Strictly adhering to the letter of the law, the committee did not favor women either. For example, Avdotia Babkina, a peasant from Podol'sk district, Moscow, was working as a housekeeper in the city of Kharkov and supporting her four children in 1880, when her husband refused to renew her passport. He had no right to do that, she complained to the Moscow Provincial Committee

71 *Sudebnyi vestnik*, no. 205 (1874): 2; TsGIAL, fond 1648, op. 1, delo 287, 190–1. See also Lazovskii, "Lichnye otnosheniia," 369.

72 TsGIAgM, fond 66, op. 2, t. 1, ed. kh. 347, sv. 338, 3–4. I read this document in 1985. By 1991 the classification system had changed. All subsequent footnotes refer to the current system of classification.

73 N.P. Eroshkin, Iu. V. Kulikov, and A.V. Chernov, *Istoriia gosudarstvennykh uchrezhdenii Rossii do Velikoi Oktiabr'skoi sotsialisticheskoi revoliutsii* (Moscow, 1965), 261.

74 See the discussion in Tikhonov, *Pereseleniia*, 122–3.

on Peasant Affairs. In the course of their twelve years of marriage, her husband had never supported her, and he would be unable to support her in the future, she claimed, because he had neither a family farm in the village nor a steady job elsewhere. He had even been in trouble with the law, condemned by a court to imprisonment ten years earlier. Without her own passport, she pointed out, she would be unable to work and support her children, and her husband was "hardly in a position to support himself; he's practically a beggar." The committee nevertheless refused her request for a passport.[75] In another case, peasant officials had for years granted a peasant wife a passport, despite her husband's protests, because he was known to treat her badly and was in and out of jail. But in 1883 he began to insist that the *volost'* elder revoke her passport, employing every argument he could think of. He cast aspersions on his wife's character – "her life in Moscow isn't quite decent," he wrote, and he claimed to require her labor in the village. "I want her to live in my father's house . . . and to share the family's labor so that I can be freed from the expense of hiring a woman worker." Almost as an afterthought, at the end of his letter he added, "I want her to live with me like a wife with a husband." The authorities denied the woman the passport.[76]

Women's lack of legal recourse put husbands in a position to take financial advantage of them. Citing the need to hire a woman worker, husbands often required payment in return for granting their wives the passport they wanted. *Obrok* is the word the documents use for this payment. In the days of serfdom, *obrok* denoted quitrent, the money or goods with which the serf fulfilled his obligations to his lord. The use of the word in this context suggests a comparable sense of ownership and obligation. Although there was no legal basis for a wife to pay *obrok*, the fact that a wife was first and foremost a worker in her husband's household provided an economic basis. If the household needed the wife's labor, it would have to be replaced, and the replacement would have to be paid, since only a wife (or a child) would labor in the fields, in the barn, in the kitchen garden, at the loom, and in the household for room and board alone.[77] So a wife who wanted to live elsewhere might come to an agreement with her husband about the sum she

---

75   TsGIAgM, fond 66, op. 1, ed. kh. 12590, 1–2.

76   Ibid., ed. kh. 14033, 10–11.

77   See, for example, the case brought for back pay by a peasant woman who had done essentially what wives do, but who received only room and board. *Trudy komissii*, 2: 515; also 509.

would send him yearly, and he had the right to revoke her passport and to bring her home if she failed to send it.

A wife on *obrok* remained in virtually absolute dependence on her husband's will. Even in cases where the husband violated village norms and tsarist law requiring him to support his wife, even when he had no need to replace his wife's labor, he retained his patriarchal authority to control her movements and to demand money from her if he chose. Two cases demonstrate the extent of even a feckless and abusive husband's authority. The first involves Praskovia Kurygina, who in 1882 brought a complaint against her husband, Fyodor, and her *volost'* elder. Condemned by a peasant court to twenty blows with a lash for his hot-tempered behavior and cruel treatment of his wife, Fyodor had refused to mend his ways and instead, began to treat his wife even more cruelly. He had also ceased altogether to tend his allotment. Praskovia turned again to the *volost'* court for help in controlling her husband, but this time the elder intervened, insisting she reconcile with her husband and submit to him. Deciding to leave, Praskovia succeeded in obtaining a six-month passport. Taking her two-year-old child along, she found a job at a rural factory. Then her husband vanished, forcing her to pay his debt of twenty-three rubles. Soon after the debt was paid, Praskovia's passport ran out, and Fyodor reappeared to demand she send him more money. When she failed to comply, he withheld the new passport with the elder's support, forcing her to leave her job. The committee also rejected her pleas, reasoning that "her complaints about her husband who beats her and offends her in every way do not merit consideration," because they were merely her side of the story.[78] The second case involved Natasha Osipova, a peasant from Kolomna district, Moscow, who complained to the Peasant Committee in 1886. About ten years earlier, Natasha wrote, she had given birth to a daughter and, right afterward, her husband drove her from the house with the baby at her breast. She sought shelter at her father's, where she lived for a while before returning to her husband and conceiving another child. Again her husband drove her out, and this time the infant died. When she requested a passport of her own, the husband insisted that she pay him thirty rubles first. He had no occupation, Natasha claimed, and lived with his mother, who supported him. Since Natasha could not come up with such a substantial sum, for the last ten years she and her daughter had remained homeless, wandering here and there, living in other people's houses, barely

78 TsGIAgM, fond 66, op. 1, ed. kh. 13465, 2–6.

able to feed themselves. The committee also rejected her plea for the necessary documents.[79]

Like these two men, other-husbands of abused or restless women were
frequently tempted to take advantage of their almost limitless power in order
to extract as large a portion of their wives' earnings as they could get,
demanding sums as high as twenty rubles a year or more, depending on the
level of the husband's greed and the wife's desperation.[80] In 1869, the *Judicial Herald* carried a story about one extreme case, a peasant couple who
had been married as serfs twenty years earlier, according to the master's will.
She had worked as a servant for years, for a time in Moscow, then in St.
Petersburg, but he continually summoned her back to their village. Presently,
he refused to approve her passport until she agreed to pay him fifty rubles,
an enormous sum for a servant, and far more than she could earn in a year
even if she spent not a kopek on herself.[81]

Informal agreements between husbands and wives had no force of law, so
the husband retained the power to recall his wife at any point. Even when a
wife sent home money she had no guarantee that a husband would honor his
part of the agreement. Ivan Gerasimov revoked his wife Anna's passport
even after she sent fifteen rubles to their village to pay the household's taxes.
Accusing Anna of abandoning the farm and living a "disorderly life" in St.
Petersburg, Ivan succeeded in bringing her home.[82] Nikonor Semechkov also
succeeded in revoking his wife's passport in 1880 for her failure to send
three shirts in addition to the twenty rubles she remitted to the village. The
fact that the community had imprisoned Semechkov four times for his
immoral behavior did nothing to diminish his authority over his wife.[83]

After 1888, it became a little easier for badly mistreated peasant wives to
obtain their independence. Deluged with stories similar to the above, of
abused and tormented wives who were being forced to remain with their

---

79  Ibid., ed. kh. 15662, 1–2.
80  See, for example, *Trudy komissii*, 2: 555, 557, 563. Also, Lazovskii, "Lichnye otnosheniia,"
    369–70; Ia. Liudmer, "Bab'i stony," *Iuridicheskii vestnik* 6 (1884): 466–7.
81  *Sudebnyi vestnik*, no. 217 (1869): 2–3.
82  TsGIAgM, fond 66, op. 1, ed. kh. 13398, 5–7, 9.
83  The committee was briefly swayed by Avdotia's plea that three shirts in addition to twenty
    rubles was too much *obrok* to ask of a working woman. The family had no right to require
    from her payments that were beyond her capacity to make. But in the end, they did not act
    on her complaint and suggested she turn to the justice of the peace, a civil court. TsGIAgM,
    fond 66, op. 1, ed. kh. 12059. Agreements reached with the help of the imperial authorities
    were more formal and often stipulated that if she paid her *obrok*, a wife must be left alone.

husbands or were exploited by them, the Ministry of Internal Affairs instructed local officials to issue separate passports to peasant women who had separated from their spouses or were clearly mistreated by them. These instructions by no means guaranteed that a woman who wanted her own passport would automatically get it. But they did provide more protection from excessive demands for *obrok*. For example, early in 1889, Aleksandra Lepekhina, a peasant woman from Kolomna district, Moscow, lodged a complaint with the Moscow Committee on Peasant Affairs. She had lived in the city of Moscow almost seven years, she wrote, and her *volost'* elder had just refused to renew her yearly passport. In place of it, he had issued her a document that allowed her to remain in the city of Moscow only by the month (*mesiachnoe svidetel'stvo*) until she came up with the eight rubles he demanded in payment of her husband's arrears. She had already complained about this to the district authorities, but they had found in favor of the elder. She protested their decision in no uncertain terms. It seems likely that the scribe who wrote her letter took a hand in crafting its contents as well. "I find . . . this decision completely unjust," the letter reads, "and for the following reasons: 1) Laws . . . were not made to obligate wives to pay *obrok* to their husbands or to pay any sort of arrears; 2) by denying me a passport and forcing me to pay my husband's arrears, the *volost'* administration deprives me of the chance to live by honest labor; and 3) since my husband constantly fails to pay his arrears . . . they are bound to grow into an enormous sum, so that every time I renew my passport, the *volost'* administration will demand that I pay not just eight rubles, but more and more each time." She requested that no further financial obstacles be placed between herself and her passport. Appealing to beliefs the authorities were likely to share concerning the unequal capacities of men and women, she asked to be freed from "having to bear a burden beyond my strength, and one that is more suitable (*prisyshche*) to a man." This time the authorities found in the woman's favor.[84]

Toward the end of the century, the State Senate tinkered with the law yet again, ruling that a husband who had neither the desire nor the ability to live with and support his wife could not deny her a passport.[85] But it seems clear that peasant officials applied this ruling selectively. This was certainly the case with Kseniia Grishina, a peasant from Tula. Soon after her marriage to her husband, Mikhail, he began to beat her without reason and to deprive

84  Ibid., ed. kh. 16894.
85  Kozhukhov, "O praktike," p. 158. A report in the St. Petersburg judiciary archives gives the decision a more liberal interpretation. TsGIAL, fond 254, op. 1, delo 13078, 11, 13.

her of food, or so she said. Finally, he tossed all her belongings on the street of their village and drove her from the house. She went to the city of Tula, where she supported herself by knitting stockings. Every so often Mikhail would come from the village, get drunk, and pay her a visit. Demanding that she give him money, he would threaten to withhold her passport. In 1911 she sued for divorce on the grounds of his adultery. While the divorce slowly made its way through Synodal courts, he made good on his threat, convincing village officials to revoke her passport and leaving her with no means to earn a living.[86] Other men were also prepared to exercise their legal rights punitively. Nikandor Tiagilev, a peasant from the agricultural province of Kursk and a railroad worker, wrote the wife he had abandoned years before that if she kept pestering him, he would request she be sent without a passport back to the village.[87] At least until the outbreak of World War I, peasant officials sometimes restricted the mobility of even abused or abandoned peasant wives at their husband's request.

Nevertheless, cities and towns continued to tempt. They offered insulted, abused, and abandoned women opportunities to earn their keep. For sexually restless women, the relative anonymity of an urban setting provided both relief from the relentless scrutiny of fellow villagers and a more varied menu of personal choices. Despite formidable obstacles of law and custom, many women who were determined enough, or desperate enough, somehow managed to get away. There is considerable evidence of women who willfully (samovol'no) left a husband's household, headed for the city, and refused to return home. In 1868, a peasant husband from Iaroslavl' complained to the volost' court that his wife not only refused to live with him but was working as a laundress in the city of Iaroslavl', where, he claimed, she had also found herself two lovers.[88] In 1872, the authorities in Mologda district, Iaroslavl', finally located a peasant wife who had fled her husband seventeen years earlier and had borne several illegitimate children during her absence.[89] In the early 1870s, the wife of Evdokim Chistiakov worked as a cook in St. Petersburg and refused to live with her husband, despite his repeated requests.[90] Natasha Trezvov, a peasant from Tver', grew tired of living with her husband in an extended family household, where they shared a roof with Aleksei's older

86  TsGIA SSSR, fond 796, op. 197, I stol, IV otd., ed. kh. 1289, 2–3, 5. See also TsGIAgM, fond 203, op. 412, delo 57, 1–2 (1906).
87  TsGIA SSSR, fond 796, op. 199, II stol, IV otd., ed. kh. 335, 2.
88  Sudebnyi vestnik, no. 95 (1869): 3.
89  Trudy komissii, 3: 40.
90  Sudebnyi vestnik, no. 3 (1874): 4.

brothers and their wives. Although she had married her husband for love, in 1890 she left him to go to St. Petersburg, where she found a job as a servant. She liked it so much that she managed to renew her passport, despite her husband's repeated requests that she return to him in the village.[91]

Occasionally, women eluded the grasp of the village by breaking the law. The passport system designed to control the mobility of peasants was circumvented with considerably frequency. Tsarist police were notoriously inefficient. St. Petersburg and Moscow nourished what appears to have been a thriving trade in counterfeit passports.[92] If they could not obtain a counterfeit passport, peasants sometimes bought someone else's legitimate one. That is the route Ekaterina Gerasimova took in 1892. A peasant from Novgorod, she was working as a servant in St. Petersburg when her husband refused to renew her passport. Already on her way back to the village, she encountered a woman who possessed a six-month passport and the two made a deal. For the price of five rubles Gerasimova bought her new acquaintance's passport and returned to her job in St. Petersburg.[93]

However they managed it, once having had a taste of urban life, some women simply refused to go back to the village. Take, for example, one peasant woman from Vladimir, whom her husband had left behind when he went off to St. Petersburg to work. She soon went off to earn wages as well. Lacking a passport, she sought work in her district town, where she did not need one. In town she found a lover and bore an illegitimate child. Tracked down by the village authorities, brought back to the village against her will, and ordered to live with her husband, the woman refused in no uncertain terms. "She recognizes no authority and refuses to submit to anyone" (*Ona znat' nikogo ni khochet, i nikomu ni podchiniat'sia*), the record of her trial states.[94] Two months after his wedding in 1900, Pyotr Zavolokin left a village in Iaroslavl' to ply his trade in St. Petersburg. Lacking a passport, his wife, Anastasia, went off to the neighboring city of Rybinsk. A year later, when her husband returned and summoned her to the village, she refused to join him. The two lived apart for seven more years, then Pyotr sued for divorce.[95] After her husband, Mikhail, was called up to serve in the Russo-Japanese War, Maria Zaitseva, a peasant from Iaroslavl', went off to work at a factory

91  *Peterburgskii listok*, no. 295 (27 Oct. 1892): 3.
92  For individual cases, see *Sudebnyi vestnik*, no. 224 (1869): 2–3; no. 8 (1870): 2–3; for the trade, no. 217 (1872): 3.
93  *Peterburgskii listok*, no. 21 (22 Jan. 1892): 2; see also *Sudebnyi vestnik*, no. 16 (1869): 2–4; *Peterburgskii listok*, no. 348 (Dec. 19, 1892): 3.
94  *Trudy komissii*, 2: 356–7.
95  TsGIA SSSR, fond 796, op. 189, II stol, IV otd., ed. kh. 5299, 4.

in Rostov, found herself a lover, and refused to return to the village.[96] Evdokiia Il'ina, a peasant from Riazan, also went off to work in the city when her husband was drafted. The record notes that there was no real need for Evdokiia to work, as her husband's family was relatively well-to-do, and she would not have been a burden. She found work as a cook and then was kept by several men in succession. Twice the husband had her brought home by force, and twice she fled back to the city. Although he had sued for divorce on the grounds of her adultery, Vasilii was prepared to reconcile. But Evdokiia refused. She felt unable to return to her former life, she said, and wanted to sever all ties to her husband. This was not his fault, however. Absolving her husband of responsibility by saying that she had nothing against him, she took the sin of adultery upon herself.[97] Her story, like others, shows that women's rebelliousness was not invariably connected to economic marginality or to troubled relations within the household. Sometimes, women simply preferred a life different from the one the village offered them.

It would be a mistake to exaggerate the numbers of rebellious peasant women who were willing to sunder forever the ties that bound them to family and community. They remained a tiny minority: Most peasant women continued to live much as their mothers and grandmothers had done. Nevertheless, the dissonant voices are worth listening to, because they tell a different story about peasant women's lives and aspirations than the one we have become accustomed to hearing, a story of individual resistance to collective pressures toward conformity. Their story is a reminder that cities attracted women whom the village did not necessarily reject.

### Conclusion

Although a proportion of women migrants such as these discontented wives, along with spinsters and widows and some marriageable women, took a one-way ticket to the city, increasing numbers of women migrants went back as well as forth. Much migration in Russia was "circular," to borrow the category suggested by historian Charles Tilly.[98] After a definite period of time, migrants returned to their point of origin, bringing their earnings and experience home with them. At the same time, migration in Russia, especially migration to the city, also displayed characteristics of the chain: Related

96  Ibid., op. 199, I stol, IV otd., ed. kh. 1057; a similar case, deriving from Tver' district, Tver', can be found in op. 189, I stol, IV otd., ed. kh. 4363.
97  Ibid., op. 189, II stol, IV otd., ed. kh. 5675, 1–3.
98  Charles Tilly, "Migration in Modern European History," in *Human Migration*, ed. William McNeill (Bloomington, Ind., 1978), 48–68.

individuals or households moved from one place to another, with people at the destination providing aid, information, and encouragement to newcomers. As was often the case with chain migration, Russian migration followed a sex-selective pattern. Initially, single males made up the vanguard; then single women followed; and finally whole families joined them. This hybrid of circle and chain meant that not only women but also families might circulate between village and city.

When women returned to the village, they were never quite the same. Earning wages outside the village broadened a woman's horizons. Even when she migrated seasonally, or stayed away only temporarily, and had experiences of a wider world that were mediated by kin and *zemliak* ties, migration might nevertheless alter a woman's outlook and expectations. One Russian historian has written that women's migration threatened "the entire patriarchal way of life."[99] It is impossible to know how substantial a threat it was, because war and revolution intervened so soon after the numbers of migrant women really began to grow. Research on other countries suggests, however, that women's migration reflected the loosening of family bonds far more than men's did, and that it not only reflected change but helped to generate it too.[100] This was certainly the case in Russia. Opportunities to earn an independent wage outside the village provided alternatives for women on the margins and added to the numbers of women who were prepared to question, even challenge, their customary lot.

99 P.G. Ryndziunskii, *Krest'iane i gorod v kapitalisticheskoi Rossii vtoroi poloviny xix veka* (Moscow, 1983), 79.
100 Fawcett, Khoo, and Smith, "Urbanization," 5.

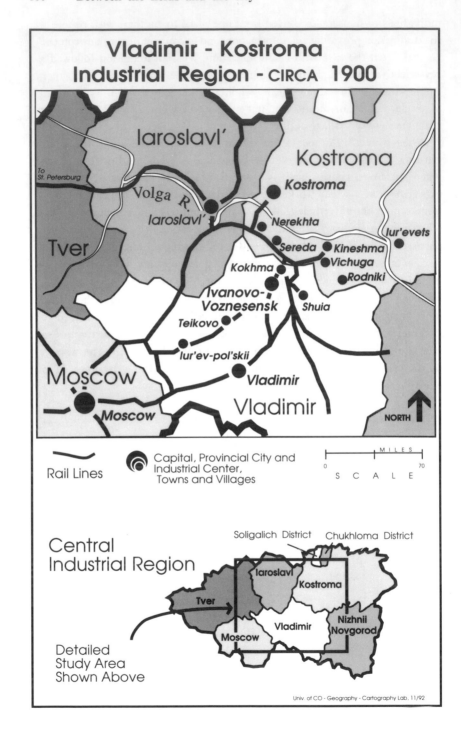

## Vladimir - Kostroma
## Industrial Region - CIRCA 1900

Iaroslavl'

Kostroma

To St. Petersburg

Volga R.

Kostroma

Iaroslavl'

Nerekhta

Iur'evets

Tver

Sereda

Kineshma

Vichuga

Kokhma

Rodniki

Ivanovo-
Voznesensk

Shuia

Teikovo

Iur'ev-pol'skii

Moscow

Vladimir

Moscow

Vladimir

NORTH

Rail Lines

Capital, Provincial City and
Industrial Center,
Towns and Villages

MILES

0       70

S C A L E

### Central
### Industrial Region

Soligalich District     Chukhloma District

Iaroslavl

Kostroma

Tver

Vladimir

Nizhnii
Novgorod

Moscow

Detailed
Study Area
Shown Above

Univ. of CO - Geography - Cartography Lab. 11/92

# 4. Between the fields and the factory

Early one evening around the turn of the century, three men lay waiting for a peasant woman to finish her shift in the textile mill where she worked near a village of Shuia district, Vladimir province. The men plotted revenge. Each of them had once been her lover, and it was she who had ended the affair each time. As soon as she appeared, they seized her, then lifted her dress and tied it over her head with a rope. Now naked below the waist, she was bound to one of the crosses in the graveyard in a ritual of public shaming. She remained there until other workers returned to the village, discovered and untied her.[1]

It was customary for peasants to humiliate publicly a woman who transgressed sexual norms. Everywhere in rural Russia, ritual shaming practices served to uphold the community's norms of morality.[2] But however customary the punishment or typical its form, the shaming that occurred that evening in rural Shuia was nevertheless unusual. For one thing, the peasant woman it targeted had conducted herself with rare effrontery. Engaging in premarital sex, enjoying a series of partners, and abandoning each when he ceased to please her, she had transgressed virtually every norm that governed the behavior of the marriageable woman. It was also unusual that personal revenge played a key role in the ritual. It was the men she had spurned, not the village community, that humiliated her. Understanding this combination of custom and novelty requires a closer look at the setting and at the lives of peasant women such as this one, who earned her modest living in a factory close to home. By the end of the nineteenth century, when this incident occurred, tens of thousands of peasant women worked in textile mills set in or near peasant villages. They engaged in labor that enabled them

1 Tenishev archive, op. 1, delo 58, 11.
2 See Stephen Frank, "Popular Justice, Community, and Culture among the Russian Peasantry, 1870–1900," *Russian Review* 46, no. 3 (July 1987): 239–65.

to earn an independent wage, but returned after work, or on holidays, to peasant households and communities where gender expectations remained much the same as they were elsewhere in rural Russia. This chapter will look at the effect of factory labor in a rural setting on the patriarchal peasant family and on peasant women's lives.

The emancipation of the serfs in 1861 initiated Russia's industrial revolution. Industrialization proceeded slowly for a few decades, then accelerated rapidly in the 1890s, encouraged by the Russian government. The rate of growth was intense. At the beginning of the twentieth century, 14,464 industrial enterprises operated in Russia; 85 percent of them established after 1861, 40 percent of them between 1891 and 1902. The factory labor force also grew apace: from about 706,000 workers in 1865 to about 1,424,700 in 1890, then to 3,743,800 by 1914. From the first, women constituted a significant minority of the industrial labor force, and their proportion grew as the numbers increased. In 1885, about one in every five industrial workers was female: about one in three by 1914. Women worked in every branch of industry, but the majority of women (over half by 1910) clustered in the textile trades.[3]

How much industrialization disrupted the peasant way of life is a question whose answer depends to some extent on where you look. While by the early twentieth century tens of thousands of peasants had left their native villages to work for wages in the factories of major cities such as Moscow and St. Petersburg, tens of thousands more found industrial employment much closer to home. Russia's industrialization did not automatically bring urbanization in its wake, as it did in most of Western Europe. Many factories, textile factories in particular, grew up in rural areas to take advantage of a cheap labor force, experienced in working wool, silk, cotton, and flax. Parts of the Central Industrial Region, where industrial or semiindustrial labor was already a familiar feature of rural life, were especially hospitable. Since the early eighteenth century, Moscow and its adjacent provinces had dominated textile production. Until 1861, most of the workers were peasant serfs laboring either in large factories or, more commonly, in their cottages or in small rural workshops. They worked the land during the short summer season, then manufactured for the remainder of the year. Women labored as well as men, spinning, carding, and weaving fabric for local factories or for

---

3 Joseph Bradley, *Muzhik and Muscovite: Urbanization in Late Imperial Russia* (Berkeley, Calif., 1985), 9–10; William Blackwell, *The Industrialization of Russia: An Historical Perspective* (Arlington Heights, Ill., 1970), 44; Rose Glickman, *Russian Factory Women: Workplace and Society, 1880–1914* (Berkeley, Calif., 1984), 84.

sale to middlemen or at the marketplace. As the textile trade expanded after
1861, mechanized factories took over many of the tasks that workers had
formerly done at home. The number of power looms increased from eleven
thousand in 1860 to eighty-seven thousand in 1890 and the mechanization of
cotton spinning proceeded even more rapidly. Large factories were built that
often employed a thousand hands or more. The factories were concentrated
in the areas where textile production had long predominated – that is, in
Moscow and its adjacent provinces.[4]

The peculiarities of Russia's development made these changes less disruptive than they were in Western Europe. The majority of factories were
located in rural areas. In the non–black earth provinces as a group, 65
percent of the factories and 65 percent of the workers were situated outside
of urban centers at the beginning of the twentieth century.[5] Moreover, small-
scale household production continued to coexist with large-scale factory
production. Factories farmed out certain tasks to cottage workers, or to tiny
village manufacturies (svetelki), where whole families worked on handlooms
with a few hired laborers. An organization of labor that located work in or
near home proved especially conducive to women's employment because, as
we have seen, women were far less likely than men to travel elsewhere in
search of wages. As a result, women represented a higher proportion of the
rural factory labor force than of the urban one until the onset of World War
I. Women who went off to work in rural factories had a different experience
than women workers in Russia's cities, or their peasant sisters who stayed at
home. In rural areas, the village mediated workers' contact with the factory
world; at the same time, unlike other peasant women, women workers earned
an independent wage. An examination of women's work in rural factories
permits a closer look at the impact of individual wage earning on peasant
women and the peasant way of life.

This chapter will focus on the Vladimir–Kostroma textile region, one
of the most highly industrialized in Russia. In Vladimir province, industry
was most heavily concentrated in Shuia district, which included the town of
Ivanovo-Voznesensk, known as "the Russian Manchester," the city of Shuia,
large industrialized villages such as Kokhma and Teikovo, and dozens of

---

4 Robert Johnson, *Peasant and Proletarian: The Working Class of Moscow in the Late Nineteenth
  Century* (New Brunswick, N.J., 1979), 13–16; Edgar Melton, "Proto-Industrialization, Serf
  Agriculture, and Agrarian Social Structure: Two Estates in Nineteenth-Century Russia,"
  *Past and Present*, no. 115 (May 1987): 69–106; B.N. Vasiliev, "Formirovanie promyshlennogo
  proletariata Ivanovskoi oblasti," *Voprosy istorii* 6 (1952): 99–117.
5 Joseph Bradley, *Muzhik* 16; P.G. Ryndziunskii, *Krest'iane i gorod v kapitalisticheskoi Rossii
  vtoroi poloviny xix veka* (Moscow, 1983), 161.

smaller settlements in the vicinity of factories. In Kostroma, where the most industrialized districts were Kineshma, Nerekhta, and Iur'ev, 86 percent of textile factories and 84 percent of workers were located outside of a city in the 1890s.[6]

In these industrial regions, workers were likely to be local in origin and to live in or near their native villages (by contrast, for example, with Moscow province, where at least half of the workforce occupied company housing by the early twentieth century). In 1897, most of the workers of Shuia, Teikovo, and Kokhma came from villages within walking distance (under ten *versts*, or about six miles) of their factory. In the Kineshma region of Kostroma, about one-third of workers lived in their own houses in 1905; another quarter rented space in villages close to factories. These factory workers remained closely linked to the peasant household.[7] Coming from villages only a short distance from their place of employment, they could visit home regularly if they did not live there. Like migrants to the major cities, the majority of these "peasant workers," as historians Douglas Holmes and Jean Quataert have entitled them, sought employment as a member of a family economy.[8] From the perspective of their household, employment in a rural factory represented only another stage in an ongoing struggle for survival, and households that had long deployed members between agriculture and wage earning were simply exploiting a new source of income. Yet even from the perspective of the household, working in a factory changed things. Craft work or domestic manufacture took place under the supervision of the head of one's own household, and the worker herself was unlikely to see the proceeds. As a *zemstvo* statistician put it, "When weaving was done in the household, the master himself handled all the income and expenses."[9] Work in a mechanized factory, by contrast, usually took place in a more structured setting, and it brought the worker an independent wage.

6  E.V. Matveeva, "K voprosu o sviazi rabochikh tekstil'chikov Kostromskoi gubernii s zemlei v 90–e gody xix veka," in *Promyshlennost' i proletariat gubernii verkhnego Povolzh'ia v kontse xix-nachale xx vv.* (Iaroslavl', 1976), 89.

7  Housing arrangements of Moscow workers are discussed in Victoria Bonnell, ed. *The Russian Worker: Life and Labor under the Tsarist Regime* (Berkeley, Calif., 1983), 21. For Shuia and Kineshma workers, see *Materialy dlia otsenki zemel Vladimirskoi gubernii* (hereafter *MOZVG*) 10, vyp. 3 (Vladimir, 1908), 61–2, and Iurii Kirianov, *Zhiznennyi uroven' rabochikh Rossii* (Moscow, 1979), 223. Also Vasiliev, "Formirovanie promyshlennogo," 114, and A.G. Rashin, *Formirovanie rabochego klassa Rossii* (Moscow, 1958), 416–26.

8  Douglas Holmes and Jean Quataert, "An Approach to Modern Labor: Worker Peasantries in Historical Saxony and the Friuli Region over Three Centuries," *Comparative Studies in Society and History* (Apr. 1986): 191–217.

9  *Materialy dlia statistiki Kostromskoi gubernii*, vyp. 4 (Kostroma, 1881). 44–5.

In the Vladimir-Kostroma textile region, tens of thousands of women experienced the difference. The number of women who worked in factories in the region increased steadily in the years following 1861; so did the percentage of women in the workforce. In Shuia district, women workers constituted about 15.5 percent of the factory labor force in 1868 and 36 percent by the mid 1880s. By 1899, over a fifth of all peasant women between the ages of sixteen and fifty-five worked in a factory, and women made up close to 41 percent of more than fourteen thousand factory workers. A decade later, women workers slightly outnumbered men in Vladimir province as a whole. In Kostroma, women comprised 35 percent of textile workers in the 1880s. Over the next decade, three-quarters of the workers entering Kostroma factories for the first time were female, so that by the early twentieth century, the proportion of women workers had grown to almost 45 percent.[10]

A sizable minority of these women workers followed in the footsteps of their fathers or mothers. In prerevolutionary Russia, the conditions of the emancipation of the serfs and comparatively late industrialization retarded the development of a hereditary proletariat. At least until 1905, a majority of Russia's workers were the first in their families to enter a factory. But workers who did inherit their status usually worked in older and comparatively small rural plants or factories rather than in large urban centers, and most of them retained their links with agriculture. In Shuia district, Vladimir, and Nerekhta district, Kostroma, at the end of the nineteenth century, about 36 percent of women workers (and over 48 percent of men) had inherited their trade.[11]

These worker-peasants inhabited a different social and cultural landscape than their brothers and sisters in Moscow and St. Petersburg or even in the industrial city of Ivanovo-Voznesensk. While they had one foot in the factory, the other was often planted firmly in villages little touched by factory production. Their mothers and fathers, or sisters and brothers lived and worked much as peasants did elsewhere in rural Russia. In the words of a *zemstvo* investigator, "Alongside the industrial city of Ivanovo, nestled villages

10  For Vladimir, Ministerstvo vnutrennykh del. Tsentral'nyi statisticheskii komitet. *Statisticheskii vremennik Rossiiskoi imperii*, vyp. 3, "Materialy dlia izucheniia kustarnoi promyshlennosti i ruchnogo truda v Rossii" (St. Petersburg, 1872), 216; Rose Glickman, *Russian Factory Women*, 79–81; *MOZVG*, 10, vyp. 3, 62. For Kostroma, see Matveeva, "K voprosu," 94.
11  The closer the factory and the younger the workers, the higher became the proportion of hereditary workers. *MOZVG*, 10, vyp. 3, 51; *Materialy dlia otsenki zemel' Kostromskoi gubernii. Sbornik statisticheskikh svedenii po Kostromskoi gubernii* (hereafter *MOZKG*) (Kostroma, 1901), 80–5; 92–6. I have averaged the rates for workers in the Pavlov and Gorbunov mill, which together employed 96 percent of women workers in Sereda.

that differed little from all Russian villages, with their straw roofs, wooden ploughs, three-field system, domestic manufacture of linen, and so forth."[12] Popular culture remained largely the same as well, as Fyodor Samoilov observed. Samoilov was born in 1884 in a village about twelve miles from Ivanovo-Voznesensk. Virtually every family in his village sent at least one of its members off to work there. But according to Samoilov, the departure of family members had little effect on those who stayed behind. The peasants were reluctant to send their children to school, and they clung to traditional beliefs in forest and house spirits and in witches and wizards. Samoilov's father worked in a factory in Ivanovo, returning home only on holidays, but the authority of the household head (Fyodor's grandfather) remained undiminished. Fyodor's mother lived with her in-laws and "suffered a lot from the despotism of the family," Samoilov wrote.[13]

In other respects, as well, the villages of the Vladimir-Kostroma textile region were indistinguishable from villages elsewhere in rural Russia. Household needs and customary expectations shaped an individual's choices, whether the individual was male or female. Most nineteenth-century sources write of households "sending" their members off to work, and this choice of language is no accident. The decision to engage in factory labor, like the decision to go to St. Petersburg or to remain at home, was rarely just an individual one. Take, for example, the experience of Aleksei Makhov. A peasant from a village in Shuia district, he had worked as a weaver for five or six years in a mill in Ivanovo; in the final year, his wife joined him to work as a weaver, too. But around 1880, Makhov's recently widowed mother forced her son, his wife, and their small child to return to the village. If Aleksei did not accede to her wishes, the mother threatened to have his passport revoked and to have him beaten for lack of respect toward parental authority. She insisted that he, the eldest son, become head of the household (*bol'shak*) and take responsibility for paying the taxes and raising his younger brother and sisters. Makhov never went back to Ivanovo.[14]

---

12 *MOZVG*, 10, vyp. 3, 1.
13 F. Samoilov, *Po sledam minuvshego* (Moscow, 1954), 11–13.
14 Because of his father's years at Ivanovo, his son Nikifor would be considered an hereditary worker. He later became a Bolshevik. Makhov represents his father as preferring the life of the factory worker but virtually forced to assume the role of peasant patriarch. Perhaps the political climate of the late 1930s, when the memoir was published, affected the narrative and led the author to exaggerate his father's proletarian inclinations and to play down his own role in his return to the peasant village. But the backing and forthing from factory to village is authentic, and there is evidence elsewhere for widowed mothers demanding that their sons return. Nikifor Makhov, *Zhizn' minuvshaia* (Ivanovo, 1939), 8.

If anything, household needs and gender expectations shaped a woman's choices even more than they did a man's. They determined whether a woman earned money, when she began to work, and how long she would labor. Almost from the first, the rhythms of women's labor were closely attuned to the needs of her family. Although peasant children everywhere contributed to the household economy according to age and ability, in these industrial regions if the mother worked in a factory, her children were likely to assume adult responsibilities at an earlier age than usual and to grow up quickly. Carrying out the instructions of their elders, six-, seven- and eight-year-old children tackled work far beyond their years. Girls could substitute for the mother in the household, not only caring for siblings as many girls did, but also preparing simple meals and tidying up the house. By the age of ten, a girl might already bear all the burdens of her mother's household. The need for daughters at home meant that they took up factory work somewhat later than their brothers did: In Shuia district at the turn of the century, about 57 percent of the male workers, as compared to 50 percent of the female, had started work before the age of fifteen.[15]

Family needs also curtailed many women's experience of waged labor away from home. Women were more likely to leave the factory before their brothers and, overall, women spent less of their lives inside the factory gates. According to *zemstvo* investigators in Shuia, the greatest proportion of laboring women (over 40 percent) remained at the factory for under three years, while the highest proportion of men (32 percent) stayed for sixteen years or more. Of the male workers, 42 percent labored ten years or longer, but only 20 percent of the women did, and the vast majority of these came from families without land. Investigators found that the majority of women workers were young and single, or married and childless. After the age of twenty, the number of factory women dropped noticeably, especially from families with land, as the women married, became *khoziaiki*, and left the factory to care for their households and to work the land, tend the children, and perhaps weave for the factory at home in their "spare time."[16]

Even in factory regions, many women earned money at home. The expansion of factory production did not drive out domestic weaving; it transformed it, as well as other processes, into putting-out work and, by reducing earnings, restricted it almost exclusively to women and children, while men sought more lucrative trades elsewhere. In the 1870s and 1880s, a woman

15 Tenishev archive, op. 1, delo 50, 5; S. Budina and M. Shmeleva, *Gorod i narodnye traditsii Russkikh* (Moscow, 1989), 128; *MOZVG*, 10, vyp. 3, 52.
16 Ibid., 53–8; Tenishev archive, op. 1, delo 5, 19–29 (Vladimir, Vladimir).

working at home made no more than four rubles a month, for fifteen to eighteen hours of work a day, six days a week in wintertime, while a woman employed at a rural textile mill earned four to eight rubles a month in the 1870s, and seven to eight rubles a month a decade later.[17] In the 1890s the differences became even more substantial, as factory wages for women rose to twelve to thirteen rubles per month, more than three times as much as they could earn at home.[18] Despite the lure of higher wages, many peasant women continued to work in their cottages because of household needs. Although the return for their labor was abysmally low – so low that handloom weavers had long since abandoned the trade in Western Europe – at the turn of the century, ten thousand pairs of poorly paid hands wove cloth, sewed buttons, and engaged in a variety of other operations in the peasant cottages of Shuia. As late as 1909, women continued to do putting-out work for local factories in the villages of industrial Kostroma.[19]

When her household had an allotment of land (as did 73 percent of the households in Shuia), domestic production was often more suited than factory production to the demands on a woman's time. At home, she could control the pace of her work: She could abandon domestic production in the spring and take it up again in the fall; she could set it aside when she had to prepare meals, to clean up the hut, or to care for the livestock. If the household badly needed the woman's cash contribution, she could make up for the interruptions by extending her working hours far into the night. Women who worked at home labored longer hours than factory workers, just about every study indicates.[20] In order to spend as much time as possible at her loom, a handloom weaver might leave other tasks like fetching water or feeding chickens to a daughter or an old woman. Sometimes, two weavers would work the same loom, one during the day, the other all night.

A listing of 107 households located in the industrial region of Kostroma province permits a closer look at the factors that shaped peasant women's working lives.[21] Based on an investigation of household budgets that the

---

17 *Materialy dlia statistiki Kostromskoi gubernii*, vyp. 3 (Kostroma, 1872), 69.
18 *MOZVG*, 10, vyp. 3, 112–14; *Trudy komissii po izsledovaniiu kustarnoi promyshlennosti*, vyp. 13 (St. Petersburg, 1885), 422–3. In 1909, women's earnings at factory work remained much the same. *Statisticheskii ezhegodnik Kostromskoi gubernii za 1908–1909*, vyp. 1 (Kostroma, 1910), 61.
19 Ibid., 58.
20 See, for example, *MOZVG*, 10, vyp. 3, 11.
21 *Krest'ianskie biudzhety po Kostromskoi gubernii*, vyp. 1: Fabrichnyi raion. Sost. N.I. Vorob'ev, N.P. Makarov (Kostroma, 1924). Each household described is numbered. For convenience, I will refer to them by number in the text. I am very grateful to Robert Johnson for sharing this source with me.

Kostroma *zemstvo* conducted in 1909, the published results differ from similar studies in that they are presented household by household instead of on an aggregate basis. The listing provides data on age, sex, literacy, kinship position, yearly income, and the nature of employment of household members. This small sample of 107 households cannot be called "typical." Smaller (and probably poorer) households are underrepresented in it and, more importantly, the list contains neither landless nor absent households. Cash income was probably underreported by peasants who were suspicious of the investigator's obligations as tax assessors.[22] Women's income, the easiest to conceal, was the most likely to be underreported. Still, industrial Kostroma has much to tell us about the rhythms of women's work and its relation to household needs in villages near rural factories.

Those rhythms differed from patterns historians have found in much of Western Europe. Despite the tendency of married women to leave the factory labor force in rural Russia, a higher proportion of Kostroma factory women were married, and a still higher proportion had children than appears to have been the norm elsewhere. In England and France, married women with children constituted a small minority of women engaging in full-time, paid employment. In Germany, childbirth prompted married women textile workers to withdraw temporarily from the labor force.[23] This practice was apparently less common in rural Russia. In the Kostroma budget study, sixteen women (almost one-half) were married and ten of them (over a quarter of the total) had one or two children, ranging in age from three weeks to ten years of age.

The numbers of working mothers demonstrate opportunity more than they do poverty. According to Louise Tilly and Joan Scott, the availability of jobs for women, combined with the insufficiency of the husband's wage, are among the most important factors prompting married women to go out to work. The textile towns of Europe offered only low-paying opportunities for men and so demonstrated high levels of women's employment.[24] Lack of opportunities for men was not the impetus in rural Russia, however. There,

---

22 Robert Johnson, "Kinship and Nonagricultural Labor in Kostroma: A Preliminary Communication," unpublished paper, presented at the Conference on the Peasantry of European Russia, Boston, 1986, 3–4.

23 See the discussion in Louise Tilly and Joan Scott, *Women, Work, and Family* (New York, 1978), 126–45, and Kathleen Canning, "Gender and the Politics of Class Formation: Rethinking German Labor History," *American Historical Review* 97, no. 3 (June 1992): 749. A somewhat different pattern is suggested by George Alter, *Family and the Female Life Course: The Women of Verviers, Belgium, 1849–1880* (Madison, Wis., 1988), 102.

24 Tilly and Scott, *Women, Work, and Family*, 130–2.

textile mills hired men as well as women and paid men the higher wage. Rather, mothers took advantage of opportunities to earn wages near home so as to enhance their household's resources. In the household survey, women factory workers often derived from households that were as strong, or even stronger, economically than others in the region, and it was the women's wages that had helped to make the difference.[25] Household number fourteen, a "middling" one, according to the census takers, is one of these. The head of the household and his wife, a forty-year-old mother of two small children, one three-years-old and the other a month old, both worked at a factory nearby. The couple had accumulated three hundred rubles in savings.[26] In well-to-do household number seventy-seven, only the twenty-five-year-old daughter-in-law worked at a nearby factory, leaving behind her four-year-old son. The fifty-eight-year-old master of the household was doing sufficiently well to have already divided off three other sons and to have provided each of them with a house and outbuildings. In one of the two cases where "need" was clearly a factor in a mother's decision to work away from home, the need was the consequence of the couple's own actions. The head, an unusually literate man, was at twenty-nine a correspondent for the provincial *zemstvo*. Six years earlier, he had separated his household from his father's, presumably under unpleasant circumstances because he had received nothing whatsoever when he left. Although in his commitment to factory labor and his failure to receive an allotment he fits the profile of a proletarian, this worker chose not to become proletarianized. Borrowing 380 rubles from the factory where he now worked as a section elder, he purchased a house and a land allotment, using his wages as a means for "repeasantization." His wife worked at the same factory as he, and they hired a woman year-round to replace her in the household and to look after their children, a six-year-old daughter and, until his death, a one-month-old son (household number sixty-two).

Proximity to the factory was an important factor in a mother's decision to work. Most working mothers were employed by factories that were walking distance away. Important, too, were reliable substitutes for the mother. Most households with working mothers contained female kin who could provide child care in the mother's absence. Both these factors appear to have been

---

25 The fact that the household census is skewed by its underrepresentation of poor and landless households may also explain the absence of the genuinely needy. In Shuia, investigators found that "strong" households were about as likely as weaker ones to send female members to the factory but made no distinctions between married and single women, or among women who were mothers, *MOZVG*, 10, vyp. 3, 44.

26 See also numbers 55, 64, 82, 87.

more important than pressing economic necessity. The exceptions are the above household (number sixty-two), which hired a woman to look after the children, and household number three, where the father, a carpenter, looked after his eight-year-old son and five-year-old daughter while his wife was off at work. All the other mothers who went out to work left households where kinswomen such as sisters-in-law, spinster aunts, or, most commonly, mothers-in-law could look after small children. Thus, the extended Russian peasant family might free mothers to engage in waged labor when the opportunity arose. But members of the extended family rarely relieved working women of all of their labor at home, since most relatives were older and lacked the necessary strength. In 1911, Dr. L. Katenina, who examined women factory workers in Sereda, an industrial village in Kostroma, noted how much factory labor added to the peasant woman's burdens. Women who lived near the factory often combined factory and fieldwork, she observed. During the summer they would return from their shift and have to labor in the fields, in addition to working around the house and taking care of their children. Having slept no more than three hours, the women could barely stay awake when they went back to the factory.[27]

The mother's work was hard on her children, too. When a peasant woman worked in a factory, child care was necessarily negligent even when relatives pitched in to help. In order to return to her work as quickly as possible, a factory woman nursed her babies only briefly. If she lived too far from the factory for a daily trip, she might leave infants and children with a family member in the village, return to the factory, and settle in an apartment or cottage with her husband. More often, the mother lived at home and could nurse an infant and care for children daily after work. This was more beneficial for the child and for the mother as well, because nursing might prevent her from becoming pregnant again so quickly.

If they consciously adopted nursing (or any other practice, for that matter) as an effort to gain control over their reproductive lives, the women of Russia's rural factory regions would have demonstrated unusual self-assertion. The number of babies Russian peasant women bore – an average of 9.4 – have led historians to conclude that they practiced contraception minimally, if at all.[28] However, factory women may have had greater incentive

27 L. Katenina, "K voprosu o polozhenii rabotnits v tekstil'noi promyshlennosti," *Obshchestvennyi vrach*, no. 3 (Mar. 1914): 439.
28 A.G. Vishnevskii, "Rannie etapy stanovleniia novogo tipa rozhdaemosti v Rossii," in *Brachnost', rozhdaemost', smertnost' v Rossii i v SSSR*, ed. A.G. Vishnevskii (Moscow, 1977), 131–3.

to limit the number of their children, because it was so much more difficult for them to care for an infant and continue to work. Educated observers believed that women in factory districts tried to limit their fertility – unmarried women in order to avoid the shame of an illegitimate birth, married women to avoid the "great misfortune," or "unavoidable evil," of an additional child.[29] Older peasant women in factory districts were convinced: "Before there was less sin, but girls gave birth more often. Now girls and widows have affairs, but don't give birth."[30] According to statisticians and ethnographers, married women practiced birth control as well. An investigator for the St. Petersburg *zemstvo* in the late nineteenth century found that factory workers had smaller families than the neighboring agricultural population, and he hypothesized that women reduced their family size by a variety of means, including sending their children to foundling homes and perhaps "measures to prevent conception."[31] In the city of Shuia, working-class wives sometimes douched after intercourse to keep from becoming pregnant.[32] But if women who worked in rural factories were trying to control their fertility, their efforts were not successful or, at least, not successful enough to affect aggregate statistics on childbearing. Birthrates in Nerekhta, an industrial district of Kostroma, were about 55 infants per 1,000 people at the turn of the century, a rate that was higher than in Kostroma province as a whole.[33] In fact, statistics suggest that the most significant factor limiting family size was infant mortality, a kind of "postnatal family planning."[34] Between 1895 and 1899, 326 of every 1,000 infants perished in the first year of life in Kostroma province as a whole; in Kineshma district, the number was 363 per 1,000, in Nerekhta, 385.[35] As was the case elsewhere in Europe, infant mortality rates in Russia were higher in areas where mothers worked long hours away from home. Especially if they were deprived of mother's milk in the first six months of life, the infants of factory workers

---

29  M. Abashkina, A.C. Iliushina, and F.F. Karpukhin, *Povest' o trekh* (Moscow, 1935), 15; M. Balabanov, *Ocherki po istorii rabochego klassa v Rossii* (Moscow, 1925–6), 159.

30  Tenishev archive, op. 1, delo 58, 3.

31  *Materialy po statistike narodnago khoziaistva v S.-Peterburgskoi gubernii*, vyp. 5, S.-Peterburgskii uezd (St. Petersburg, 1885), pt. 2, 44–5; 48–9.

32  G. Popov, *Russkaia narodno-bytovaia meditsina po materialam "Etnograficheskogo biuro" Tenisheva* (St, Petersburg, 1903), 328.

33  Z.G. Frenkel', "Osnovnye pokazateli, kharakterizuiushchie dvizhenie naseleniia v Kostromskoi gubernii v tri poslednie piatiletiia (1891–1905)," *Trudy IX gubernskago s"ezda vrachei Kostromskoi gubernii*, vyp. 3 (Kostroma, 1906): 78–83.

34  Regina Schulte, "Infanticide in Rural Bavaria in the Nineteenth Century," in *Interest and Emotion: Essays on the Study of Family and Kinship*, ed. H. Medick and D. Sabean (Cambridge, England, 1984), 91.

35  *Obshchestvennoe i chastnoe prizrenie v Rossii* (St. Petersburg, 1907), 289.

died at rates far higher than the infants of peasant women from the same locales who remained at home after their children were born. The limited sample suggests that the infants of women factory workers in the villages of industrial Kostroma were more likely to perish, too.[36] Of the 23 children the census listed as under one year, 6 (26 percent) had died during the period of investigation. Four of the mothers were factory workers.

If concern for her infant's life figured in a mother's decision to stay at home, however, it did so only indirectly and in combination with other factors. Generally, mothers in the villages of industrial Kostroma stayed home when there were no other adult women in their household to substitute for them; when they had more than two children to care for, or when their children became old enough to start earning money themselves. Some of these mothers earned money at home. Domestic manufacture occupied thirty-eight of the women who stayed home. A still larger number of women contributed to their households exclusively in kind, laboring in the fields and around the house and yard, and earning no income at all. Their occupational profiles differed from men's. Men rarely engaged exclusively in fieldwork; instead, they combined it with *kustar'* and other trades that paid as well as factory labor. In the Kostroma households 61 percent of the women, but only 27 percent of the men over the age of ten, engaged in no form of paid work.[37]

Like a snapshot, the household census does not tell us much about either the past or the future of the people it represents. It is likely, however, that substantial numbers of the women who did not earn money in 1909 had once worked for wages, or would do so later on in their lives. In that respect, the census captures only some, but by no means all of the flexibility of women's (and indeed, men's) labor as it shifted in response to internal household needs and external opportunities. Here, another look at a few representative households might be helpful. Household number ninety-seven in the village of Nerekhta consisted of a couple in their fifties, their daughter of twelve, their married son of thirty and his wife, also thirty, and their three children. Such complex family households of six to ten people made up 47.7 percent of the Kostroma household list and 34.7 percent of the households in the 1897 census.[38] The head of the household worked as a carter: In October and November, he chauffeured the village policeman about; then from December

---

36 On women workers in general, see I.S. Veger, "K statistike smertnosti detei fabrichnykh rabochikh," *Vrach* 40 (1899): 1157. It is impossible to know whether the Kostroma investigators recorded all recent infant deaths. The numbers may have been even higher.
37 Johnson, "Kinship and Nonagricultural Labor," 9.
38 Ibid., 14.

to February, he brought wood to a nearby factory. The son was employed year-round as a spinner in a factory. The daughter-in-law had been a weaver at that same factory, but had left it the previous fall to weave at home and to care for her children, six, three, and eleven months old.[39] Another exemplary household was simpler in composition. Consisting of seven people, the household was headed by a twenty-four-year-old who was employed stamping goods at a factory almost fourteen miles away. His fourteen-year-old brother was apprenticed as a roofer, and his eleven-year-old brother worked as a shepherd in a village about six and a half miles away. In addition to tilling their allotment and caring for her two daughters, aged three and one, the *khoziaika*, aged twenty-five, wove linen at home from November to May, then went off with her forty-nine-year-old widowed mother-in-law to spread gravel on the banks of the Volga. In these households, as in others, it was the needs of the family economy that determined the work women did and where they did it.

This was as true of single women as of married ones. Whether or not she lived at home, a female factory worker continued to be part of her family's economy and to hand over a portion of her wages. In Shuia, 86.3 percent of all women workers (and 87.8 percent of men) gave part of their wages to their families. Even when they came from households with no allotment of land, over three-fourths of women workers gave some money to their families. The Kostroma household listing suggests similar practices in the relatively few instances where it indicates how women disposed of their earnings. A nineteen-year-old girl from Iur'evets-Podol'skii district supported her alcoholic father, three younger brothers, and two younger sisters on the wages she earned at a factory three miles from home, to which she walked every day in warm weather, and where she lived in winters, returning home only on holidays (household number twenty-two). A twenty-seven-year-old spinster, who lived and worked as a servant in the city of Nerekhta, contributed a portion of her wages to her household, headed by her twenty-three-year-old brother (household number forty-seven). Two sisters from Kineshma, aged twenty and twenty-one, employed as weavers and presumably residing near a factory over ten miles from home, received their food from the household of their twenty-four-year-old brother, whose debts they apparently had helped to pay (household number fifty-nine).[40] A married couple from Nerekhta had a similar arrangement. He was thirty-two, she thirty-three, and both worked at a factory in the village of Sereda and sent the major

39 Household number ninety-six is very similar.
40 See also household number eighty-six.

portion of their wages to his father, at fifty-three the master of a well-to-do household of four, which supplied the couple with food products from home (household number ninety).

All of this suggests that the peasant family economy had adapted relatively smoothly to the new circumstances of wage and factory labor. Sending a woman to work in a nearby factory was greatly preferable to allowing her to travel to a distant city, where she might experience long separations from kin and community. Local industry thus enabled the men of her household to reap the benefits of a woman's labor without losing control over her person. In Shuia, an important determinant of whether women worked in a factory was how close it was to the village. The more accessible the factory, the more likely that a woman would work there. "The closer you come to the city of Ivanovo or Shuia, the larger the amounts of land that remain uncultivated, because all hands have gone off [to work in the factory]."[41] Only the poorest households were exempt from the general rule that the further away the factory, the more unwilling the men of the household were to allow women to go off by themselves. Women, especially single women, worked very close to home unless other family members could accompany them to the factory or they belonged to a household that was so poor that they had no choice, or so well off that they could spare a horse for the woman to ride to work and perhaps a child to bring her food from home.[42]

In villages of industrial Kostroma, too, distance operated as a restraining factor. In Sereda, 5,036 women engaged in factory work in 1900; half of them came from neighboring villages, and another 47 percent derived from the district of Nerekhta. A quarter of these women workers lived at home.[43] Judging from data in the Kostroma household survey, when women lived away from home, in dormitories or rented rooms at the factory where they worked, others from their family usually lived there, too. Two of the married women workers appear to have lived at home; the other 14 were employed in the same factory as their husbands. Single women worked in the same factory as either their mothers or fathers (household numbers 30, 44, 84) or other siblings (household numbers 59, 66). Or they lived at home or worked close enough to visit on holidays and perhaps receive food from the

---

41 *MOZVG*, 9, vyp. 3, Iur'ev district (Vladimir, 1908), 15.

42 Even the women who lived in a working-class district of Ivanovo derived from the local peasantry, and the few who had traveled from far away usually came as members of a family. *MOZVG*, 10, vyp. 3, 49–50; 105.

43 Of all women workers in Nerekhta, 87 percent worked within their native district. *MOZKG*, 80–5; 92–6.

household (household numbers 22, 48, 88, and 102). The residence of two more single women remains unclear (household numbers 39 and 95). Only one woman, a thirty-two-year-old spinster working in St. Petersburg, seems to have separated herself entirely from her village (household number 70). Focusing as it does on the household, rather than the factory settlement, the household listing may exaggerate the number of factory women living in family situations. For example, at the end of the nineteenth century, 18.7 percent of 555 women workers were not living with their families in Kokhma, an industrial village in Vladimir. If we look at small urban settings, the proportion of women on their own becomes even higher.[44] Nevertheless, the percentages remain much lower than in the cities of Moscow and St. Petersburg. The question of women workers on their own will be addressed in the following chapter. The practice of women living with family members seems congruent with what we know about women's migration to work in textile mills elsewhere in Europe, where they often moved with the entire family. And in rural Russia as well, even when women lived on their own, migration usually remained an "integral part of a familial economic and moral order."[45]

In some other respects, too, the proximity of industry had only a minimal impact on the peasant way of life. Rates and ages at time of marriage serve as one example: They are virtually identical with patterns found elsewhere in rural Russia. In Sereda, for example, three-quarters of factory women aged twenty to twenty-nine (1,410 women) were married, the same proportion as in Russia as a whole. Marriage rates in Nerekhta and Iur'evets-Podol'skii districts of Kostroma (although not in Kineshma), were higher than in Kostroma province as a whole.[46] This pattern of early and nearly universal marriage contrasts with the one that Robert Johnson found in urban Moscow. According to his calculations, migrant and factory women in that city adapted themselves to an urban pattern, marrying later or not at all.[47]

---

44 *MOZVG*, 10, vyp. 3, 363–410.
45 Leslie Page Moch and Louise Tilly, "Joining the Urban World: Occupation, Family, and Migration in Three French Cities," *Comparative Studies in Society and History* 27, no. 1 (Jan. 1985): 33. A. Gordon Darroch, "Migrants in the Nineteenth Century: Fugitives or Families in Motion?" *Journal of Family History* 6 (Fall 1981): 257. In Kokhma, for example, 56 percent of peasant women workers living without their families sent a portion of their wages home to the village, *MOZVG*, 10, vyp. 3, 360–1.
46 *MOZKG*, 80–5; 92–6; Frenkel', "Osnovnye pokazateli," 78–83.
47 Robert Johnson, "Family Relations and the Rural-Urban Nexus: Patterns in the Hinterland of Moscow, 1880–1900," in *The Family in Imperial Russia*, ed. David Ransel (Urbana, Ill., 1978), 271.

Courtship is another example of the tenacity of the peasant way of life. Many of the courtship practices of peasants near rural factories are identical to those found elsewhere in rural Russia. In Teikovo, where most women workers lived in their native village, courtship took place in groups.[48] In the evenings after a long day's work, the youths and maidens would gather together, dancing and singing *chastushki* to the music of the accordian.[49] The "rough courtship" practices that existed in many of the villages of Shuia are indistinguishable from practices found in parts of Novgorod and Riazan that had no local industry.[50] Youths would grab playfully at a maiden's breasts and genitals and make bawdy jokes about sexual relations. And in villages near rural factories, the double standard remained firmly entrenched.

Nevertheless, individual wage earning did alter some aspects of village life. For example, the fact that the young earned wages exaggerated the importance of clothing in courtship. Clothing became a crucial measure of a maiden's worth – the more elegant and expensive (*modno*), the better.[51] More troubling to observers of village life, some women took advantage of their wages to claim greater sexual latitude for themselves, as did the woman whose story introduced this chapter. Discussions of women's morals in villages near factories tend to be somewhat contradictory. On the one hand, accounts invariably report increased sexual license; on the other, they suggest an ambivalent reaction on the part of the peasant community – condemnation in some cases, tolerance in others. What seems clear is that while peasants might disapprove of premarital sex, the money a woman could contribute to her in-law's household inevitably reduced the significance of her virginity in the calculations of her future in-laws. Judging by the money women saved, these contributions could be substantial. In Vladimir province as a whole, 4,839 factory women (approximately 12 percent of the total) averaged savings of 169 rubles apiece in 1898; in 1904, 12,015 factory women had set aside comparable amounts.[52]

What a woman had saved and could earn increased her value to her

---

48 On the origins of women workers, see *MOZVG*, 10, vyp. 3, 302, 306.

49 Makhov, *Zhizn' minuvshaia*, 75–7.

50 See Barbara Alpern Engel, "Peasant Morality and Pre-marital Relations in Late Nineteenth-Century Russia," *Journal of Social History* 23, no. 4 (Summer 1990): 700.

51 Tenishev archive, op. 1, delo 5, 21; delo 59, 2 (Shuia, Vladimir); delo 6, 7 (Vladimir, Vladimir); delo 23, 30 (Melenki, Vladimir).

52 *Otchet gosudarstvennykh sberegatel'nykh kass po sberegatel'nym okrugam* (St. Petersburg, yearly); number of working women in 1897 from N.A. Troinitskii, ed., *Chislennost' i sostav rabochikh v Rossii na osnovanii dannykh pervoi vseobshchei perepisi naseleniia Rossiiskoi imperii 1897 g.* (St. Petersburg, 1906), 1: 16.

spouse's household. As measured by expenditures on weddings, women were more highly valued in industrial regions than in outmigratory ones. Weddings represented an investment, and they cost the groom's side much more than the bride's. By contrast with areas of substantial male outmigration, where the custom of dowering daughters with expensive items had become widespread by the end of the nineteenth century, bride-price remained more financially significant in the villages of industrial regions. Young women generally brought only clothing and bedding with them when they married, whereas grooms paid the bride's parents substantial sums to "redeem her" (*na vykup*), compensating the household for the loss of her earning power. As Steven Hoch has noted, the amount of bride-price is a measure of a woman's worth.[53] Men paid a bride-price ranging from thirty to sixty rubles, depending on their resources. They also spent money on the wedding ceremony, paying twenty-five to thirty rubles for wine, and between five and thirty rubles to the parish priest for conducting the ceremony. In some parishes, the clergy levied a special tax on weddings. For a wedding, expenditures by the groom's side averaged between fifty and a hundred rubles, and between twenty and forty rubles by the bride's.[54]

When peasant families spent such sums, they expected the new bride to earn it back at the factory. So long as she worked hard and turned the money over to the family, many people were prepared to overlook a woman's behavior even when they did not approve of it. The young were reportedly even more accepting. As early as the 1880s, the virginity of the bride had ceased to be significant in the eyes of her contemporaries in some villages near rural factories. "If everyone fasted, there would be no one to christen," the young were heard to say.[55] Everyone placed the blame for loosened morals on the availability of factory labor. "Girls lose their virginity more frequently now, thanks to factory life," as one peasant put it.[56] If worse really came to worst, peasants said, and a woman bore an illegitimate child, she could send it to the foundling home in Moscow (at a cost of thirty rubles for

---

53  Tenishev archive, op. 1, fond 5, 26–7; fond 59, 4; I. Dobrotvorskii, "Krest'ianskie iuridicheskie obychai v vostochnoi chasti Vladimirskoi gubernii," *Iuridicheskii vestnik*, 6–7 (1889): 325–6, 336; Steven Hoch, *Serfdom and Social Control in Russia: Petrovskoe, a Village in Tambov* (Chicago, 1986), 100–1.

54  Dobrotvorskii, "Krest'ianskie iuridicheskie," 336; P. Leont'ev, "O krest'ianskikh svad'bakh v osen' i zimu 1904–5 gg.," *Vestnik Vladimirskago gubernskago zemstva*, no. 23–4 (1905): 13.

55  Dobrotvorskii, "Krest'ianskie iuridicheskie,' 336.

56  Tenishev archive, op. 1, delo 58, 11–12; delo 59, 3 (Shuia, Vladimir). See also V.P. Semenov, ed, *Rossiia: Polnoe geograficheskoe opisanie nashego otechestva*, 11 vols. (St. Petersburg, 1899) 1: 109–10 and Dobrotvorskii, "Krest'ianskie iuridicheskie," 336.

transport, higher than the prevailing rate elsewhere) or even keep it, leaving it in someone else's care and maintaining herself and the child with her wages. Everyone seemed convinced that morals around the factories had become looser. In the words of an ethnographic correspondent, "Here in the factory regions it is considered no crime for a girl to lose her virginity." "Only one or two girls out of a dozen are virtuous when they marry," the local peasants asserted, expressing both their disapproval and their acceptance of the unavoidable.[57]

However, illegitimacy statistics suggest that both the peasants and the ethnographic correspondents who reported their words may have exaggerated the effect of factory labor on women's sexual behavior. To be sure, illegitimacy statistics are not a satisfactory way to measure the sexual behavior of unmarried women. They are still less satisfactory in the Russian case, where the incidence of illegitimacy was always underreported, and the methods of gathering statistics haphazard.[58] Nevertheless, illegitimacy statistics do serve to indicate trends and to provide a basis, however shaky, for comparison. Judging by the numbers, it seems unlikely that unmarried women in Shuia or Nerekhta were engaging in premarital sex in substantially larger numbers than in other rural areas. Between 1885 and 1899, for every 1,000 babies born, about 3.5 were illegitimate in Shuia and about 2.7 in Nerekhta.[59] These illegitimacy rates were considerably lower than those in Moscow and St. Petersburg. On the other hand, the figures do indicate some weakening of community control over sexual behavior: Rates in Shuia and Nerekhta districts were higher than in other districts of Vladimir and Kostroma provinces and higher than in rural Russia as a whole.

Women's wage-earning opportunities might also reduce peasant husbands' authority over their wives, according to the complaints of men from villages in industrialized regions that married women had become harder to handle. In the 1870s, wives behaved so "dissolutely" in villages of Ivanovo canton, Shuia district, that husbands had to turn them out of the household or even drag them before the *volost'* court. Empowered by custom to discipline wives as they pleased, husbands rarely turned to the *volost'* court for help in

57 Tenishev archive, op. 1, delo 58, 10, 12; delo 68, 1–3. (Shuia, Vladimir).
58 For the reasons why they are not, see the discussion in Peter Laslett, "Introduction," in *Bastardy and Its Comparative History*, ed. Peter Laslett et al. (Cambridge, England, 1980), 1–65; and David Ransel, "Problems in Measuring Illegitimacy in Prerevolutionary Russia," *Journal of Social History* 16, no. 2 (Winter 1982): 111–15.
59 Calculated from reports in Russia. Ministerstvo Vnutrennykh Del. Tsentral'nyi statisticheskii komitet, *Statisticheskii vremennik Rossiiskoi imperii* (also known at times as *Sbornik svedenii po Rossii* and *Ezhegodnik Rossii*).

dealing with them; the fact that men did in these villages indicates their loss of authority in the household.[60] Moreover peasant men in industrial districts (and only in industrial districts) particularly objected to a law, enacted in 1863, that freed women from corporal punishment and forbade peasant courts to flog women. In Nerekhta, Kostroma, the men complained "They [the women] don't want to live at home, and they abandon their husband for days on end. Flogging would do them good." In Shuia, the peasants claimed that because women could no longer be beaten by decision of the court, women no longer feared anyone, and had become drunken and dissolute. The men placed the blame squarely on factory employment. "Factory life has spoiled the women completely. The wife has become separated from the husband. She has a husband at home and a lover at the factory," they declared.[61] Anecdotes from the close of the century suggest that at least some married women in factory districts continued flagrantly to misbehave. An ethnographic correspondent from Shuia relates the story of one woman who had betrayed her husband with a series of lovers from the first days of their marriage. At first, the husband would beat her, but this had no effect. As he himself put it, "A man would need a hundred fists like mine, and even so, he couldn't knock all the nonsense out of her." The woman whose shaming began this chapter continued to conduct herself after her marriage as she had before it, despite her husband's frequent beatings.[62]

Nevertheless, complaints about wayward women should be treated with caution. Everywhere in Europe, middle-class observers registered concern about the moral consequences of factory employment for women. In Russia, such concerns led educated observers to condemn as immoral peasant practices that they might have overlooked or interpreted differently in an exclusively agricultural setting. In peasant culture, bawdy stories, sayings, and songs were commonplace, but when I. Dobrotvorskii, writing for the *Judicial Herald* in 1889, noted the prevalence of "unprintable songs and sayings" in the villages of Shuia, he attributed them to the influence of factory work. A decade later, an ethnographic correspondent similarly explained the "liberties" (*vol'noe obrashchenie*) boys and girls took with one another, although, as we saw in Chapter 1, overtly erotic practices could be found in many parts

---

60 A.A. Titov, "Iuridicheskie obychai sela Nikola-Perevoz, Sulostskoi volosti, Rostovskago uezda," *Vestnik Iaroslavskago zemstva*, no. 181–3 (July–Sept. 1887): 49.

61 *Trudy komissii po preobrazovaniiu volostnykh sudov*, 7 vols. (St. Petersburg, 1874) 2: 10, 18, 35; 3: 320.

62 Tenishev archive, op. 1, delo 58, 9–12.

of rural Russia.[63] Peasant men joined middle-class men in articulating concerns about the influence of factory behavior on female morals, but peasants
were troubled not by bawdy behavior but by their conviction that a woman's
freedom from male control almost inevitably eventuated in the woman's
sexual license. It is likely that their anxieties about losing control over women
led men of both groups greatly to exaggerate the impact of wage earning on
women's sexual behavior before and after marriage, although as we have
seen, their concerns about loosening morals were not entirely groundless.
Still, it is worth remembering that most women went out to work for the
sake of the family economy. The women's workdays were long, their working
conditions hot and dirty and highly unsanitary, with cotton dust thick in the
air. Machinery remained unguarded and industrial accidents were commonplace. The factory administration certainly did not spoil their women workers with politeness, as one woman physician put it. After decades of work, a
fifty-year-old woman looked more like a feeble seventy-year-old. Working
conditions were hardly "luxurious," despite the claims of some middle-class
observers.[64]

In their discussion of worker-peasants, Holmes and Quataert have contended that while cleavages exist between the sexes and across generations,
grim social and economic circumstances nevertheless "enforce familial interdependence."[65] This was surely the case in Russia, too, despite the cases
dragged before the *volost'* courts, or reported by ethnographic correspondents. Nevertheless, the evidence in this chapter suggests that when people
who had woven, spun, or otherwise manufactured goods together in the
household left it to work for wages at nearby factories, things could change,
although not so much as they changed when people migrated to a major city.
To the physician L. Katenina, who studied the factory women of Sereda
on the eve of World War I, they seemed ignorant and downtrodden, true
daughters of the village. Yet the women had greater access to written culture
than women in exclusively agricultural areas. However low the literacy rates
of rural factory workers by urban standards, they compared well with the
literacy rates of the general peasant population. At the turn of the century in
Sereda, 40 percent of women workers between fifteen and nineteen were
considered literate, twice the rate of Russia as a whole. Literacy rates in

---

63 Dobrotvorskii, "Krest'ianskie iuridicheskie," 336; Tenishev archive, op. 1, delo 58, 12.
64 On conditions in rural factories, see Katenina, "K voprosu," 439–41. "In the factories,
   workers earn a lot and live very luxuriously," wrote a correspondent for the Kostroma
   *zemstvo* in 1908. *Statisticheskii ezhegodnik Kostromskoi gubernii* (Kostroma, 1909), 60–1.
65 Holmes and Quataert, "An Approach to Modern Labor," 194.

Shuia were slightly higher.[66] Moreover, by the early twentieth century, elements of a modern culture had found their way into some village environments. Surveying the reading habits of Vladimir peasants, Aleksei Smirnov found that peasants in villages near rural factories were more prone than others to read books by well-known authors and less likely to turn to religious or moral tales. In these villages, the average peasant home library consisted of 15 books (although two of the ninety households he surveyed had 130 and 146 books apiece), and the demand for books was growing. V.A. Andreev, who studied workers' budgets in Sereda in 1911, wrote that six of the eighteen families he queried had purchased books and journals, although the workers spent considerably more on religion, which remained a significant factor in their lives. And in addition to paying visits, going hunting or to family celebrations such as weddings and christenings, the villagers in Sereda might attend a local cinema, too.[67]

The earning power of young couples also changed their status in the household. While it did not do away with rural patriarchy, factory wages sometimes altered its distribution, mostly to the benefit of junior males, to some extent democratizing patriarchy, to borrow a term from Judith Stacey.[68] This is in contrast to the districts of Kostroma from which men migrated to St. Petersburg to work. There, the redistribution of family authority benefited older women. Marriage in industrial Kostroma often coincided with "separation from the paternal or fraternal family unit," with the new husband becoming head of his own household.[69] In only one household (out of 107) in industrial Kostroma did married brothers reside together. Eleven of the household heads, 11.1 percent of the total, were younger than thirty. In the 67 households of outmigratory Kostroma, by comparison, there were 5 households with coresident married brothers, and only five (8 percent) of the household heads were under thirty. More telling still is the gender of household heads. In industrial Kostroma, widowed mothers were numerous, but only one of them headed her own household, and she was the forty-six-year-old mother of a seventeen-year-old son (household number six). The other

---

66 Katenina, "K voprosu," 446. Literacy rates for Shuia were calculated on the basis of the 1897 census; for Sereda, they were calculated from *MOZKG*, 83–4; 95–6.

67 Aleksei Smirnov, "Kniga vo Vladimirskoi derevne," *Vestnik Vladimirskago gubernskago zemstva*, no. 5–6 (1905): 57–8; V.A. Andreev, "Rabochie biudzhety po issledovaniiu 1911 g." *Materialy dlia otsenki nedvizhimykh imushchestv v gorodakh i fabrichnykh poselkakh Kostromskoi gubernii. Tom 1, Statisticheskie svedeniia o Seredskom fabrichnom raione Nerekhtskogo uezda*, vyp. 2 (Kostroma, 1911), 36–7.

68 Judith Stacey, *Patriarchy and Socialist Revolution in China* (Berkeley, Calif., 1983), 224–7.

69 Johnson, "Kinship and Nonagricultural Labor," 11.

widows lived in households that their sons headed, even if (in one case) the son was only twenty. In outmigratory Kostroma, at least ten widows (16 percent) headed viable complex family households, 3 of those households containing grown-up, married sons with children, and 3 more, coresident, married sons, one as old as thirty-five.[70]

Of course, it is unlikely that a young wife mourned the loss of her mother-in-law's authority any more than she would have mourned the loss of her father-in-law's, and in that sense younger women benefited from wage labor, too. An early and dramatic example of what this might mean appeared in the *volost'* court records of Ivanovo district, where all the peasants worked at local factories. In 1871, a father and his son came into conflict over the daughter-in-law, who wanted to visit her own family. The father refused her permission; the son allowed her to go anyway and gave her some money to cover the cost of the travel. This insubordination infuriated the father so much that he beat the son, who then abandoned the father's household to live on his own with the wife.[71] This shifting of loyalty from the extended to the nuclear family contributed to the breakdown of the larger household. Elsewhere in rural Russia, discontented women often took the initiative in bringing about household separations. While authority might remain in the husband's hands, in the "small" family household, consisting of husband, wife, and children, the woman was at least free from the authority of her in-laws. When his uncle and his father divided the household after their mother's death, Fyodor Samoilov's mother was especially pleased, but even the children breathed more easily.[72] Moreover, when women left simpler households to work in factories, it sometimes caused gender distinctions to blur. If the men stayed home, they fetched the water, fed the livestock, and took on many of the tasks customarily fulfilled by women, cooking included.[73] To the extent that the authoritarian, extended family gave way to a more "companionate" sort of marriage, the life of a wife probably became a little easier.

Wage earning permitted the young more latitude in establishing a household of their own. If the father refused permission, the son might separate on his own (*samovol'no*), and if there was no place for him in the village, he could take off with his wife for the factory, as did two married couples in the Kostroma budget sample, who had "firmly established themselves" at

70 D.N. Zhbankov, *Bab'ia storona* (Kostroma, 1891), 103–10. I have counted only widows who were identified in the census as *khoziaika vdova*.

71 *Trudy komissii*, 2: 15.

72 Samoilov, *Po sledam minuvshego*, 21–2.

73 Budina and Shmeleva, *Gorod i narodnye*, 175.

the factory and no longer sent money to their fathers (household number eighty-nine). A correspondent for the Vladimir *zemstvo* summed up the change succinctly: "When everyone worked together, it was not hard to share the income, but when a worker earns the money himself [*sic*], then he wants to keep it for himself and his own family."[74]

Was the worker-peasant family dissolving then, disrupting the longstanding, cyclical rhythms of peasant household formation and dissolution?[75] On the basis of household composition in industrial Kostroma the answer would surely be no, or perhaps more accurately, not very often. Of the twenty-one married couples where the wife was (or had recently been) a factory worker, only three had separated against the *bol'shak*'s will, while fourteen more remained part of a complex family household. (Fourteen more households were simple, but evidently as a result of natural, not forced, fissioning.) Factory work, like domestic manufacture, could become part of the rhythm of the peasant household. Consider the experience of the Samoilovs'. Several years after happily setting up a household of their own, they found that they could not live off their tiny plot of land. In 1895, primarily at the insistence of the mother, the family sold their cow and horse, gave up their land, locked up their hut, and taking along their chickens, moved to the city of Ivanovo-Voznesensk. Both parents found work as weavers, and when Fyodor became old enough, he started to work as well. But they all disliked the noise and filth of the factory and the dusty, smelly streets of the working-class district. Besides, on their combined earnings of thirty-three rubles a month, there was never enough to eat. So after several years in Ivanovo, the older Samoilovs and their smaller children returned to the village, reclaimed their land, and moved back into their hut, leaving Fyodor in Ivanovo to work and to contribute to the family economy. Winters, his father would join him, stopping work only when his second son became old enough to earn factory wages, too. The Samoilovs' experience suggests how problematic the label "proletarian" could sometimes be. Although many historians would have considered them to be proletarians when they closed up their house and moved their entire family to work in Ivanovo (a household in the city being an important criteria of proletarianization), for the Samoilov family, factory

74  *Obzor Vladimirskoi gubernii v selsko-khoziaistvennom otnoshenii za 1899*, vyp. 3 (Vladimir, 1900), 33–4.
75  See A.V. Chayanov, *The Theory of Peasant Economy* (Madison, Wis., 1986); Teodor Shanin, *The Awkward Class: Political Sociology of Peasantry in a Developing Society, Russia 1910–1925* (Oxford, 1972).

labor remained part of the peasant household's struggle for survival.[76] Yet the evidence also indicates that even when it remained part of a household strategy, factory labor could broaden cultural horizons and bring subtle shifts in the authority relations within the peasant household. It strengthened the position of the younger adults of the household vis-à-vis the older generation, permitting somewhat greater female self-assertiveness and enabling discontented young wives more easily to escape the power of their in-laws; but most of all, it seems to have empowered junior males. As the peasant family demonstrated its ability to adapt to new economic circumstances, rural patriarchy was modified, but it nevertheless remained intact.

76 Samoilov, *Po sledam minuvshego*, 21–39. Samoilov himself took part in the unrest in Ivanovo in 1905 and went on to become a Bolshevik.

# 5. On their own in the city

In 1884, Evdokiia Kiseleva left her village in Riazan to live and work in St. Petersburg, where her sister already resided. Within a year she had conceived an illegitimate child; she would bear at least three more over the following years. In 1902, eighteen years after her arrival in the city she was still illiterate and earned ten rubles a month for her work as a domestic servant. On these wages, she rented a tiny room, which she shared with her four children. The story of Aleksandra Kondrat'eva, a peasant woman from Novgorod, is similar. She lost her father when she was thirteen, and shortly afterwards in 1886, she moved to St. Petersburg. She found work at the Shtiglitz factory, and at some point, she began to live with a man. At the age of twenty she bore him a child and then bore another five years later. The father abandoned the family after the birth of yet another child, leaving Aleksandra with an unnamed illness that forced her to quit working at the factory and to hire out on a daily basis. In 1901, after fifteen years of life in the city, Aleksandra was still unable to read or write. She and her children lived in a corner of a room, which they shared with two other families.[1]

Kiseleva and Kondrat'eva's stories are virtually indistinguishable from the stories of hundreds of other young, unattached peasant women who came to the city to seek their fortunes and wound up conceiving illegitimate children. In St. Petersburg, over 8,000 women bore illegitimate children every year between 1886 and 1895, and about 9,000 did the same in Moscow in the early 1890s. Statisticians for the St. Petersburg city yearbook estimated that during those years, of every 100 single women aged twenty-one to thirty, 9.5 bore illegitimate children.[2] At the turn of the century, illegitimacy rates in both Moscow and St. Petersburg numbered slightly over one-fourth

---

1 TsGIA SSSR, fond 1409, op. 15, ed kh. 1053; 1102.
2 The figures are from *Statisticheskii ezhegodnik S.-Peterburga* and *Dannye o rodivshikhsia i brakov v g. Moskve*, both published yearly. The Moscow figures are exclusive of children delivered to the foundling home.

of live births, down a little from earlier years.[3] These rates were roughly the same as rates in Paris, and although they were lower than rates in some other European cities such as Vienna (50 percent), Prague (50 percent), Rome (45 percent) or Stockholm (40 percent), they were far higher than rates in London (4 percent) and higher than rates in other Russian cities and towns.[4] Illegitimacy rates in Moscow and St. Petersburg were over ten times higher than the rates in Russia's villages, where illegitimacy rarely exceeded 2 percent.

When single women migrated to the city, it often disrupted the balance between productive activity and reproduction that characterized peasant marriage. The married couple formed the basic labor unit in the village. Everywhere in peasant Russia, a married woman made a vital contribution to the family economy at the same time she raised her children. As we saw in Chapter 2, women's contribution to the family economy was even more vital in the provinces of the Central Industrial Region from which most migrants to Moscow and St. Petersburg originated, because male migrants so often left the fieldwork in the hands of their wives. Keeping their wives and children in the village permitted many men who migrated to the city to marry and raise a family on their meager wages.

However, these very circumstances – the importance of the wife in the village and the enormous expense of life in Russia's major cities – condemned most women migrants to spinsterhood and put many at risk of bearing illegitimate children. In Russia as elsewhere in Europe, migrant women were in a precarious position in the city, and nonmarital pregnancy served as evidence of that precariousness; it was the "biological manifestation of their economic and social vulnerability."[5] But women's vulnerability had a unique dimension in Russia, because such a high proportion of their migrant male counterparts were unavailable for marriage in the city. Although migrant men far outnumbered women in Russia's cities, a substantial proportion of these men were unable to marry a woman in the city because they already had a village wife or would someday acquire one. Trying to explain why rates of marriage were so much lower in Russia's cities than in other cities like Berlin, Stockholm, and Vienna, a statistician for the city of St.

3 David Ransel, "Problems in Measuring Illegitimacy in Prerevolutionary Russia," *Journal of Social History* 16, no. 2 (Winter 1982): 111–23.
4 Rachel Fuchs and Leslie Page Moch, "Pregnant, Single, and Far from Home: Migrant Women in Nineteenth-Century Paris," *American Historical Review* 95, no. 4 (Oct. 1990): 1009–10.
5 Ibid., 1009.

Table 5.1. *Total number of marriages and illegitimate births in working-class Moscow*

| District | 1895 | | 1899 | | 1901 | | 1905* | |
|---|---|---|---|---|---|---|---|---|
| | Marriages | Illegit. Births | Marriages | Illegit. Births | Marriages | Illegit. Births | Marriages | Illegit. Births |
| Iakimanskaia | 207 | 225 | 301 | 265 | 263 | 236 | 265 | 431 |
| Piatnitskaia | 337 | 352 | 466 | 372 | 390 | 332 | 386 | 415 |
| Serpukhovskaia | 196 | 155 | 216 | 184 | 224 | 233 | 235 | 336 |

| District | 1906 | | 1907 | | 1910 | |
|---|---|---|---|---|---|---|
| | Marriages | Illegit. Births | Marriages | Illegit. Births | Marriages | Illegit. Births |
| Iakimanskaia | 315 | 284 | 325 | 471 | 347 | 382 |
| Piatnitskaia | 507 | 610 | 432 | 292 | 458 | 223 |
| Serpukhovskaia | 305 | 228 | 291 | 291 | 294 | 326 |

* The fact that marriage rates rose noticeably in some working-class districts during 1905 will be discussed in Chapter 7.
*Source*: *Dannye o rodivshikhsia i brakakh v r. Moskve* for relevant years.

Petersburg pointed to his city's vast migrant population, and to "the completely circumstantial sojourn of most of these residents, who have neither a stable place in the capital nor stable interests. All of their interests are at home, where their fiancée lives, while in the city they find temporary wages, and the struggle for a crust of bread."[6] But even migrant workers who enjoyed more stable positions often returned to the village when the time came to marry. Vanka Korovin was typical. After several years of apprenticeship in the metalworking trade, he married a village woman according to his father's wishes, then left her in the village and returned to work in the city.[7] Male workers sometimes put it this way: "They brought me to St. Petersburg in a basket [as a child] and now I'm going off [to the village] to marry."[8] This meant that the odds were against a migrant woman's bringing courtship to the successful conclusion of marriage. The picture emerges sharply in Tables 5.1 and 5.2, which compare the number of illegitimate births with

6 *Statisticheskii ezhegodnik S. Peterburga. 1885* (St. Petersburg, 1886), 12.
7 R.E. Zelnik, ed., *A Radical Worker in Tsarist Russia: The Autobiography of Semën Ivanovich Kanatchikov* (Stanford, Calif., 1986), 50–4.
8 Quoted in A. Shuster, *Peterburgskie rabochie v 1905–1907 gg.* (Leningrad, 1976), 31.

Table 5.2. *Marriage and illegitimacy rates in working-class St. Petersburg (per thousand)*

| District | 1902 | | 1905[*] | | 1909 | |
|---|---|---|---|---|---|---|
| | Marriages | Illegit. Births | Marriages | Illegit. Births | Marriages | Illegit. Births |
| Aleksander-Nevskii 1 | 5.07 | 3.5 | 6.4 | 5.0 | 5.2 | 5.8 |
| Aleksander-Nevskii 2 | 5.54 | 4.9 | 5.4 | 7.16 | 6.3 | 6.6 |
| Aleksander-Nevskii 3 | 5.22 | 6.2 | 5.2 | 5.35 | 7.0 | 6.1 |
| Vasilevskii Island 2 | 7.14 | 6.7 | 11.1 | 7.3 | 7.5 | 5.5 |
| Vasilevskii Island 3 | 6.82 | 9.7 | 9.3 | 8.8 | 4.9 | 4.2 |
| Vyborg 1 | 5.07 | 11.2 | 7.4 | 6.5 | 6.3 | 4.7 |
| Vyborg 2 | 7.26 | 10.2 | 8.0 | 10.33 | 8.3 | 7.7 |

[*] The fact that marriage rates rose noticeably in some working-class districts during 1905 will be discussed in Chapter 7.
*Source*: Calculated from *Statisticheskie ezhegodniki S.-Peterburga*.

marriages in some working-class districts of Moscow and St. Petersburg. Only as men shifted their loyalty to the city, and/or began making enough money to afford to marry there, would the situation really change. Meanwhile, as they struggled to forge a personal life in the circumstances of the city, single women more often found themselves victims than beneficiaries of economic and social changes.

The vast majority of single women who bore children in the city had migrated from peasant villages like Kiseleva and Kondrat'eva had done. The proportion of women steadily grew as waves of peasant migrants inundated the cities of Moscow and St. Petersburg after the emancipation of the serfs, causing the cities almost to triple in population by the outbreak of World War I. In 1869, there were 300 women for every 1,000 men among peasant migrants to St. Petersburg; by 1900, the proportion had grown to 368 per 1,000, and to 480 by 1910. The numbers of women increased even more markedly in Moscow, where there were 394 women for every 1,000 peasant men in 1871, but 650 per 1,000 by 1902.[9] A substantial minority of peasant women were young when they arrived in the city, and most of these were

9 Calculated on the bases of the urban censuses. By 1900, there were 667 peasant women for every 1,000 peasant men in St. Petersburg; in 1902, there were 656 migrant women for every 1,000 migrant men in Moscow.

single. In 1882, close to 24 percent of peasant women living in Moscow were aged fifteen to twenty-five; by 1902, the proportion of peasant women in this age group had dropped to 23 percent, but their actual numbers had more than doubled. It is impossible to determine both age and marital status of Moscow's peasant population from the census, but the census shows that in 1902, 87.5 percent of migrant women between fifteen and nineteen were single, and 45 percent of migrant women aged twenty to twenty-nine. By the early twentieth century, slightly over a quarter of women peasants in St. Petersburg were between sixteen and twenty-five years old; 86 percent of peasant women between sixteen and twenty were single, as were 53 percent of the women between twenty-one and twenty-five. A decade later, in 1910, the proportions remained much the same.[10]

The enormous hardship that drove village women to seek their fortunes in the city bore particularly heavily on the young and the single. Even as peasant patriarchy controlled women's sexuality and restricted women's choices, it generally tried to protect women from the vagaries of the market-place and to ensure that courtship led to marriage. To be sure, even when their members left the village peasant families tried to sustain traditional patterns to the best of their ability; most women traveled as a member of a family, for example, whereas most men went to the city alone. Parents in the city might arrange a daughter's marriage. That was what happened to Natalia Agafonova, a peasant from Kaluga who worked as a typesetter and lived with her parents in Mary's Grove, in Moscow. In 1901, her father forced her to marry a craftsman employed in a cart-making shop. Taisa Slovachevskaia, another printworker in Moscow, successfully resisted pressures to marry according to her mother's wishes, but only after her mother had tried to betroth her to several master craftsmen in succession, each of them substantial looking, "their beards divided in two, a gold chain bouncing on their bellies."[11] Family ties and, to a lesser extent, ties to *zemliaki* not only facilitated a woman's adaptation to urban life (as they did for men) but also extended the supervision that in the village had ensured a woman's chastity. Nevertheless, as out-of-wedlock pregnancies demonstrate, in a substantial

---

10 *Perepis' Moskvy 1882 g.*, vyp. 2 (Moscow, 1885), Table 1; *Perepis' Moskvy 1902 g.* vyp. 1 (Moscow, 1904), 12–13; Robert Johnson, "Family Relations and the Urban-Rural Nexus: Patterns in the Hinterland of Moscow, 1880–1900," in *The Family in Imperial Russia*, ed. David Ransel (Urbana, Ill., 1978), 268; *St. Peterburg po perepisi 15 Dekabria 1900 g.*, vyp. 1 (St. Petersburg, 1903), 125–9; 262–306; *Petrograd po perepisi 15 Dekabria 1910 g.* (Petrograd, 1914), ch. 1, 10.

11 TsGIA SSSR, fond 1412, op. 212, delo 31, 7; Taisa Slovachevskaia in *Proidennyi put': Sbornik* (Moscow-Leningrad, 1925), 155–7.

number of cases such supervision was either lacking or insufficient. An examination of the circumstances surrounding illegitimacy in urban Russia provides a window into the lives of unattached migrant women and a way of exploring their particular vulnerability, as well as their new opportunities, in a time of rapid economic and social change.

### Introduction to the city

Moving for the first time from the village to the city could be difficult for both sexes, but women experienced the transition in gender-specific ways. In almost every respect, women who migrated to the city were in a weaker position than men. Most peasant women were poorly equipped for living in an urban world. Especially if she derived from a province with longstanding patterns of migration to Moscow and St. Petersburg, a woman was unlikely to have stopped and worked at a smaller town before coming to the city.[12] Almost everything she encountered would therefore appear unfamiliar. Instead of single or two-story wooden cottages strung along an unpaved village road, inhabited by people she had known since childhood, as she left the railroad station or entered through city gates the newcomer would see "huge, multi-storied houses . . . stores, shops, taverns, beer halls, horse-drawn carriages going by, a horse-drawn tramway – and all around . . . crowds of bustling people, rushing to unknown destinations for unknown reasons."[13] In these surroundings, women migrants were far more likely than men to have trouble making their own way, being hampered by their inability to decipher the lettered street and shop signs that by the late nineteenth century had replaced pictures in the central parts of the cities. In 1897, only 17 percent of all peasant girls aged ten to nineteen could read; the older the woman, the less likely she was to be literate. In terms of literacy, women from the Central Industrial provinces such as Iaroslavl', Tver', Kostroma, and Moscow were better prepared for urban life than their sisters from the agricultural regions. Nevertheless, the majority even of these could neither read nor write.[14] A decade later, the literacy of women migrants had greatly improved, thanks to advances in primary education. Still, it remained much

---

12 For a discussion of the reasons for direct migration, see Joseph Bradley, *Muzhik and Muscovite: Urbanization in Late Imperial Russia* (Berkeley, Calif., 1985), 120–2.

13 Zelnik, ed., *A Radical Worker*, 7.

14 For literacy rates in general, see A.G. Rashin, *Naselenie Rossii za 100 let* (Moscow, 1956), 293.

lower than men's. Of the migrant women who arrived in St. Petersburg between 1906 and 1910, 60 percent were literate, compared to 87 percent of the migrant men.[15]

For both sexes, it made an enormous difference to have a contact in the city or a job already waiting. Rarely did a young peasant woman go off to an unfamiliar city unaccompanied by kin or *zemliaki*; when she did, she often knew someone in the city who would help her to get established. The heroines of late nineteenth-century novels and short stories, like their real-life counterparts, rarely ventured forth alone. In N.P. Leikin's novel *Out to Work* (*Na zarabotkakh*), maidens left the village together with married women, whom their mothers urged to supervise them. Or women found shelter with a kinswoman or *zemliachka* in the difficult early days, as did Agafia, the heroine of S.T. Semenov's novella "The Soldier's Wife," who stayed with her aunt, a servant, when she first arrived in Moscow.[16]

Women forced to fend entirely for themselves from the first were likely to be widows or orphans, or the daughters of households so desperately poor that they were unable to provide even the most elementary protections for their members. Lacking urban connections, a woman would have to spend some of her precious kopeks on a bed in a flophouse for however long it took her to find a job. And she would have to make her own way in an unstable and overcrowded urban job market, without training or skills and, often, without even the ability to read and write. Unfortunates like Feodosiia Sharygina sometimes made the newspapers. Sharygina, a thirty-year-old peasant woman from Riazan, unsuccessfully sought a position in St. Petersburg for two months before she despaired and threw herself from a bridge into the Fontanka canal. She had spent all her money and had neither contacts in St. Petersburg nor a means to return to her village.[17]

Even the more fortunate risked ending up at the very bottom of the urban job market. They could be seen first thing in the morning, standing in Nikol'skii Market (see Figure 5) or Haymarket Square in St. Petersburg, or in Khitrov Market in Moscow, waiting to be hired for day labor, for seasonal work in gardens, for unskilled factory labor, or, most frequently, for domestic service. A woman seeking a job might turn to a private employment agency, or if she had the money for such an investment, she might place an

---

15 *Petrograd po perepisi . . . 1910 g.*, ch. 1, 19–20.
16 Nikolai A. Leikin, *Na zarabotkakh: Roman iz zhizni chernorabochikh zhenshchin* (St. Petersburg, 1891), 18–19; S.T. Semenov, "Soldatka," in *V rodnoi derevne* (Moscow, 1962), 61–90.
17 *Zhenskii vestnik* 2 (26 June 1905): 319. See also *Peterburgskii listok*, no. 108 (22 Apr. 1894): 3.

Fig. 5. Waiting to be hired at Nikol'skii Market, St. Petersburg, early
twentieth century. (Courtesy of the Library of Congress.)

ad in a newspaper. Advertisements that ran in the popular *Peterburgskii Listok*
suggest the modesty of the potential servant's aspirations. "A village girl
wants to find a position as servant for a small remuneration." "I am looking
for a position as servant in a small family." They also hint at the low level
of specialized skill required: "I seek a position as servant or cook," "I seek a
position as servant or nurse." After 1905, women could also use an urban job
registry. Domestic servants monopolized over half of their business.[18]

Many a migrant woman practiced an economy of makeshift, taking whatever work she could get as she maneuvered to keep bread on her table and
a roof over her head in a labor market oversupplied with unskilled and
semiskilled female hands. Hers was a life of desperate insecurity, of penny-
pinching and hunger, as she tried to subsist between one job and the next.
Having a relative willing to provide shelter could be vital in a hungry time.

18 David Ransel, *Mothers of Misery: Child Abandonment in Russia* (Princeton, N.J., 1988), 165.
   On private hiring agencies, see *Peterburgskii listok*, no. 165 (19 June 1894): 3.

Such women's work identities were necessarily fluid; they defy the neat categories that urban censuses offer us. Take Anastasia Nikolaeva, a thirty-two-year-old migrant from Iaroslavl', who first gave her profession as cape maker, but in 1911 was supporting herself as a day laborer. Irina Petrova, a twenty-two-year-old migrant from Novgorod was a cook, she said, but was employed as a laundress in 1912. Maria Shvedova, from Kostroma, worked at the Shaposhnikov factory in 1908 but earned her living as a laundress in 1916.[19] The job identities of many women who bore illegitimate children were probably just as changeable, despite the efforts of officials to pin them firmly down: About 46 percent of unwed mothers were servants, statistical yearbooks tell us; another 30 percent were factory workers or unskilled laborers; an additional 15 percent were craftswomen.[20]

Many men faced uncertain employment opportunities, too, but women experienced particular difficulties. While it would be foolish to place much faith in census counts of unemployment, which undoubtedly underestimated the numbers of men and, especially, women unsuccessfully searching for work, the censuses are all we have, and they do provide at least a sense of the numbers. The St. Petersburg census of 1900 indicates that although men far outnumbered women in the urban labor force, women were far the more likely to be unemployed: 6,795 women, 6,470 of them servants seeking a position, said they were temporarily out of work, as compared to 2,527 men. These 6,795 women constituted about 4.5 percent of the entire female workforce of the city that year.[21] Moreover, even when women found work, whatever their trade, they earned one-half to two-thirds of what men did, barely enough for survival. In addition, women workers were personally as well as economically vulnerable, liable to sexual as well as economic exploitation.

When a Russian peasant woman went to the city, she left village restrictions and protections behind her. Historians have recently argued that industrialization and urbanization did not necessarily atomize workers or break up families. In the words of Leslie Moch and Louise Tilly, "joining the urban world . . . was often a collective family experience."[22] However, in Russia, where families also migrated together or in a chain to the city, once

19 TsGIA SSSR, fond 1409, op. 15, ed. kh. 2503; TsGIAL, fond 251, op. 1, ed. kh. 2, 304–6; ed. kh. 3, 177–9. The records of philanthropic organizations from which these examples are drawn are replete with evidence of the fluidity of women's occupational identities.
20 *Statisticheskii ezhegodnik S.-Peterburga. 1900* (St. Petersburg, 1903), 20–21.
21 *St. Peterburg po perepisi . . . 1900*, vyp. 2, 90–102.
22 Leslie Moch and Louise Tilly, "Joining the Urban World: Occupation, Family, and Migration in Three French Cities," *Comparative Studies in Society and History* 27, no. 1 (Jan. 1985): 55.

she got there if a woman needed to earn a living, she usually had to venture
out on her own. This was especially true of the women working as domestic
servants, the vast majority of whom lived with their employers and not with
kin. More surprisingly, other categories of women workers also lived apart
from their families. The census of 1897, the only one to tabulate such data,
revealed that an extraordinarily high proportion of working women (excluding
servants) lived on their own. In St. Petersburg, where one-third of working women were married, 86 percent of all working women lived alone and
apart from their families. Although the proportion of married women was
slightly higher in Moscow, the proportion living alone was even larger than
in St. Petersburg, close to 93 percent. Only 6.5 percent of working women
in Moscow, and 12.5 percent of them in St. Petersburg were members of
families living with their families, and an unknown proportion of these
women were wives, not daughters. And in the textile trades, where migrants
predominated among women workers, the proportion living with family
members was lower still. Judging by the residency pattern at 14/2
Nizhegorodskaia Street in 1908–10, women migrants who did reside with
family members were far more likely to live with a sibling than a father.
Under 5 percent of working women migrants lived with a brother or a sister
at that address; none resided with their father. The mother was in residence
in one instance – the Panteleev family in apartment forty-four. The family
had migrated from Rybinsk, Iaroslavl', and the fifty-five-year-old mother
depended on the earnings of her three sons, thirty-one, twenty-two, and
twenty, all single and unskilled laborers, and of her two daughters, Evdokiia,
twenty-nine, a tailor, and Ekaterina, thirty, a midwife and masseuse.[23]

The numbers of women living on their own suggest that even as Russian
migrants were more likely than their Western European counterparts to
keep one foot in the village, they were also far less likely than their counterparts
elsewhere to have the shock of migration to the city cushioned by the family.
To be sure, many women migrants who lived apart from the family kept
contact with family members, who might offer protection. For example, in
the early 1860s the father of one fifteen-year-old servant girl lodged a complaint with an urban justice of the peace (*mirovoi sud*) about his daughter's
employer. Although the girl had been hired to nurse the employer's child,

---

23 N.A. Troinitskii, ed., *Chislennost' i sostav rabochikh v Rossii na osnovanii dannykh pervoi
vseobshchei perepisi naseleniia Rossiiskoi imperii 1897 g.* (St. Petersburg, 1906), 1: 46–7; 66–7.
In apartment 58, Pavel Kulikov, a migrant from Tver', lived with his three sisters, Elena,
twenty-nine, a servant; Anna, twenty-three, a tailor; and Zinaida, fifteen, their dependent.
In apartments 32, 61, 69, and 72, migrant laboring brothers and sisters also lived together.
Brothers often shared a roof, too.

the employer had forced her to serve wine to his guests and to drink with them. Fearful for the daughter's moral well-being, her father succeeded in having her released from the position, then placed her in another, "with good masters."[24] Other women without kin managed to locate near people from their village, *volost'*, or district. Nevertheless, living near *zemliaki* or even kin was not the same as living with family, as illegitimacy rates attest. The patriarchal authority and community cohesion that successfully controlled women's sexuality in the village, holding illegitimacy at under 2 percent of overall fertility in rural Russia in 1897, was difficult to re-create in the urban setting. *Zemliak* ties provided a poor substitute for close kinfolk, and *zemliaki* lacked the clout of a village community. Without fathers, mothers, or brothers to shield or restrain them, women became more vulnerable to sexual harassment or seduction and perhaps freer to dispose of their sexual favors as they chose, even in the absence of firm guarantees for their own future. Migrant women also lacked the means to enforce a seducer's promise of marriage, and in the city even a father had no power to protect them. Consider the case of a fourteen-year-old peasant servant who had become the lover of the son of her employer, a merchant, and had borne a child and sent it to a foundling home. Her father took the youth to court in 1886, contending that the young man had raped his daughter before falsely promising to marry her in order to convince her to become his lover. Lacking the leverage to press for marriage, he sued for financial support for his daughter but failed to obtain it.[25] Neither kin nor the *zemliak* community could muster the resources that a tightly knit peasant village might mobilize to protect its women from seduction and abandonment.

The odds of finding a husband in the city were not favorable for the migrant woman. Not only were substantial numbers of migrant men committed to marriage in the village, but even otherwise available men sometimes avoided marriage altogether, despite peasant beliefs that all men and women should marry. Male migrants to the city were more prone than villagers to stay single. In St. Petersburg, close to 20 percent of male workers between forty and fifty-nine remained bachelors; in Moscow, 14 percent of male workers, and 17 percent of male migrants. By comparison, only 10 percent of all Russian men in that age group failed to wed.[26] Economics accounted for most of these lifelong bachelors: They lacked land in the village and

24 V.N. Nikitin, *Mirovoi sud v Peterburge: Stseny v kammerakh sudei i podrobnyia razbiratel'stva* (St. Petersburg, 1867), 169–70.

25 *Sudebnaia gazeta*, no. 17 (1887): 2–3.

26 For Moscow, see Robert Johnson, "Family Relations," 268; on St. Petersburg, S. Bernshtein-Kogan, *Chislennost', sostav i polozhenie Peterburgskikh rabochikh* (St. Petersburg, 1910), 62.

made too little to provide for a family in the city. As a result, a substantial proportion of working women married late or remained single. Although 82 percent of all Russian women between twenty and thirty-nine were married in 1897, of the factory women in that age group, only 44.3 percent were married in St. Petersburg and 60 percent in Moscow.[27] Even these low numbers cannot be taken as evidence of successful urban courtship, because an unknown proportion of these married factory women had wed in the village and started work thereafter.

Despite the disadvantageous situation, village patterns of early and nearly universal marriage encouraged women migrants to nurture unrealistic expectations about whether and when they would wed. Economics reinforced this predisposition. Men's earnings were much higher than women's and could ease a woman's poverty, improve her diet, and put a greater distance between the woman and the streets. Marriage also provided a form of social security in a society that made no systematic provision for sickness or old age. Peasants expected their children to care for them and support them when they became too old to work. Some women also had romantic aspirations. "I wanted to marry for love," remembered Taisa Slovachevskaia. But many more, recognizing their need for a man's support and protection, surely took a practical approach, as did M. Abashkina, a textile worker. When she married at seventeen she believed "like all [her] friends" that she would "take refuge behind her husband's back as behind a stone wall" (*za muzhninoi spiny, kak za kamennoi stenoi*).[28] These expectations and needs contributed to illegitimate births by making women more vulnerable to seductive promises of marriage, and/or more willing to settle for a consensual union.

Their relatively advantageous position in the urban sexual economy tempted working men to play around, and all the more so as many working men held working women in low regard. Some of these, the more politically aware and active, feared that a "backward" woman would prevent them from participating fully in the workers' movement. Among such workers, the "prevailing wisdom" was that the woman worker was "a creature of a lower order," an extension of the peasant milieu and an obstacle to the development of men. In their circles, "a negative attitude toward the family, marriage, even women in general was viewed as a necessity."[29] Others were simply contemptuous

27 Bernshtein-Kogan, *Chislennost'*, 62; Johnson, "Family Relations," 268.
28 Taisa Slovachevskaia, *Proidennyi put'*, 158; M. Abashkina, A.C. Iliushina, and F.F. Karpukhin, *Povest' o trekh* (Moscow, 1935), 15.
29 Reginald Zelnik, "Russian Bebels: An Introduction to the Memoirs of the Russian Workers Semën Kanatchikov and Matvei Fisher," *Russian Review* 35, no. 3 (1976): 277–8. Zelnik provides a sensitive discussion of why some workers might want to avoid marriage.

and occasionally expressed that contempt through sexual harassment. One woman worker in a paper box factory, for example, complained of how "the men [workers] treat the women workers and apprentices as if they were street prostitutes. All the time one hears from them [nothing but] insults and obscene propositions." She told the story of one male worker exposing himself to the women·and of another raping a young woman worker.[30] The higher his level of skill and education, the more scornful a man was likely to be. Metalworkers, the elite of Russia's workforce, were among the worst offenders. "Women predominated among [textile workers]," recalled the metalworker Aleksei Buzinov, "and we showed our contempt for them at every opportunity."[31] His attitude was partly the result of stratifications within the labor force, particularly between the two major industrial groups, metalworkers (almost entirely male) and textile workers (over 50 percent female by the early twentieth century). But even male textile workers looked down on their female co-workers. As the Soviet historian of the Prokhorov textile factory put it, "Relations between male and female workers were unequal and unhealthy. They called the women's dormitory the cattle-yard, and the name stuck."[32]

Such collective attitudes surely derived in part from peasant men's suspicions of women on their own and their equation of women's freedom from male control with women's sexual license. The comic genres of popular urban entertainment licensed physical aggression toward women; and the domination of women was a frequent theme in the bandit novels so popular among the urban masses. Jeffrey Brooks hypothesizes that such themes may have appealed to readers "uncomfortable with the loosening of traditional family ties and with the novelty and confusion that increasing geographic and social mobility brought to relations between the sexes."[33] In life as in fiction, women unprotected by family and community were especially vulnerable. They might be victimized by the kind of casual harassment that L.D. Krylova and her mates suffered. Workers at the Prokhorov factory in Moscow and residents of its dormitory, the women lived right next door to

30 Quoted in Rose Glickman, *Russian Factory Women: Workplace and Society, 1880–1914* (Berkeley, Calif., 1984), 205.
31 A. Buzinov, *Za nevskoi zastavoi: Zapiski rabochego Alekseia Buzinova* (Moscow-Leningrad, 1930), 20.
32 S. Lapitskaia, *Byt rabochikh trekhgornoi manufaktury* (Moscow, 1935), 77.
33 Catriona Kelly, "'Better Halves'? Representations of Women in Russian Urban Popular Entertainments, 1870–1900," in *Women and Society in Russia and the Soviet Union*, ed. Linda Edmondson (New York, 1992), 21; Jeffrey Brooks, *When Russia Learned to Read: Literacy and Popular Literature, 1861–1917* (Princeton, N.J., 1985), 188.

drunken "hooligans" who would occasionally seize one of the women, drag her into the courtyard, and do "what they pleased" with her. One spring, when the women went out in a group to stroll in a nearby meadow, a group of teenage boys attacked them "like a herd of dogs," catching one of the women and tying her skirt above her head.[34] This was the way that peasants customarily punished dissolute women. Its apparently gratuitous application to a young factory woman out with her friends for a walk may only indicate a traditional practice unmoored from its roots. More likely it represents a perception that women without kin or husband were morally suspect and fair game. The anthropologist Andrei Simic observed similar attitudes to women on their own in urban Yugoslavia.[35]

Men who conceived of women as a lower order of being tended to view relations with them as a contest from which a man should take what he could get. In the words of Maxim Gorky, "For the real-life working man, women were only a source of amusement – but a dangerous one: With women one always had to be cunning, or else they would get the upper hand and ruin one's life."[36] In the metalworking factory where A. Buzinov was employed, young men boasted daily and in great detail about their sexual conquests. It is with a touch of envy that the metalworker Semyon Kanatchikov describes Stepka, a good-looking and popular metalworker, who was "like a fish in water in female company." To the admiration of his friends, he would unceremoniously "tear off the flowers of pleasure."[37]

The scarcity of available men, the antipathy of some to marriage, and the widespread contempt for women compounded the problem of men's low wages and the economic obstacles to family life and made courtship especially perilous for women in the city. Rates of urban marriage remained low. During the last decade of the nineteenth century, the average rate of marriage for every 1,000 inhabitants in Russia was 9, whereas in Moscow, marriage rates remained under 5.3 per thousand in this period. St. Petersburg averaged 6.4 marriages per 1,000 inhabitants between 1887 and 1896; 6 per 1,000 in 1899, and 5.9 per 1,000 in 1900.[38] In most working-class districts,

---

34 L.D. Krylova, *Zapiski tkachikhi* (Moscow, 1932), 19–20.
35 Andrei Simic, *The Peasant Urbanites: A Study of Rural-Urban Mobility in Serbia* (New York, 1973), 84.
36 Maxim Gorky, *My Apprenticeship* (Harmondsworth, England, 1976), 315. See also Simic, *The Peasant Urbanites*, 84.
37 Buzinov, *Za nevskoi zastavoi*, 26–7; Semën Kanatchikov, *Iz istorii moego bytiia* (Moscow-Leningrad, 1929), 50.
38 A. Shuster, *Peterburgskie rabochie*, 23. Rates in Moscow calculated on the basis of *Statisticheskii ezhegodnik goroda Moskvy* (Moscow, 1913), 23, 25.

marriage rates were still lower, with the exception of the second section of Vasilevskii Island, where the Putilov metalworks were located, and the second section of Vyborg district, one of the most distinctively "working-class" areas of St. Petersburg. In both these sections, the presence of substantial numbers of women factory workers who were able to earn a steady wage after marriage and even after childbearing sometimes tipped the balance in favor of marriage in the city.

Such variations in the rates of marriage suggest the usefulness of distinguishing among migrant women on the basis of their occupations. While in general migrant women lacked the "economic clout" to marry partners of their choice, there were substantial differences between women engaged in domestic service and women engaged in factory work, the two most common occupations of peasant women migrants. Each occupational group will be treated separately and at some length.

### Domestic servants

Domestic service was the most common occupation for women in urban Russia. There were over 92,000 women servants in St. Petersburg at the turn of the century, as compared to 57,848 women working in all branches of industry. In Moscow, servants comprised 28 percent of independently employed women in 1902, and 25 percent in 1912. Although Moscow's industrial sector had grown considerably by then, servants still outnumbered factory workers two to one.[39] In Russia, as elsewhere in Europe, domestic service had advantages as well as drawbacks, although the advantages have eluded the attention of both historians of Russian women and most of the servants' own contemporaries. Upper-class observers were particularly scathing. Liberals, leftists, and feminists concurred that domestic service was the most degraded form of women's work. Their negative evaluation is captured by the title *White Slaves* (*Belye nevol'niki*), which the feminist Evgeniia Turzhe-Turzhanskaia gave to her pamphlet on the plight of the domestic servant.[40]

There was certainly much to criticize. A servant's wage was low, her position often insecure, her work neverending. The fewer the servants, the more work a woman would have to do. Over half of the households in Moscow and St. Petersburg that hired a servant employed only one.[41] She

39 Glickman, *Russian Factory Women*, 60–1; Ransel, *Mothers of Misery*, 164–5.
40 Evgeniia Turzhe-Turzhanskaia, *Belye nevol'niki* (Smolensk, 1906).
41 David Ransel, "Problems in Measuring Illegitimacy," 122.

would be on call twenty-four hours a day, rising at 6:00 A.M. to light the stove and clean the house. She prepared all the meals and did the washing up, ran errands, and answered the door. She had little time to broaden her intellectual or cultural horizons, or to taste the fruits of urban life: Typically she was allowed time off two days a month. The servant was more subject to the personal power of her employer than any other woman worker. A servant who got sick was likely to lose her job; a servant who broke things paid for the damage from her wages; a servant who failed to obey promptly risked losing the references she needed to gain another position. Her living conditions were often demeaning as well. Unlike her counterparts in England and France, who usually slept in a garret room, in congested urban apartments the Russian servant often had no place at all to call her own. She spent the night behind a screen in a passageway or in the kitchen, or even by the bedside of her employer.[42] Her position may also have been more difficult because Russian society was more authoritarian, serfdom had ended so recently, and the rights of the individual, especially the lower-class individual, were so little respected. In the words of the liberal weekly *Nedelia*, the Russian servant suffered particular abuse because Russia was "still too close to serfdom, when servants were mute and powerless slaves."[43]

For all its shortcomings, however, domestic service offered real advantages, especially for women who were more comfortable in a familiar, patriarchal domestic setting. When women took up the trade, it was not necessarily because they lacked other options. Literacy figures, low as they are, suggest that service may have been a choice as often as it was an unavoidable necessity. According to the census of 1902, women servants in Moscow enjoyed a literacy rate of 27 percent, higher than factory women (19.3 percent) and much higher than day laborers (11.5 percent). And the overall turnover rate in the profession was lower than it was among factory workers, although servants appear to have changed positions much more frequently in search of more humane employers or better working conditions. The duration of time domestics spent at a particular position can be ascertained, if imprecisely, from the register of the building at 14/2 Nizhegorodskaia Street –

---

42 On the servant in Russia, see L.N. Lenskaia, *O prisluge* (Moscow, 1908); P.F. Kudelli, *Rabotnitsa v 1905 g. v S.-Peterburge* (Leningrad, 1926), 43; Glickman, *Russian Factory Women*, 60–1; and Ransel, *Mothers of Misery*. On Europe, see John Gillis, "Servants, Sexual Relations, and the Risks of Illegitimacy in London, 1801–1900." *Feminist Studies* 5, no. 1 (Spring 1979): 142–73, and Theresa McBride, *The Domestic Revolution: The Modernization of Household Work in England and France* (London, 1976).
43 *Nedelia*, no. 24 (1897): 741–2.

imprecisely, because the register extends only over two to three years and thus cannot track servants who began work before the record begins or toward the end of the period covered. Some domestics in residence for under a month may have been between jobs and staying with friends or kin, while others were genuinely employed in the building. Still, such records do provide a sense of the peripatetic nature of servants' lives: Less than a third of the eighty-eight servants residing at that address had served there for over a year, and close to a third came and went within three months. However, most of the servants who left that address found work as a servant at another one. Urban censuses confirm the fact that many women continued to work as servants for years. In 1902, about 30 percent of migrant women employed as domestics in Moscow had worked at their trade more than eleven years (although not necessarily for the same employer), by comparison with about 25 percent of factory workers. Domestic service was not necessarily a way station en route to the factory, and although it was certainly crowded with newcomers, it was far from the exclusive preserve of the greenhorn.[44]

Service provided a roof over one's head and a steady diet, and if the servant could endure the demeaning treatment, the long hours, and the lack of freedom, her work brought economic benefits, too. In the words of a German woman who had worked many years as a servant, "The servant girls have it much better than the working woman. . . . Servants and maids can live well off their employers."[45] Domestic servants were shielded from slow seasons that left seamstresses and other needlewomen out of work and from the cyclical depressions that laid off factory workers. To be sure, their wages were low when compared to other women's: An experienced servant might earn five to six rubles a month at the close of the century, less than half of what a poorly paid woman factory worker received. On the other hand, the domestic spent none of her income on food or shelter, which absorbed the bulk of the factory woman's wages. After sending a portion to her family in the village, the servant could spend the rest on clothing, or save, a kopek at a time, toward marriage, hard times, or age and infirmity. Russian servants shared with servants elsewhere a propensity to save: They set aside larger sums of money than any other category of urban worker. In 1898, 31,352 women servants in St. Petersburg province, close to one-third of the servant

---

44 Joseph Bradley, *Muzhik*, 151–2; 176. I have used Bradley's figures but made my own calculations as to length of service.
45 "Frau Hoffman, Retired Maid," in Alfred Kelly, ed., *The German Worker: Working-Class Autobiographies from the Age of Industrialization* (Berkeley, Calif., 1987), 359.

Fig. 6. A cook in a St. Petersburg household, circa 1913. (Courtesy of Tsentral'nyi Gosudarstvennyi Arkhiv Kinofonofotodokumentov.)

population, had managed to save an average of 140 rubles apiece, according to the records of the state saving bank.[46] The number of servants who had set money aside was actually larger, because some servants distrusted the bank and preferred to keep their savings with them in a locked trunk, or to entrust

46  *Otchet gosudarstvennykh sberegatel'nykh kass po sberegatel'nym okrugam za 1898* (St. Petersburg, 1899), 120–1.

the money to their friends.[47] It is true that in the city such savings would not take a woman far. When she had grown too old to work, a servant who had amassed 150 to 200 rubles over a lifetime of toil could at best rent herself a cot for two or three years. But were other laboring women in a more favorable position at the end of their working days?[48]

Their savings enabled some servants to provide themselves with a dowry and return to the village to marry. It was much harder to find a mate in the city. Not only did servants face the same disadvantageous marriage market as other lower-class women, but also their occupation was particularly difficult to pursue after marriage (although some pursued it nonetheless). Russian masters and mistresses demanded celibacy of servants, restricted their time off to a minimum, and forbade them to entertain male guests.[49] While a woman's savings could enhance her value in courtship negotiations, the fact that if she continued to work, the couple would have to live apart after marriage and would be unable to raise children, must often have tipped the odds against her. Only a minority of migrant men earned enough to support a wife in the city, and fewer still made enough to support children, as Chapter 7 will show. These circumstances destined most servants to spinsterhood.

They did not, however, prevent women from courting. Evenings, they might slip off in their employers' absence and pay a visit to a pleasure garden or receive a suitor in the kitchen. Her working conditions circumscribed a servant's contacts with men, although the degree depended on residential segregation. While most families had only one servant, the servant was rarely isolated. In the crowded and expensive housing of Russia's major cities, a middle-class couple who hired a maid-of-all-work might live in only one or two rooms of an apartment with many rooms. Next door might dwell another couple, or a group of students, who hired a servant too. A high proportion of the middle-class occupants of 14/2 Nizhegorodskaia – physicians, teachers, *chinovniki* – appear to have occupied no more than a room or two. This meant that a single apartment might have as many as three or four servants

47 On informal savings, see for example, *Peterburgskii listok*, no. 22 ( June 1893): 3; no. 189 (14 July 1894): 3; no. 67 (1 Mar. 1894): 3.
48 N.K., "Iz nabliudenii sotrudnitsy popechitel'stva," *Trudovaia pomoshch*, no. 4 (Apr. 1901): 473. On the advantages of service elsewhere, see Gillis, "Servants," 147, McBride, *The Domestic Revolution*, and Christine Stansell, *City of Women: Sex and Class in New York* (New York, 1986), 157.
49 Lenskaia, *O prisluge*, 11–12. This was a common practice in other countries, too. See Gillis, "Servants," 150; Sarah Maza, *Servants and Masters in Eighteenth-Century France: The Uses of Loyalty* (Princeton, N.J., 1983), 132–3.

working for different employers. And if the socially heterogenous building at 14/2 Nizhegorodskaia Street is at all typical, in the apartment next door might dwell skilled workers, while upstairs in the garret apartments of the same building, artisans, unskilled workers, and laborers rented themselves a corner. So a servant might become involved with a man whom she met through her work, or more often, a man who lived in her building. Sofia Litvin, a twenty-one-year-old peasant migrant from Vitebsk, served as a chambermaid in the Shemetov eating house in St. Petersburg, when she fell in love with a railroad worker who ate there every day.[50] A woman who washed dishes at the buffet of the Baltic Station in St. Petersburg became engaged to a manservant who worked there, too.[51] Servants, as well as chimney sweeps, plumbers, and yardmen, were barred from using the formal entryways of their buildings, but they might meet and court on the backstairs. Ivan Anan'ich, the apprentice of a watchmaker, Fink, met and courted the chambermaid who worked upstairs in a house on Bol'shoi Prospekt in St. Petersburg.[52] A chambermaid took up with a manservant employed in the same building.[53] Another serving woman became involved with a worker who lived upstairs.[54]

Despite, or perhaps because of, restrictions that enforced constant contact between the servant and her social betters, serving in a well-to-do household sometimes raised a young woman's aspirations. While he was courting the chambermaid, the apprentice watchmaker Ivan Anan'ich felt he had to dress himself well and to bestow on her presents. In order to purchase clothing, trinkets, candy, and flowers, Anan'ich pilfered and then pawned his employer's property. Before he was discovered, he had taken several of his employer's gold watches, a ring, and finally an overcoat.[55] Grusha Sherstiannikov was very proud of the fact that she had once been the housekeeper of some great "lords," and considered her marriage to a semiliterate patternmaker a failure. "Why, there were once real gentlemen who wanted to marry me," she would shout at her husband when she was angry.[56] Such aspirations made serving women especially susceptible to seductive promises of marriage from men of a higher social status. For example, Nikolai Zabolotskii, the son of a merchant, promised to marry his father's servant, the twenty-three-year-old

50 *Peterburgskii listok*, no. 247 (9 Sept. 1893): 3.    51 Ibid., no. 254 (16 Sept. 1893): 4.

52 Ibid., no. 264 (26 Sept. 1893): 4.    53 Ibid., no. 165 (19 June, 1894): 3.

54 *Rossiiskoe obshchestvo zashchity zhenshchin. Otchet o deiatel'nosti obshchestva* (St. Petersburg, 1911), 58.

55 *Peterburgskii listok*, no. 264 (26 Sept. 1893): 4.

56 Zelnik, ed., *A Radical Worker in Tsarist Russia*, 57.

Matryona Tolstaia, and even took an oath before witnesses. But he forgot his promises as soon as she submitted to him. Lacking the legal or social leverage to make him honor his word, Matryona turned to the Synod of the Russian Orthodox Church in 1883. She wanted to marry her seducer, or failing that, to receive financial compensation for her dishonor. The church was unable to help her.[57] Serving women had good reason to be wary of "real gentlemen" offering marriage. Still, occasionally a serving woman did achieve a modest upward mobility, marrying a man with sufficient means to support her, or using her nest egg to free herself from the need for service. A chambermaid wed a shoemaker and became the mistress of his small shoemaking shop. O. S., who derived from a landless household, worked for five years as a chambermaid in furnished apartments and accumulated sufficient savings that when she married a yardman, they could invest two hundred rubles to open a wineshop in the village.[58]

But the vast majority were not so fortunate. The age range of servants suggests that in Russia, servanthood was rarely a temporary stage in life. In Russia's cities, most servants were single, and at the end of the nineteenth century, the majority were no longer young; their average age was thirty-three to thirty-six.[59] In Moscow in 1902, only 12 percent of domestics were under twenty, and another 27.5 percent were under twenty-five.[60] The age distribution of domestics, as well as their comparatively high rates of illegitimacy, suggests that servants were much more likely to conceive a child out of wedlock than to find themselves a husband.

A significant minority of domestic servants bore illegitimate children. In the 1890s, over 8,000 women bore illegitimate children every year in St. Petersburg, about 9,000 in Moscow. Slightly under half of these women were domestic servants, which means that every year one of every 200 servants in St. Petersburg, and one of every 150 in Moscow, gave birth to an illegitimate child. In order to avoid pregnancy, a woman would have had to avoid sex with a man altogether. In the absence of reliable means of contraception, women who engaged in sexual relations before marriage risked pregnancy every time. By the early twentieth century, women in cities might resort to abortionists, or so physicians believed.[61] However, the servants,

57  TsGIA SSSR, fond 796, op. 164, II stol, IV otd., ed. kh. 1979, 1–2.

58  *Komu pomogaiut gorodskaia popechitel'stva?* (Moscow, 1897), 14, 28–9.

59  Figures cited in Ransel, *Mothers of Misery*, 165.

60  *Glavneishie predvaritel'nye dannye perepisi goroda Moskvy 31 Ianvaria 1902 g.*, vyp. 6 (Moscow, 1907), 52.

61  See the discussion in Laura Engelstein, "Abortion and the Civic Order: The Legal and Medical Debates," in *Russia's Women: Accommodation, Resistance, Transformation*, ed. Barbara Clements, Barbara Engel, and Christine Worobec (Berkeley, Calif., 1991), 185–207.

laundresses, unskilled factory workers, and poorly paid craftswomen who comprised the vast majority of women bearing illegitimate children either could not afford their services or did not know of them. As a result, women who wanted male companionship but were in a poor position to negotiate a marriage remained at risk of unwed motherhood.

Once a woman bore an illegitimate child, her bargaining position became even weaker. In a given year, only a minority of the servants bearing illegitimate children were inexperienced newcomers to the city. Most were in a position to know better. For example, in the first months of 1890, of the 103 unwed servant women bearing children in the St. Petersburg Maternity Home, about two-thirds (67) already had at least one other child, and 30 percent had more than two. The proportions were virtually identical among women in other occupations.[62] As historian George Alter has noted, such multiple births often indicated women's lack of leverage in courtship. "Once a woman has had a sexual relationship in a courtship that failed to result in marriage, the sexual bargaining in later courting becomes even more difficult. Her subsequent partners will expect sexual intercourse earlier in the relationship, and they will be less likely to interpret sexual activity as a sign of commitment. Thus, women who have engaged in sexual activity in unsuccessful courtships are increasingly at risk of becoming unwed mothers in later courtships."[63]

Becoming pregnant was usually a disaster for the servant. If a servant's employer learned about the pregnancy, it almost invariably cost her the job. Disapproving parents or kin would be reluctant to take her in; if she were visibly pregnant, she would be unable to find work as a servant. The servant Agafia Golubeva lost her job when her pregnancy was discovered. She turned to her mother, but the mother, a factory worker, was so scandalized by the pregnancy that she beat her daughter and refused to allow her to take shelter in the mother's apartment.[64] With no other resources, either the pregnant servant would have to hire herself out by the day, doing laundry, washing floors, picking rags, earning perhaps forty-five kopeks a day for her labor, or she would be forced to use up her savings and then sell her

---

62 One of these women claimed to have borne sixteen children, another, eleven. See TsGIAL, fond 145, op. 1, ed. kh. 112. For overall fertility, see the *Statisticheskii ezhegodnik S.-Peterburga*, yearly. As the number of newcomers to the city increased in the 1890s, the proportion of unwed mothers bearing children for the first time increased as well, but it nevertheless remained under half at least until 1900.

63 George Alter, *Family and the Female Life Course: The Women of Verviers, Belgium, 1849–1880* (Madison, Wis., 1988), 118.

64 I. Kor, ed., *Kak my zhili pri tsare i kak zhivem teper'* (Moscow, 1934), 23; see also *Sudebnyi vestnik*, no. 232 (1874): 2–3.

belongings for rent and food. Cases that appeared in newspapers suggest the lengths to which a pregnant servant might go to keep a roof over her head. One woman had held her position for seven months. Although pregnant, she had managed to conceal her state and to fulfill all her duties uncomplainingly. The employers had nothing but good things to say about her. The servant had worked hard, and her behavior was exemplary in every respect. However, had they known she was pregnant they would have fired her. But no one had noticed. The lady of the household was sickly, so the servant slept by her bed every night and every day drew her bath. Drawing the bath required her to lug forty buckets of water to and from the bathtub. This would have been "practically impossible" for a pregnant woman, the husband was certain. In fact, the servant had drawn the bath on the very day that she gave birth. There was no indication that she found the work any more difficult than usual. And the only night she slept alone was the night she bore the child. Complaining of a headache, she had asked to sleep in the kitchen.[65] A few employers must have been prepared to overlook their servants' pregnancies: For example, one thirty-eight-year-old cook worked until the very last moments and was back at her job within the week.[66]

Getting help from the father was difficult. Russian law, designed to uphold the integrity of the patriarchal family, offered little of use to the unwed mother. A woman involved with a married man could make no claims at all upon the father of her child. If her lover was single, her position was only a little more favorable. In order to obtain financial support for a child, a woman had to have compelling evidence that the man she named really was the father and that her own personal conduct had otherwise been "blameless" during the period the child was conceived. A law of 1902 expanded the responsibilities of the father of an illegitimate child by obliging him to provide support until the child's maturity, but the law made it no easier for the mother to make her case and obtain assistance.[67] In any event, women of the laboring classes, migrant women especially, had neither the knowledge nor the resources to initiate the necessary lawsuits. Dependent on what they could earn as domestics, the vast majority of unwed mothers were financially on their own. It is no wonder, then, that so many servants abandoned their

65 The case was reported at length in *Sudebnyi vestnik*, no. 153 (1876): 2.
66 See TsGIAL, fond 251, op. 1, delo 7, 489–91.
67 V. Volzhin, "O protivozakonnom sozhitii," *Iuridicheskii vestnik* 4 (1890): 646–63; "Peterburgskie deti," *Peterburgskii listok*, no. 28 (1870): 1; D.I. Orlov, "Zadachi Pirogovskoi komissii po prizreniiu pokinutykh detei," *Zhurnal obshchestva Russkikh vrachei*, no. 1 (1903): 17; Berenice Madison, "Russia's Illegitimate Children Before and After the Revolution," *Slavic Review* 22, no. 1 (Mar. 1963): 82–95.

children to urban foundling homes and to almost certain death.[68] Servants were far more likely to give up their infants than other laboring women. As late as 1910, servants constituted at least half of abandoning mothers; David Ransel has speculated that their proportion must at times have run as high as 80 percent.[69] Unable to find a marriage partner in the city, the servant was equally unable to combine work and motherhood.

### The factory worker

As demonstrated by their higher marriage rates and lower rates of illegitimacy, the woman factory worker was in a better position than the servant to negotiate a courtship successfully. Yet in some respects, the two groups of women were quite similar. Both derived from the peasantry. Both were entirely dependent on the stability of their employment and their own continuing good health and ability to work. Factory women also faced the structural disadvantages that the servant and other migrant women encountered in the urban marriage market. Nevertheless, in other, apparently crucial respects, the workers' situation differed from the servants'. These differences and their impact on women workers' efforts to negotiate a personal life in the urban setting, will be developed below.

As Russia industrialized, the number of women engaged in factory labor increased dramatically. Women made up a growing proportion of a rapidly expanding workforce, comprising almost one-third of the factory labor force by 1913.[70] Women's wages varied according to the trade and how long they had worked at it. In St. Petersburg in 1896, the average wage of a woman textile worker was twelve to sixteen rubles a month, more than twice the wages of a servant; tobacco workers earned thirteen rubles, confectionary workers, twelve.[71] These wages amounted to one-half to two-thirds of men's. The woman worker could not count on shelter, however inadequate, as the servant could. Nor, as we have seen, was she likely to live with other family

---

68 Ransel, *Mothers of Misery*, discusses at length the high proportion of infant foundlings who perished. There is some evidence that abandoning mothers tried to keep track of their children. Women bearing illegitimate children in the St. Petersburg Maternity Shelter who clearly had sent earlier children to the Foundling Home claimed to know how many of these children were still alive. Perhaps this was merely wishful thinking; however, V.G. Gerasimov, a foundling sent from St. Petersburg to be raised in rural Finland, writes that his mother came from the city several times to visit him when he was seven. V.G. Gerasimov, *Zhizn' russkogo rabochego. Vospominaniia* (Moscow, 1959), 15–16.
69 Ransel, *Mothers of Misery*, 167–8.        70 Glickman, *Russian Factory Women*, 86.
71 M.I. Pokrovskaia, "Peterburgskaia rabotnitsa," *Mir bozhii*, no. 12 (Dec. 1900): 35.

members. Rather, she had to depend on her own resources and ingenuity to locate housing in a city where it was both scarce and enormously expensive. As the population in Moscow and St. Petersburg skyrocketed, housing, already inadequate, failed to keep pace. The price of a roof over her head rose more quickly than a worker's income. Housing costs in Moscow hit the working class especially hard, because the one-room apartments typically occupied by workers cost more per square foot to rent than larger ones. And by the turn of the century, the cost of housing made St. Petersburg the most expensive major city in all of Europe.[72] In both cities, people crowded into cellars and attics; kitchens were partitioned into cubicles and rented. Cot and corner apartments proliferated. In these, beds filled practically every available inch of space, and strangers lived side by side. People even shared a bed.[73] To rent a room in a working-class district of St. Petersburg in the 1890s cost anywhere from five to eight and a half rubles a month, about half of a woman's wages. A room of her own was an inaccessible luxury for the laboring woman; many could afford only a corner. It cost one and a half to two rubles to rent a corner in the 1890s; a decade later, rents had risen for even the most undesirable housing, and women paid two and a half rubles for a corner in a basement, three and a half rubles for a corner in a kitchen, and between four and a half and six rubles for a corner in other rooms of an apartment.[74]

Factory housing could save money and protect a woman from the indiscriminate mixing of unattached men and women that was unavoidable in cot and corner apartments. Factory housing was more common in Moscow than in St. Petersburg. It was usually barracks-style: Dormitories consisted of enormous rooms, with plank beds laid side by side or in tiers. They left no room for furniture or personal affects, no room at all for privacy. Employers who provided housing for their workers generally exercised paternalistic control over them outside the workplace as well as within it. They might impose curfews on workers or require attendance at church.[75] Despite the restrictive character of this paternalism, women who had recently migrated from the countryside probably experienced paternalism as a comforting

---

72 James Bater, *St. Petersburg: Industrialization and Change* (Montreal, 1976), 111–12, 173–81, 328.
73 Ibid., 335–6; Bradley, *Muzhik*, 348–9.
74 I base these amounts on rents cited in philanthropic records.
75 Bradley, *Muzhik*, 202–4; Victoria Bonnell, ed., *The Russian Worker: Life and Labor under the Tsarist Regime* (Berkeley, Calif., 1983), 20–3.

reminder of the village, rather than as an unwarranted intrusion on their personal freedom. Company housing perpetuated a peasant mentality in other ways as well. It separated workers from the rest of the urban population and cushioned the impact of city life. Women textile workers who lived in company housing in St. Petersburg "remained strictly protected from outside influences by their 'benevolent' masters."[76] A decreasing minority of urban workers lived in these circumstances, however – about 28 percent of Moscow's industrial workforce, about 9 percent of St. Petersburg's by the end of World War I.[77] This left the majority of women workers free to arrange their own lives and to encounter the city for themselves, unlike their servant sisters.

Most women workers had to fend for themselves. When, meager wages in hand, a woman looked for housing, she had to consider more than its cost. Young unattached women, especially, tried to avoid indiscriminate corner-cot arrangements, which put them in sexual jeopardy. Either they shared a room with a married couple, as did one twenty-three-year-old textile worker who paid four rubles a month for her corner in 1912; or they lived with other women.[78] Sometimes, women formed an artel, a distinctively Russian arrangement that in an urban context usually denoted a living and eating collective composed of workers from the same village or district. Newcomers were especially likely to form artels, and men more likely to form them than women. Under the rubric "households of artels, workers, and servants living separately from their employers" in the census of 1897, artels absorbed about 10 percent of the entire female population of Moscow (as compared to 25 percent of the male) and about 4.4 percent of St. Petersburg's female population (as compared to 15 percent of the male). Because the census incorporated into this category households consisting of as few as two unrelated individuals, these percentages doubtless include rooms shared by a few woman friends, such as the room a twenty-two-year-old textile worker rented with two other women in 1912. For three rubles a month, she had a bed to herself, while her two friends who shared a bed paid less. Like other working women, these textile workers lowered their housing costs by doing

76 S. Kanatchikov, *Iz istorii moego bytiia*, 1: 80.
77 Iurii Kirianov, *Zhiznennyi uroven' rabochikh Rossii* (Moscow, 1979), 230–1. Kirianov does not separate men and women in these figures. The year is 1918, late for this study, but the only year after 1897 for which he provides aggregate figures.
78 Pokrovskaia, "Peterburgskaia rabotnitsa," 35; *Trudy Pervago vserossiiskago zhenskago s''ezda pri Russkom Zhenskom Obshchestve v S.-Peterburge 10–16 Dekabria 1908* (St. Petersburg, 1909), 329–33.

their own cooking and cleaning.[79] The male lodger required from his land-lady a variety of services for which he had to pay: She swept his part of the room, washed the floor, made his bed, and laundered his clothing. To avoid these expenses, women workers spent part of Saturday cleaning and evenings after work doing their wash.[80] Even so, as a group they wound up paying more than men did. In St. Petersburg, single women workers spent twice as high a proportion of their income on housing as men did, and they also spent more in absolute terms.[81]

Factory work provided migrant women with a modicum of independence and allowed for far more self-development than domestic service did. For all the hardships and uncertainties, the low wages and repetitive toil in often demoralizing circumstances, earning a wage of her own and living on her own (unlike many craftswomen) allowed the factory worker to shape her own life to a degree that was unthinkable in the village, even in villages near rural factories, and to feel "the ground of independence" beneath her feet, in the words of Taisa Slovachevskaia, a weaver.[82]

For example, factory women took pride in their living conditions and tried to make them homelike. With their hard-earned kopeks they might purchase a lamp, a mirror, a few sticks of furniture, and inexpensive crockery.[83] Their beds were neat, covered with a clean sheet, the pillow encased in a clean pillowcase. A male worker, by contrast, rarely spent money on bedclothes and was willing to sleep on a filthy mattress and pillow.[84] Even when women lived as an artel, they frequently tried to spruce up their environment by placing flowers on the windowsill and hanging pictures on the wall.[85]

The feminist physician Maria Pokrovskaia, a sympathetic chronicler of working women's lives, thought that the woman worker's concern for her personal environment resulted from what a contemporary feminist would call sex-role socialization. She wrote that mothers taught daughters, not

79 N.A. Troinitskii, ed., *Obshchii svod po imperii rezul'tatov razrabotki dannykh pervoi vseobshchei perepisi naseleniia proizvedennoi 28 Ianvaria 1897 g.* (St. Petersburg, 1905), 22–3; *Trudy Pervago . . . zhenskago s"ezda,* 329–33. One apartment at 14/2 Nizhegorodskaia, number 29, was occupied exclusively by servants.

80 TsGIAL, fond 1037, op. 1, delo 68 (manuscript of Maria Pokrovskaia), 24.

81 Glickman, *Russian Factory Women,* 117; M. Davidovich, *Peterburgskie tekstil'nye rabochie* (Moscow, 1919), 32.

82 T. Slovachevskaia, *Povest' rabotnitsy i krest'ianki* (Moscow, 1921), 157.

83 *Trudy Pervago . . . zhenskago s"ezda,* 329–33.

84 Pokrovskaia, "Peterburgskaia rabotnitsa," 35.

85 D.P. Nikol'skii, "Shlissel'burgskii prigorodnyi (fabrichnyi) uchastok S.-Petersburgskago uezda v sanitarnom otnoshenii," in *Vos'moi sanitarnyi s"ezd Sanktpeterburgskoi gubernii,* vyp. 3 (St. Petersburg, 1901), 251.

sons, to be neat and clean, and when men and women started to live by themselves they continued the behavior they had learned as children.[86] But surely this is only part of the story. The "home" in which most working-class women were raised was a peasant cottage. On the rare occasions that commentators on peasant life refer to peasant women's neatness or cleanliness, they remark it in terms of "progress" or "change," never as an ordinary circumstance of peasant life, especially of the impoverished peasantry from which most laboring women derived. More than sex-role socialization, women's attempts to create decent living conditions for themselves suggest rising expectations of life and a growing sense of personal dignity.

This is certainly what observers would have said had the women been men. According to M. Davidovich, the more progressive the male worker, the more physical space he required. Actually, in terms of their domestic arrangements, one of the few realms over which laboring people exercised control, women far more commonly than men demonstrated the "awakening of the individual and the broadening of his requirements and needs" that often signifies to labor historians the emergence of a working class more conscious of its social and political interests.[87] Perhaps the reason that historians have overlooked the broadening of women's requirements is that, as in the above quotation, they conceived of the working class as generically male. Or perhaps it is because women's heightened expectations of life did not lead to demands for social and political transformation, except in relatively rare cases, and remained limited to the sphere of marriage, home, and family that custom and tradition assigned them. On the other hand, as Rose Glickman has shown, the obstacles to organizing women workers were formidable, and by no means least among these obstacles was the fact that male workers tended to regard working-class organizations as purely male terrain.[88] In any case, the way that factory women organized their living arrangements indicates that while their wages were barely enough to live on, factory wages nevertheless enabled working women to assert control over their lives in a way that would have been impossible in the village.

Women factory workers also took particular pleasure in clothing. In the 1870s, this had led populist agitators to despair about organizing them.[89]

---

86 M.I. Pokrovskaia, "O zhilishchakh rabochikh peterburgskikh prigorodov," *Vestnik obshchestvennoi gigieny, Sudebnoi i prakticheskoi meditsiny*, Mar. 1896: 208.
87 K.A. Pazhitnov, *Polozhenie rabochego klassa v Rossii*, 3 vols. (Leningrad, 1924), 1: 84. See also B.N. Vasiliev, "Formirovanie promyshlennogo proletariata Ivanovskoi oblasti," *Voprosy istorii*, no. 6 (1952): 99.
88 Glickman, *Russian Factory Women*, chap. 6.
89 A.A. Ul'ianovskii, *Zhenshchiny v protsesse 50-ti* (St. Petersburg, 1906), 65.

Fig. 7. At the flea market, Moscow, 1902. (Courtesy of the Library of Congress.)

Thirty years later, although women workers' cultural level had risen considerably, their interest in clothing remained fundamentally unchanged. The migrant woman who had worked for a while in the city was even more demanding than the newcomer. Single women spent more money on clothing in absolute terms than single men did, and clothing represented a far higher proportion of a woman's budget – about 20 percent. Of course, much of women's clothing was neither new nor particularly elegant. For everyday use, the woman worker simply went to the bazaar and exchanged her worn-out clothing for secondhand but still serviceable wear. But when they went out on the town, many single women workers preferred something finer. To afford a pair of boots or an attractive dress, women sometimes skimped on food. In order to dress themselves up, Iraida Kommissarova and her girlfriends, all textile workers, were prepared to go hungry.[90] In 1908, an elegant, rose-colored cashmere dress, trimmed with white, machine-made lace and rose-colored satin ribbons cost the eighteen-year-old weaver P.T. Galkina three rubles. She paid a seamstress to copy it from a magazine.[91] Mikhail Isakovskii, whose sister migrated to Moscow from Smolensk to work in a textile mill, remembers that to buy the fashionable sack (sak) was the dream of young women workers like his sister. The sack was an overcoat cut a special way. It might take years for a textile worker to save enough money to buy one, because the women earned so little. "And women saved," he recalled, "because you could not live without a sack. Women workers had endless conversations about buying a sack. And if they bought one, they wrote to the village at once, to tell everyone that the long-desired sack had been purchased."[92] In Russia, we find no complaints about working women wearing "outlandish hot-looking dresses" in their free time, such as their sisters wore in New York City; nor did women workers don the "disorderly" shop-floor fashions of the German spinner or weaver. Instead, Russian working women adopted the clothing displayed in shopwindows and on the pages of fashion magazines, that is, the garb of the new middle class. In thus assimilating into the urban milieu they democratized fashion and, consciously or not, rejected the class distinctions that continued to govern social relations in the city.[93]

In other ways, too, living in the city might raise a working woman's expectations of life. After work, the factory woman's time was her own. Newcomers to the city were likely to spend their leisure much as they had in the village. For example, men and women textile workers at the Pal' textile mill in St. Petersburg, mainly migrants from Novotorzhok and Kashin districts of Tver', would walk out together in groups, the women attired in broad-sleeved peasant sarafans.[94] In Moscow, young textile workers would gather to do circle dances near the Presnia Gate and in the

90 In O.N. Chaadaeva, ed. *Rabotnitsa na sotsialisticheskoi stroike: Sbornik avtobiografii* (Moscow, 1923), 128–9. See also *Trudy Pervago . . . zhenskago s"ezda*, 332–3.

91 M.N. Levinson-Nechaeva, "Polozhenie i byt rabochikh tekstil'noi promyshlennosti Moskovskoi gubernii vo vtoroi polovine xix veka," in *Istoriko-bytovye ekspeditsii, 1949–50*, ed. A. Pankratova (Moscow, 1953), 165–6.

92 M.V. Isakovskii, *Na el'ninskoi zemle* (Moscow, 1975), 198.

93 C. Stansell, *City of Women*, 164; Katherine Canning, "Gender and the Politics of Class Formation: Rethinking German Labor History," *American Historical Review* 97, no. 3 (June 1992): 756–7. On dress as a means to assimilate into urban life, see Diane Koenker, "Urban Families, Working-Class Youth Groups, and the 1917 Revolution in Moscow," in *The Family in Imperial Russia*, 290.

94 A.G. Boldyreva, "Minuvshie gody," in *V nachale puti. Vospominaniia peterburgskikh rabochikh*, ed. E.A. Korol'chuk (Leningrad, 1975), 250.

square in front of the Prokhorov factory barracks.[95] "Village beauties" spoke a different language than skilled and citified workers. A metalworker like Ivan Babushkin felt you had to know how to approach such a woman and how to strike up a conversation on a subject of interest to her. Even to try might be risky: Fistfights over women were common in the working-class community.[96] Collective courtship practices reminiscent of village life probably helped to protect factory women's chastity in an urban setting.

Other pleasures drew the woman migrant more deeply into urban life. At Christmas, Carnival, and Easter, a carousel would go up near one working-class suburb of St. Petersburg.[97] In some parts of the city, the seasonal funfairs (*narodnye gulianiia*) became far more elaborate. During Shrovetide, clowns performed, trained bears danced, barkers shouted from balconies to attract customers, and crowds of people jammed the streets and squares. For a few kopeks, you could ride a carousel, a swing, or a Ferris wheel, or watch a puppet performance of Petrushka. In August 1893, thousands of lower-class residents of St. Petersburg attended a festival that took place at the Tsaritsyn meadow, following a religious procession from the Alexander-Nevskii Monastery to St. Isaac's Cathedral. Without spending a kopek, people could listen to the singing, ride on a carousel, and watch popular plays at open-air theaters. Contests and games began at 5:00 on the dot: The men tried to ascend a greased pole and to keep their balance while running along a log that turned beneath their feet.[98] Muscovites enjoyed similar entertainments. "On Sundays, the pavements [in working-class regions of Moscow] are packed with people of the lowest orders . . . and the sound of the inevitable accordian accompanies the singing of popular songs," a commentator wrote in the 1880s. Agafia, the shy heroine of Semenov's novella "The Soldier's Wife," began actually to like living in Moscow when she allowed one of her co-workers at a laundry to coax her into attending a fair near Maiden's Field. She really enjoyed watching a performance of Petrushka, listening to the singers, and eating cheap sweets. After that, she started to look forward to

95 V. Iu. Krupianskaia, "Evoliutsiia semeino-bytovogo uklada rabochikh," in *Rossiiskii proletariat. Oblik bor'ba gegemoniia*, ed. L.M. Ivanov (Moscow, 1970), 283.

96 I.V. Babushkin, *Vospominaniia Ivana Vasilievicha Babushkina, 1893–1900* (Leningrad, 1925), 40.

97 P.P. Aleksandrov, *Za Narvskoi zastavoi. Vospominaniia starogo rabochego* (Leningrad, 1963), 11.

98 *Peterburgskii listok*, no. 238 (31 Aug. 1893): 2; also Aleksandrov, *Za Narvskoi zastavoi*, 11, and Iu. A. Dmitriev, "Gulian'ia i drugie formy massovykh zrelishch," *Russkaia khudozhestvennaia kul'tura kontsa xix-nachala xx veka (1895–1907)* (Moscow, 1968), 248–61.

her days off and the chance to stroll with her friends in the streets and the parks, taking in the pleasures of the city. This led her to spend much less of her free time with the aunt who had sheltered her when she first came to Moscow.[99]

There is no way of knowing how many women workers (or laundresses or even servants) took advantage of these opportunities for inexpensive pleasure, but there can be no question that thousands of men and women did. Soldiers and skilled workers were the first to attend the performances but, increasingly, women composed part of the audience, too.[100] One pleasure garden that opened in the spring of 1896 in the midst of a densely settled working-class district of St. Petersburg provided entertainment for about twelve thousand people on Sundays and holidays. It was patronized primarily by the young and by families, who could enter the park without paying anything, listen to a wind orchestra, watch acrobats and clowns, and sit in the back of the open-air theater. Twenty kopeks would buy a front seat.[101] During the decade of the 1890s, tens of thousands of people, primarily from the laboring classes, enjoyed a mixture of traditional fare, variety shows, plays, readings, dances, and concerts at fairs and pleasure gardens in both Moscow and St. Petersburg.

Their experiences in the city could broaden women's cultural horizons. While some women workers at the Pal' textile mill walked out in their sarafans, others attended the theater from time to time. One of them responded at great length to a questionnaire aimed at ascertaining audience response to plays. The fact that the respondent was a woman, but nevertheless used the masculine pronoun when she referred to the worker in the abstract, suggests the degree to which virtually everyone conceived of the working class as generically male, women workers included. In her words, the theater was a place where "the worker can forget his position, and become totally absorbed in what he sees and hears." Plays left her refreshed and energized, she wrote. She enjoyed relating the plots to people who had not seen the performances and discussing what happened with those who had. Attending plays had even helped her to understand her own faults, like talking about an absent girlfriend behind her back.[102] Her interest in the theatre was by no

---

99   Quoted in Kelly, " 'Better Halves?' ", 10; Semenov, "Soldatka," 69–71.
100  *Russkie narodnye gulian'ia po rasskazam A. Alekseeva-Iakovleva* (Leningrad, 1948), 114.
101  Ibid., 110.
102  N. Mikhailovskii, "Literatura i zhizn'," *Russkoe bogatstvo*, no. 6 ( June 1896): 55. One nineteen-year-old woman worker at the Maxwell factory went twice to the theater in 1907, paying forty-five kopeks apiece for her tickets. *Trudy Pervago . . . zhenskago s'ezda*, 332.

means atypical. By the early twentieth century, drama circles had become enormously popular among working women and men. Between 1900 and 1905, there was a "virtual epidemic" of workers' theaters in the factories of St. Petersburg and Moscow, including the Prokhorov and Tsindel factories, where substantial numbers of women were employed. After 1905, youth clubs offering cultural diversions proliferated in the working-class districts of both cities. Women workers were particularly drawn to the romantic possibilities they offered.[103]

Their broadened horizons and growing self-assertion may have enabled some women workers to resist seductive promises in return for sexual favors. Certainly, their steady wages and the fact that they could continue earning money even after they married, and even after they had children, gave them advantages in the urban marriage market that their servant sisters lacked. Still, their advantage was relative, not absolute, because the deck was stacked against them, too. Marriage and illegitimacy rates from some working-class districts of St. Petersburg and Moscow provide a rough index of their relative success (see Table 5.1 and Table 5.2). For St. Petersburg, particularly noteworthy are the second section of Vasilevskii Island and the second section of Vyborg district. From the turn of the century onward, marriage rates in both sections far exceeded the norm for the city, which was about 6 marriages per 1,000 people. In Vasilevskii Island 2, more women married than bore an illegitimate child, whereas in Vyborg 2, the reverse remained the case until after the Stolypin reforms: For every 73 women who married in 1902, another 102 bore illegitimate children. The Stolypin reforms of 1906–7 made it easier for young peasant workers to sever their ties to their villages. The fact that marriage rates rose thereafter is further evidence of the connection between high rates of illegitimacy and migrant men's links with their native villages. However, while the reforms increased a woman's odds of a successful courtship in the city, they by no means guaranteed success, as the figures in Table 5.1 and Table 5.2 indicate. Marriage rates went up in a number of working-class quarters, Vyborg 2 in particular. But illegitimacy rates as a proportion of live births declined only slowly. In Moscow, in two of the working-class districts surveyed, the number of illegitimate births grew more rapidly than the number of marriages; while in many working-class districts of St. Petersburg, illegitimate births continued to outnumber weddings as late as 1909. That year, the balance finally

103 Diane Koenker, "Urban Families, Working-Class Youth Groups," 289, 297–8; also Slovachevskaia, *Povest'*, 159.

shifted in favor of brides in Vyborg 2: For every 83 women who got married, another 77 gave birth to illegitimate children.

Statistical surveys rarely reveal the occupations of unwed mothers with any precision. One exception is the St. Petersburg statistical yearbook for 1886, the only one I have found that listed factory women separately from unskilled laborers. That year, only 3.7 percent of women giving birth to illegitimate children in St. Petersburg were factory workers, about half of them tobacco workers. In 1890, factory workers constituted approximately 6.7 percent of working women in the city. As the number of factory women increased, their rates of illegitimacy may have grown. The physician M.P. Krivoshein delivered babies in a maternity home which served a working-class clientele and was situated in the Vyborg district of St. Petersburg. In the 1890s, he wrote, most of the women he attended were factory workers or craftswomen and almost two-thirds of them were single.[104]

Some of the factory women bearing illegitimate children were involved in consensual relationships. Krivoshein found that an unwed factory woman was far more likely than a servant to keep her child, and the relatively small numbers of women workers among abandoning mothers indicates that this remained the case well into the twentieth century.[105] On her skimpy wages, a woman worker could support herself and her child only at the most marginal level; most, I suspect, counted on the assistance of the father. Anthropologists have noted that consensual unions are one of the characteristics of an impoverished urban milieu, in which sexual partners are matters of individual choice rather than the result of an effort to amalgamate kin groups.[106] Such unions were likely to have been more common in Moscow and St. Petersburg than in Paris, London, or Berlin, because of the numerous obstacles to marriage in urban Russia. Exactly how common they were it is difficult to say. G.I. Arkhangel'skii, attempting to assess life in St. Petersburg on the basis of the first thoroughgoing urban census, estimated that in 1869 as many as a quarter of the single women in the city lived in "civil marriage," although he carefully noted that he was only guessing.[107] In the 1890s, the investigator N. Nikol'skii found consensual unions to be "common" in the

---

104 M.P. Krivoshein, *O prizrenii rozhenits v gorodskikh rodil'nykh priiutakh S.-Petersburga* (St. Petersburg, 1897), 7.
105 Ibid., 7; Ransel, *Mothers of Misery*, 170.
106 Edwin Eames and Judith Goode, *Urban Poverty in Cross-Cultural Context* (New York, 1973), 172–81.
107 G.I. Arkhangel'skii, "Zhizn' v Peterburg po statisticheskim dannym," *Arkhiv sudebnoi meditsiny*, no. 2 (June 1869): 73–4.

industrial Shlisselburg suburbs of St. Petersburg, where illegitimacy rates ranged from 9 to 12 percent of live births.[108] At the close of the century, two census takers tried to estimate the number of such unions on the basis of their own observations. They had collected data in the third quarter of the Narva district, an entirely working-class region containing a number of factories and several textile mills. About 9 percent of the twenty-six hundred workers whom they queried acknowledged living in "civil marriages"; they supposed that the numbers were actually larger. They found that workers in common-law unions were for the most part relatively recent migrants to St. Petersburg from Smolensk, Riazan, Tver', Iaroslavl', and Novgorod. They belonged to the "least cultured" layer of their class. Whereas in 1900, 68 percent of peasant men in St. Petersburg and 35 percent of peasant women could read, in their sample, only 38 percent of the men and 30 percent of the women were literate. These couples clustered at the lower end of the wage scale, the men earning between twenty and twenty-four rubles a month, the women, between twelve and fifteen.[109]

People have offered differing explanations for these consensual unions. The census takers, for example, thought migrants failed to marry because marriage cost money and also because migrants did not value marriage as highly as villagers did. It is certainly true that for many, perhaps the majority, poverty was the primary obstacle. A survey of St. Petersburg metalworkers, conducted in 1909, showed that 46 percent of men earning less than one and a half rubles a day were single, as compared to only 21 percent of men earning two and a half rubles a day. In their petitions requesting legitimation of children born before the wedding, migrant peasant couples often cited poverty or lack of means as the reason they had waited to wed.[110] But common-law unions were not invariably the consequence of poverty. Diane Koenker has surmised that more conscious and urbanized working-class couples may have preferred common-law marriages to the ritual of a church wedding.[111] Joseph Bradley has drawn attention to an additional factor that kept a proportion of cohabiting couples from marrying: The man was married to a village woman or lived apart from his wife in the city. In his

---

108 Nikol'skii, "Shlissel'burgskie," 271–5. Servants were rare in this working-class section of town.

109 *St. Peterburg po perepisi . . . 1900*, vyp. 1, 168–9; M. and O., "Tsifry i fakty iz perepisi Sankt-Peterburga v 1900 g.," *Russkaia mysl'* 23, no. 2 (Feb. 1902): 75–6.

110 *Soiuz rabochikh po metallu. Materialy ob ekonomicheskom polozhenii i professional'nom organizatsii peterburgskikh rabochikh po metallu* (St. Petersburg, 1909), 86. For petitions, see, for example, TsGIAL, fond 225, op. 1, delo 3157, 3167, 3155, 3156, 3162.

111 Koenker, "Urban Families," 291.

words, "transitory and consensual unions were common means of coping
with long separations" of husband and wife.[112]

According to ethnographic correspondents, married male migrants became involved in liaisons relatively often. Observed a correspondent from
Zubtsov, Tver', husbands sometimes "take up with women when they live
elsewhere for most of the year – in the city, at the factory, and so forth."[113]
"Some of the *Pitershchiki* forget their [rural] family and start another in the
capital," wrote a correspondent from Galich, Kostroma.[114] Married migrants
from Smolensk who took up with women workers or servants in St. Petersburg
sometimes abandoned their village wives, considering them "filthy peasant
women (*babenki*)" by comparison with their new and citified love.[115] Occasionally, the liaisons of married men became part of the historical record.
For example, the investigation of a strike at the Nikol'skaia textile mill in
1885 revealed quite incidentally that one of the men accused of instigating
the action, the weaver Luka Ivanov, had been living with a peasant woman
who had borne him a daughter. Although he had begun a second family, he
still maintained relations with his village wife and had spent a couple of days
with her in the village following his first arrest and exile in 1883.[116] Liaisons
were also an informal solution to the difficulties of divorce in Russia.[117] But,
of course, if the man was already married, his consensual partner had no
chance at all of obtaining the legal guarantees and no assurance of obtaining
the financial resources that marriage was supposed to provide.

Even when consensual unions occurred in the absence of legal or financial
obstacles to marriage, the woman was in a relatively weak bargaining position, lacking the social and economic leverage to induce a lover to marry her.
Two historians of the Parisian lower classes have argued that consensual
unions were based on women's economic, legal, and physical vulnerability,
and that the woman was likely to perceive such a relationship as a failed
courtship.[118] Many lower-class Russian women of peasant background undoubtedly shared these perceptions. Peasants strongly condemned consensual unions and the female partner in particular. Such attitudes carried over
to the city. According to the Soviet historian Sima Lapitskaia, even when

112 Bradley, *Muzhik*, 226–7. Separation of couples in the city will be discussed in Chapter 7.
113 Tenishev archive, op. 1, delo 1726, 10–11.
114 Ibid., delo 588, 20–1. See also delo 1781, 17.
115 Ibid., delo 1702, 23–5; also delo 1695, 11, and Nikol'skii, "Shlissel'burgskie," 237.
116 A.N. Pankratova, ed., *Rabochee dvizhenie v Rossii* (Moscow-Leningrad, 1952), v. 3, ch. 1,
    173–5.
117 See, for example, TsGIA SSSR, fond 796, op. 189, II stol, IV otd., ed. kh. 5389.
118 Cited in Fuchs and Moch, "Pregnant, Single, and Far from Home," 1018.

consensual unions were long lasting and stable, factory workers regarded them as a shame (*pozor*) for the woman and treated her contemptuously. "Civil marriage elicited everyone's jeers and condemnations," she writes. The women would use insulting nicknames to refer to working women in common-law marriages.[119]

In their own way, educated Russians were equally dismissive of such unions. Society's lack of recognition or support for the makeshift domestic arrangements of the urban poor emerges in a case brought before the St. Petersburg court in 1903. M.S. Baklagin, a peasant migrant from Iaroslavl', brought the case on behalf of his "wife," Pelageia Kucherova, a peasant migrant from Novgorod. While the two were away from home at their work as tailors, their two-year-old son, Boris, had run across the railroad tracks and been run over by a train. Because the child had been harmed so severely that he might be "unable to support his parents in their old age," Baklagin claimed compensation from the city. Investigation revealed that the couple was unmarried and that Boris, the youngest of five children, was "illegitimate." Although it was never demonstrated that Baklagin was not Boris's father, the fact that he and Kucherova were unmarried enabled the court to dismiss his suit. Concluding that Baklagin had "no parental relation with the family of the victim," the court ruled that he "has no right to make any claim on the city government" on the family's behalf. The published record leaves unclear Baklagin's motives for bringing the case. However, all educated parties, including the man who reported the case, were convinced that he was out for what he could get for himself. In their eyes, Baklagin had neither legitimate ties to nor responsibility for the family he claimed as his own.[120]

Lack of support from the larger society or the working-class community meant that the woman in a consensual union could not make the claims of a wife. Unwed mothers could never count on a lover's assistance or on obtaining adequate support. Why else would an unmarried thirty-two-year-old factory worker with three children work up until the very last days of pregnancy, resuming work within three weeks, when her lover, a knife grinder, earned thirty-five rubles a month? Or another factory woman, thirty years of age, live with three children in a corner when her lover, a tradesman, earned a ruble a day? Evfrosiniia Kuteinikova, an unskilled laborer from Tver' who earned seven rubles a month, managed to obtain only an

---

119 Lapitskaia, *Byt rabochikh*, 77. See also Tenishev archive, op. 1, delo 1726, 11 (Zubtsov, Tver').
120 "O mirovom okonchanii," *Izvestiia Sanktpeterburgskoi gorodskoi dumy*, no. 2 (Jan. 1904): 3.

additional three rubles from the father of her child, a tailor.[121] Although, like the tailor, a father might "help" the mother of his child, the woman had no real legal claim on him, and both the man and the woman knew it.[122] Observing one longstanding liaison between two textile workers, the sociologist E. Kabo wrote in 1928, "One feels something is not quite stable in this household. It seems as if the husband is not a permanent member but a temporary visitor in the family. He gives his family only a small part of his salary and even though he earns much more than his wife, he contributes much less, not even enough to cover the cost of his food."[123] In the absence of the socially and religiously sanctioned bond of marriage, there was nothing to ensure the man's continuing loyalty, or his economic support, except his own goodwill, and nothing to keep him from leaving. When they grew tired of the woman, or burdened by her children, men were free to pick up and leave, as had Aleksandra Kondrat'eva's lover in the brief history that introduced this chapter.[124]

Materially, the position of the unwed mother was probably no worse than that of a widow or abandoned wife with small children. They all lived lives of the direst poverty, huddling in crowded corners with their children, eating far less than other working women, going about in rags. Pre-revolutionary Russia had no public welfare system; the assistance offered to the single mother by both public and private philanthropic organizations did not meet pressing needs, especially the desperate need of women who struggled alone to support their children. But abandoned wives and widows had other resources to draw on. Village kin were more willing to take in legitimate children than illegitimate ones; parents, aunts, and uncles were more willing to shelter and assist a bereaved wife than a woman abandoned by her lover. An unmarried woman had no claim on the resources of her lover's kin, as a widow might have on her husband's. As a result, the unwed mother would find herself in the same isolation from kin and community that had enabled someone to seduce her in the first place. Asked why she had borne and raised three illegitimate children when she complained they were like a noose around her neck, one lower-class woman explained, "I had the first because I was stupid, and when the father of the child abandoned me, I was alone,

---

121 TsGIAL, fond 251, op. 1, ed. kh. 3, 540–1.
122 The word "help" appears frequently in these records, even in cases where couples appear to cohabit. See ibid., ed. kh. 3, 16–18; 55–7.
123 E. Kabo, *Ocherki rabochego byta: opyt monograficheskogo issledovaniia domashnego rabochego byta* (Moscow, 1928), 29.
124 See, for example, the cases in TsGIA SSSR, fond 1409, op. 15, ed. kh. 104, 1640, 2569.

tied down and did not know what to do. So I tried to find another bread-winner, and then he left me, this time with two children. I couldn't cope with them all, and found myself a third."[125]

Despite the risks of abandonment and destitution, a substantial minority of single women migrants struck up sexual relations with men. Some of them counted on marriage; others, recognizing the odds against a legal union, nevertheless preferred a consensual relationship to no relationship at all. There were good reasons for this choice. Apart from the very elusive questions of personal companionship and sexual pleasure, ongoing liaisons could bring tangible benefits. To have the income that a man could provide eased to some extent working women's poverty and put a greater distance between the woman and the streets. Some women in consensual unions ceased to earn wages altogether, at least for a while. Of the 141 peasant women who bore illegitimate children at the St. Petersburg Maternity Home early in 1890, 20 (14 percent) did not work for wages and gave their trade as "housewife."[126] Given the odds against an urban marriage, many women, especially older women, were in no position to be fussy. If a working woman was sometimes "quarrelsome, jealous, and possessive of her man," as early socialist propagandists found them to be, it is not hard to understand why. In addition to a modicum of comfort and support, a man's income could mean a hot meal and perhaps a bit of meat once or twice a week, instead of the eternal bread, milk, and cucumbers that composed the diet of most single women workers.

But perhaps most importantly, illegitimacy rates in urban Russia point to a profound difference between the experiences of migrant women and migrant men. Confronted by formidable obstacles to marriage in urban Russia – the high cost of urban living, low wages, and the tenacity of village ties – men had an option that few women enjoyed, because of women's responsibility for child care. A man could marry in the village and leave his wife and children there as he continued to migrate and to contribute to the family economy. The fact that so many men chose that option stacked the odds against a migrant woman's finding a husband and having a family in the city. The situation was not hopeless. Some migrant women managed to overcome these structural disadvantages to negotiate a courtship in an urban setting,

125 E.P. Kalacheva, "Bezplatnyi narodnyi detskii sad, ustroennyi E.P. Kalachevoi," *Trudovaia pomoshch* 5 (May 1901): 649.
126 Only four of these unmarried "housewives" were recorded as dispatching their babies to the foundling home. Sixty-five percent of married peasant women giving birth listed their trade as "housewife."

and their numbers grew after 1906. Nevertheless, as rates of illegitimacy and infant abandonment attest, even as late as 1909 a woman who gambled with her chastity in the hope of forming an enduring liaison was almost as likely to lose as to win. Thus, the transition from an agrarian society to a more modern, urban one offered some migrant women unprecedented opportunities for self-development and self-definition; but it condemned many others to lives of celibacy or unwed motherhood, depriving them of the modest pleasures and satisfactions that their peasant mothers had known.

# 6. Women on the margins/ marginalizing women

The question of prostitution is an important one in the history of women of the laboring poor in late nineteenth-century Russia because of the perspective it provides on efforts to regulate the behavior of women who migrated to cities in search of wages and the effect of those efforts on the women themselves. Like the majority of urban women, most women who became prostitutes belonged to the lower classes and had traveled to the city from somewhere else. Their occupational and personal profiles are in many respects indistinguishable from those of thousands of other migrant peasant women who struggled both to make a living and to find a mate in Russia's major cities. The primary difference between many women alleged to be prostitutes and other servants, craftswomen, unskilled laborers, and the like was that those alleged to be prostitutes lived closer to the margins of urban life and behaved in ways that brought them to the attention of special police, who were empowered to scrutinize the sexual behavior of lower-class women. As a result of their brush with the authorities, the lives of women suspected of prostitution are far better documented than the lives of other migrant peasant women. Information about them offers insights into the processes that marginalized women; it also highlights the circumstances in which the peasant family economy and patriarchal control of women's sexuality might fail to function.

Prostitution, both casual and professional, became widespread in urban Russia in the decades between the emancipation of the serfs and the outbreak of World War I. As in London, Paris, Milan, and other large cities of Europe and the United States, in Russia the process of urbanization and industrialization brought into the city unprecedented numbers of unattached women. Dependent for their livelihood on what they could earn themselves, many migrant women found it difficult to find steady work and to live on the wages. In the city women encountered many more temptations than they

166

had in the enclosed world of the village and, as we have seen, sometimes insuperable obstacles to legal union. Whether or not they wound up becoming prostitutes (and only a small minority did so on a professional, full-time basis), the option of exchanging sex for money or favors was ever-present in working women's lives. Urban popular entertainments often portrayed men using material resources as a means to convince women to give in to men's sexual demands. If she barely subsisted on her wages and yearned for a good time after her long day, a woman might also exchange sex for a warm meal, a scarf, an evening on the town, or other "treats."[1] Most women who exchanged sex for money or favors would have preferred to choose the timing and the circumstances. In the words of one prostitute, "Then a girl could sell herself only when she pleased, and when she pleased, she could stop."[2]

Such flexibility was difficult in Russia, as it was in much of Western Europe.[3] Having placed herself beyond the reach of the patriarchal village, a woman considered a prostitute found herself in the power of agents of the patriarchal state. Russia had a system of regulation that was supposed to confine the spread of venereal disease by registering women as prostitutes. Based upon the French model, the Russian system began operation in 1844. It was greatly expanded following the emancipation of the serfs in 1861, in response to the rising number of women living by themselves in the city. Medical officials of the Ministry of the Interior, who believed that venereal disease, syphilis in particular, threatened to assume epidemic proportions, attributed the threat mainly to unattached women newly on their own (and not necessarily professional prostitutes). The women primarily responsible for spreading syphilis were "soldiers' wives, living apart from their husbands, women who sell gingerbread, pears, and the like on the streets, and

1 Catriona Kelly, " 'Better Halves'? Representations of Women in Russian Urban Popular Entertainments, 1870–1910," in *Women and Society in Russia and the Soviet Union*, ed. Linda Edmondson (New York, 1992), 17–18. For a discussion of the practice of treating in New York City around the turn of the century, see Kathy Peiss, " 'Charity Girls' and City Pleasures: Historical Notes on Working-Class Sexuality 1880–1920," in *Power of Desire: The Politics of Sexuality*, ed. Ann Snitow, Christine Stansell, and Sharon Thompson (New York, 1983), 74–87.

2 *Soiuz zhenshchin'*, no. 1 (June–July 1907), 9 (copy preserved in the Central State Archive of the October Revolution [TsGAOR], reference: fond 516, op. 1, ed. kh. 6).

3 On France, see Jill Harsin, *Policing Prostitution in Nineteenth-Century Paris* (Princeton, N.J., 1985); on Italy, Mary Gibson, *Prostitution and the State in Italy, 1860–1915* (New Brunswick, N.J., 1986); on Germany, Richard Evans, "Prostitution, State, and Society in Imperial Germany," *Past and Present*, no. 70 (Feb. 1976): 106–29; and on England, Judith Walkowitz, *Prostitution and Victorian Society: Women, Class, and the State* (Cambridge, England, 1980).

vagrant women of various sorts . . . and also women factory workers."[4] The
solution was to cast the net broadly and to register as prostitutes as many
suspect women as possible.

Registration as a prostitute severely restricted women's freedom of movement. Registered women were obliged to appear periodically for a genital
examination by a physician. If they were found to be infected with venereal
disease, they were required to enter a hospital for prolonged treatment.
Registered women who failed to appear regularly for their examinations
risked incarceration in the workhouse or a house of correction. To prevent
women from avoiding examination, the law required registered women to
surrender their passports to the appropriate authority. In return they received a "yellow ticket" that clearly identified their trade and strictly controlled their activities. It forbade them to visit the main streets or squares of
their cities, to walk with women friends on the street, or even to stand in the
entryways of their apartments.[5] By substituting the "yellow ticket" for the
passport a woman needed to rent an apartment or find a job, registration
made it more difficult for her to return to the milieu of the respectable poor.
As Laurie Bernstein puts it: "Women who registered . . . had nothing to
show prospective landlords or employers but their embarrassing licenses."[6]

The system of regulation empowered those who enforced it to set the
boundary between casual sexuality and professional prostitution and to judge
who transgressed it. In most cities, this meant that a Medical-Police Committee, composed of physicians, supervised the system, while it was enforced
by special police agents who in 1890 received thirty rubles a month to keep
an eye on avowed prostitutes and to apprehend "clandestine" ones in the
section of the city they patrolled.[7] The agents had the authority to apprehend suspect women on the streets and during periodic roundups they

4  Mikhail Kuznetsov, *Prostitutsiia i sifilis v Rossii* (St. Petersburg, 1871), 203. On syphilis, see
   Laura Engelstein, "Morality and the Wooden Spoon: Russian Doctors View Syphilis, Social
   Class, and Sexual Behavior, 1890–1905," *Representations*, no. 14 (Spring 1986): 169–208. The
   surveillance of prostitution was established by a network of overlapping laws and authorities,
   some deriving from the central government, others in the hands of the localities. See L.F.
   Ragozin, ed. *Svod uzakonenii i rasporiazhenii pravitel' stva po vrachebnoi i sanitarnoi chasti v
   Imperii* (St. Petersburg, 1895–6) (Prilozhenie k st. 164, 63–163. The development of this
   legislation is discussed in Laurie Bernstein, "Sonia's Daughters: Prostitution and Society in
   Russia," Ph.D. diss., University of California, Berkeley, 1987.
5  M. Kuznetsov, "Istoriko-statistichcskii ocherk prostitutsii v Peterburge v 1852 g. po 1869
   g.," *Arkhiv sudebnoi meditsiny i obshchestvennoi gigieny* 6, no. 1 (Mar. 1870): 75, 77–8.
6  Bernstein, "Sonia's Daughters," 22.
7  A.I. Fedorov, "Prostitutsiia v S.-Peterburge i vrachebno-politseiskii nadzor za neiu," *Vestnik
   obshchestvennoi gigieny, sudebnoi i prakticheskoi meditsiny* 13 (Jan.–Mar. 1892): 49–50.

conducted in the flophouses, taverns, and other places where the disreputable poor dwelled and disported themselves. The way the law defined a prostitute gave agents considerable latitude: women who "trade[d] in vice" (*promyshliaiut nepotrebstvom*) or who "made debauchery into a trade" (*obrativshie rasputstvo v promysl'*). Apprehended by the police, a woman became subject to an examination for venereal disease. If the examination revealed that she was infected, she was hospitalized immediately, and if this was her second hospitalization, and if the police could demonstrate that the woman "made an industry of depravity," she was registered as a prostitute. Even women who plied the trade casually and intermittently (or perhaps not at all) risked encountering the police and becoming registered as "professional" prostitutes. As Laurie Bernstein has noted, this gave local authorities carte blanche in supervising the activities of working-class and poor women, which the authorities sometimes used to harass and even to blackmail women.[8] The low wages of the police agents made bribery and corruption almost inevitable.

Toward the end of the century, attempts to reform the system curtailed a few of the arbitrary powers over women but left most fully in force. In response to widespread abuses, in 1892 the State Senate ruled that the police could neither examine women nor register them without their agreement. But the police retained the right to investigate women and to command their presence before the Medical-Police Committee, so the system continued to operate much as it had done earlier. After 1892 as before, police agents encouraged yardmen (*dvorniki*) and landladies to keep an eye on unattached women. Ordinary citizens could send anonymous letters to the authorities, denouncing a woman as a prostitute, thereby bringing her to the attention of police agents. Although the surveillance of a suspected prostitute was supposed to be secret, the agents would query her yardman and others concerning her behavior. In St. Petersburg, police agents often "invited" a suspect to appear before the Medical-Police Committee, where she would be pressured to register as a prostitute. By casting doubt upon a woman's reputation, police agents could put a job or a relationship in jeopardy, thereby increasing the likelihood that the woman would abandon her resistance.

Although all lower-class women were potentially suspect, women without jobs were particularly vulnerable to involuntary registration and women without a male guardian (whether father, husband, or lover) were more

8 Laurie Bernstein, "Yellow Tickets and State-Licensed Brothels: The Tsarist Government and the Regulation of Urban Prostitution," in *Health and Society in Revolutionary Russia*, ed. Susan G. Solomon and John F. Hutchinson (Bloomington, Ind., 1990), 49.

vulnerable still. A typical candidate for police harassment was an unemployed servant or craftswoman, living alone or with a female relative, and with no visible means of support. Women who engaged in unruly behavior or defied notions of acceptable female sexual conduct also put themselves at risk. If a woman kept company with a man and returned home with him late at night, or if people saw her with different escorts at a place of public amusement, or if she spent time with friends in a tavern, she was likely to come to the attention of the police. Once she had, she would find it difficult to resist pressure to register as a prostitute, despite rulings aimed at protecting her from involuntary registration.

Case histories from Medical-Police archives illustrate how the process of registration might unfold. The first, quite typical, concerns Maria Bykova, an eighteen-year-old migrant peasant from Chukhloma, Kostroma. In 1893, Bykova came to the attention of the St. Petersburg Medical–Police Committee, which instructed one of its agents to "gather accurate information about her behavior, occupation, and material resources." Bykova was then living with her married sister on Liteinyi Prospect. According to the agents' reports, Bykova had no occupation and was frequently away from home in the evening. The agent consulted the yardman, who told him that Bykova lived with her sister intermittently, when she was between positions as a servant, and that she frequently changed jobs, which, as we have seen, servants commonly did. On the basis of this circumstantial evidence, the agent concluded that Bykova's conduct was extremely suspicious and that, in general, she was a "bold girl" (*bystraia devushka*). In his opinion, her behavior "resembled a prostitute's," and he predicted that if she did not soon find another position, she would openly become one. The prediction came true, aided, perhaps, by his surveillance, which may have compromised her reputation. Bykova found a position as a servant but two weeks later registered as a prostitute.[9]

The registration of a second woman, Glafira Printseva, is recorded in much greater detail and is unusual only in the fact that Printseva tried hard, but without success, to avoid becoming a professional prostitute. Printseva was a nineteen-year-old migrant from Kashin, Tver'. She first came to the attention of the police in June 1897, when she was detained at eight in the evening for disorderly conduct in a public place. An agent was instructed to find out whether she was registered and, if she was not, to keep tabs on her. Over the next few months, he proceeded to investigate her lifestyle, with the

9 TsGIAL, fond 593, op. 1, delo 547.

assistance of the local police, her yardman, and others who knew her. The agent learned that Printseva rented a room that cost fifteen rubles a month but had no definite occupation, that she often left her room about six in the evening to visit a tavern or cheap hotel and, he was convinced, to pick up men. She would return after midnight, and sometimes the following morning, accompanied by a man. Although she never took the man to her room, the agent concluded that this was evidence that she "traded in vice." About six months after her initial apprehension on the streets, Printseva was "invited" to appear before the St. Petersburg Medical-Police Committee, and the police in her quarter were instructed to take appropriate measures should she fail to show up. What followed can be told in Printseva's own words. Illiterate herself, she must have prevailed upon someone or paid someone to write a letter in her name and in her self-defense. "No one has caught me doing anything," the letter began,

> and although I'm currently without a position as a servant, I'm seeking one. In the beginning of this month [December] an agent of the Medical-Police Committee appeared in the house where I live and summoned me to the stairway. He demanded that I take a blank [the infamous yellow ticket] and when I refused, he handed me a note written in pencil, declaring that I had to appear before the Committee. Then he left. I paid no attention to the note and did not go. After a few days, I received a summons to the Committee. When I appeared before the chair of the Committee to learn the reason for the summons, he told me that the agent had reported that I was a prostitute, and that I must take a blank. But since I am not and never have been a prostitute, I refused outright to take it, declaring that should I ever be known to practice such a profession, then he could persecute me, but not now. Then, on December 18, I was summoned to the local police station and forced to sign a statement that I would appear at the Committee and take a blank on the nineteenth. Such insistent demands by the chair of the Medical-Police Committee cannot make me into a prostitute, but they can make me unhappy.

The letter was addressed to the chief of St. Petersburg's police, whom she asked to investigate the matter, because, she insisted, the Committee did not have the power to force her to become a prostitute.

The fact that Printseva was correct in terms of the law made no difference in practice. The state and its agents could and did circumvent the law with impunity. Printseva's letter was ignored, the harassment of her continued. In practice if not by law, the Committee enjoyed the power to force Printseva to abandon the identity of a woman who was temporarily out of work, and who occasionally exchanged sex for money or drinks, and to assume the identity of a registered prostitute, despite her efforts to resist this. On December 29, 1897, Printseva "voluntarily" registered and submitted to the surveillance of the Medical-Police Committee. Over the next eight years, she would leave prostitution and then return to it several times.[10]

Only compelling evidence that someone else had authority over a woman offered reliable protection from such pressures. If she found a steady job she could escape registration or, better still, if she kept company with one man, rather than several.[11] Once she had come to the attention of the police, it was exceedingly difficult for a woman to free herself from their scrutiny. Lacking such protection, some women simply left town. Epistimiia Aleksandrova, a twenty-year-old migrant to St. Petersburg from Ostashkov, Tver', was one of these. Aleksandrova, a tailor, engaged in sex with a man who afterward informed on her to the police, alleging she had given him a venereal disease. "Invited" to appear before the Medical-Police Committee early in April 1909, she quickly packed up and returned to her village.[12]

That this system, so onerous for the lower-class women it targeted, should prove so useful to the historian who seeks to study them is ironic to say the least. The problem of prostitution attracted considerable attention not only from the officials and police agents who sought to regulate it but also from people who opposed regulation. Toward the close of the century, physicians and reformers of various political stripes used the fight against syphilis and the regulation system as a basis from which to conduct their own struggle against autocracy's bureaucratic regime.[13] To pursue this struggle, both sides accumulated a formidable array of data on the economic, social, and family status of prostitutes, utilizing information drawn from registration records, from interviews that recorded life histories, and, after 1889, from a census of prostitutes registered throughout the Russian empire.[14]

The data is far from flawless. Directed at women who were no longer under the patriarchal authority of serf owner, father, or husband, the system of regulation had political implications from the outset. Whether or not it was intended as "a system of controlling women, not disease," as Laura

10  Ibid., delo 584, 16–17; see delo 587 for a similar story.
11  See ibid., delo 643 and 645, for hundreds of cases of women who were investigated but not registered by the Medical Police. They avoided registration mainly because they were living with or engaged to men who would vouch for them, or because they had steady employment.
12  Ibid., delo 645, 71–2. Printseva had threatened to return to her village too.
13  See Engelstein, "Morality," 189–95; Bernstein, "Sonia's Daughters," chap. 7.
14  "Prostitutsiia v Rossiiskoi Imperii po obsledovaniiu 1 Avgusta 1889 g.," in *Statistika Rossiiskoi Imperii*, ed. N.A. Troinitskii, vol. 13 (St. Petersburg, 1891).

Engelstein has maintained, control of women was certainly the outcome.[15] As a result, women who confronted the regulators had every reason not to trust them. Russian prostitutes may or may not have been the habitual liars that A.J.B. Parent-Duchatelet, the most influential nineteenth-century writer on prostitution, found Parisian prostitutes to be, but as he himself observed, a woman confronting the census taker, the physician, the policeman, or even the reformer had good cause to be suspicious and to conceal as much as she revealed.[16] Little of the information available on prostitutes is verifiable. Her passport could serve as an independent source for a woman's social background and province of origin, but the only way an investigator could learn about a prostitute's previous profession, age at first intercourse, or why she had taken up the trade was from the woman's own words. Archival records suggest the fluidity of women's work identities as they sought a different status for themselves or struggled to make ends meet in an uncertain job market. Glafira Printseva said she was a servant at first, but two years later, when she registered for the second time, she claimed to have been working as a folder (fal'sofshchitsa) in a printshop, and the fact that her file contains a printed card giving her name and profession suggests she told the truth. A woman who worked as a dishwasher at one point might declare herself a seamstress at another; cigar makers turned into fringe makers, or unskilled laborers.[17] Despite these and other limitations, aggregate data on prostitution does shed light on the lives of women on the margins of lower-class life, about the sources of their marginality, and about the impact of efforts to subject them to regulation.

This chapter will focus on the city of St. Petersburg because both published and archival sources that treat prostitution there are unusually abundant and unusually detailed. They include two intensive studies conducted by physicians. One of these physicians, Dr. Pyotr Oboznenko, is not easy to categorize politically. He began his career as a zemstvo physician, served in the Medical Department of the Ministry of Internal Affairs, and then on the staff of the Kalinkinskaia hospital for syphilitics, where he collected data on 4,220 registered prostitutes. Despite his involvement with the system of regulation, his views evolved from moderate to highly critical endorsement of it. The other physician, Dr. Aleksandr Fedorov, was a leading advocate of regulation. During his service on the Medical-Police Committee of St. Petersburg, he gathered information on 2,552 registered women, selecting

15 Engelstein, "Morality," 195.     16 Cited in Harsin, Policing Prostitution, 116.
17 TsGIAL, fond 593, op. 1, delo 546, 592, 596.

the records of 143 "at random" for closer examination. In an article published in 1892, he included eight pages of tables, providing data on each woman's social origins, former occupation, age at registration, relationship with parents, age at first intercourse, the age and status of the woman's first sexual partner, and what prompted her to take up the profession in the first place.[18] On the basis of this data, it is possible to sketch the socioeconomic and personal profiles of St. Petersburg's prostitutes around the turn of the century.

Information that could be obtained from the passport is the most reliable and, therefore, a good place to begin: This information included social estate, permanent residence, marital status, age, and date of entry into the city. The overwhelming majority of urban prostitutes derived from the laboring poor, and the highest proportion were ascribed to the peasantry: 49.6 percent according to Fedorov's study, 47.6 percent according to Oboznenko's. This was a higher percentage than in the urban population as a whole (45.6 percent). If soldiers' wives and daughters are incorporated into the category of peasants, as they were in the St. Petersburg census of 1890, then the proportion of peasant prostitutes is higher still – *soldatki* comprised 13 percent of Fedorov's sample and 7.3 percent of Oboznenko's.[19]

After the peasantry, *meshchanki* supplied the greatest number of prostitutes. Like the peasantry, the *meshchanstvo* was an officially designated, hereditary estate. It included the urban lower orders and a petty bourgeoisie that ranged from poor to middling status. The *meshchanstvo* was more likely to incorporate artisans, peddlers, and small shopkeepers than wage laborers. *Meshchanki*, 28.4 percent of St. Petersburg's female population in 1890, made up 33 percent of Fedorov's sample; Oboznenko, separating *meshchanki* from the daughters of artisans, found 30.1 percent of the former and 1.5 percent of the latter. As compared to 74 percent of the entire female population of St. Petersburg in 1890, 95.6 percent of registered prostitutes came from peasant or *meshchanstvo* background according to Fedorov's sample, and 86.5 percent according to Oboznenko.[20] Not surprisingly, in St. Petersburg

18 On Oboznenko and Fedorov's stance in the debate on prostitution, see Engelstein, "Morality," 189–90. P.E. Oboznenko, *Podnadzornaia prostitutsiia S.-Peterburga po dannym politseiskago komiteta i Kalinkinskoi bol' nitsy* (St. Petersburg, 1896); Fedorov, "Prostitutsiia," 37–76.

19 *S.-Peterburg po perepisi 15 Dekabria 1890 goda* (St. Petersburg, 1892), pt. 1, fasc. 1, 70–1; for figures on prostitutes, see Fedorov, "Prostitutsiia," 65. Fedorov's figure is drawn from all 2,552 registered women he studied and not from the smaller sample in the tables mentioned above. Oboznenko, *Podnadzornaia*, 21.

20 *S. -Peterburg po perepisi . . . 1890*, pt. 1, fasc. 1, 70–1, for the general data; Fedorov and Oboznenko for the data on prostitutes.

as elsewhere in Europe, lower-class women were disproportionately represented among the population of prostitutes.

Although ascription to the peasantry did not necessarily mean that a woman was raised in a rural area, Fedorov tells us that most of the peasants were in fact migrants who came from St. Petersburg and neighboring provinces.[21] Judging by the data in Table 6.1 at least, a peasant or *meshchanka* who came to St. Petersburg from the Baltic and northwesternmost provinces of Russia (Lifland, Estland, Kovno, Vitebsk, Novgorod, Pskov, Olonets) was somewhat more likely to end up as a registered prostitute than a woman of the same estate who had migrated from provinces further east or south. More importantly, the numbers in Table 6.1 suggest that by removing a woman from the parental and communal supervision that both protected and controlled her, migration itself might put a woman at risk: The proportion of registered prostitutes who had been born elsewhere than the city of St. Petersburg was higher than the proportion of migrants in the lower-class female population.[22]

Wherever they came from, most women who became registered prostitutes were neither adventuresses nor victims in any straightforward sense.[23] And it was relatively rare for "young naive peasant girls entering the large cities at railway stations" to be lured into prostitution by "ubiquitous" brothel recruiters.[24] This is not to deny that such recruiters existed. Men as well as women made a practice of enticing women into the trade, the men by seducing them and then putting them on the streets. In Oboznenko's survey, fifty-four of the women queried responded that they had been talked into prostitution by procurers.[25] One such procurer attempted to ensnare the revolutionary Olga Liubatovich in 1878. Returning to St. Petersburg from abroad, Liubatovich encountered an "elderly, plainly dressed woman" at the railroad station. Underground and with nothing but a few kopeks to her name, Liubatovich allowed herself to be lured to a cheap rooming house.

---

21 Fedorov, "Prostitutsiia," 41.

22 The fact that women from Tver' were somewhat more prone to become registered prostitutes than migrants from Iaroslavl' may be another reflection of the economic differences between the two provinces.

23 To be sure, there existed villages such as Orok, in Rzhev district, Tver' province, where according to a *zemstvo* statistician "drunkenness and debauchery" were so well developed that some of the local women intentionally went off to work as prostitutes. *Statisticheskoe opisanie Rzhevskago uezda, Tverskoi gubernii* (Tver', 1885), 103.

24 Rose Glickman, *Russian Factory Women: Workplace and Society, 1880–1914* (Berkeley, Calif., 1984), 68.

25 Oboznenko, *Podnadzornaia*, 23–4. On pimps, B.I. Bentovin, *Torguiushchaia telom. Ocherki sovremennoi prostitutsii* (Moscow, 1907), 196–8.

Table 6.1. *Peasants*, meshchanki, *and prostitutes in St. Petersburg, by place of birth*

| Place of Birth | Percent of Peasants | Percent of *Meshchanki* | Percent of Prostitutes | Total Prostitutes* |
|---|---|---|---|---|
| St. Petersburg city | 24.0 | 49.1 | 23.1 | 995 |
| St. Petersburg province | 10.0 | 22.5 | 19.4 | 834 |
| Novgorod | 10.0 | 2.9 | 13.5 | 583 |
| Tver' | 16.5 | 3.1 | 10.5 | 451 |
| Pskov | 3.9 | 1.5 | 5.2 | 224 |
| Lifland | 0.8 | 2.4 | 4.5 | 196 |
| Estland | 0.7 | 1.6 | 3.1 | 135 |
| Iaroslavl' | 8.2 | 2.4 | 3.5 | 152 |
| Vitebsk | 2.0 | 1.3 | 2.6 | 110 |
| Smolensk | 3.2 | 0.6 | 2.3 | 99 |
| Olonets | 1.5 | 0.4 | 2.3 | 99 |
| Moscow | 2.7 | 1.5 | 1.8 | 78 |
| Vologda | 1.6 | 0.5 | 1.5 | 64 |
| Kostroma | 2.5 | 0.9 | 1.3 | 57 |
| Arkhangel | 1.3 | 0.3 | 1.2 | 50 |
| Kovno | 0.4 | 0.8 | 1.2 | 51 |
| Riazan | 2.6 | 0.5 | 0.8 | 36 |
| Kaluga | 1.7 | 0.6 | 0.5 | 21 |
| Tula | 1.5 | 0.4 | 0.4 | 19 |
| Vladimir | 0.6 | 0.2 | 0.4 | 18 |
| Orel | 0.3 | 0.2 | 0.4 | 17 |
| Tambov | 0.4 | 0.2 | 0.3 | 11 |
| TOTAL | | | | 4,307 |

* These include all the prostitutes Oboznenko studied and are undifferentiated by estate. They add up to a larger total, 4,307, than the one he cites elsewhere in his article. He does not explain why. Because the percentages have been rounded off to the nearest tenth, they do not add up to 100.
*Source*: *S.-Peterburg po perepisi 15 Dekabria 1900 goda* (St. Petersburg, 1903), fasc. 1, 82–4; P.E. Oboznenko, *Podnadzornaia prostitutsiia S.-Peterburga po dannym politseiskogo komiteta i Kalinkinskoi bol'nitsy* (St. Petersburg, 1896), 19–20.

When her kopeks ran out, she ate the rolls and drank the tea her landlady offered her, but she fled after the building's yardman suggested "insolently" that Liubatovich "get acquainted" with some young men living in the same house.[26] Still, the fifty-four women lured into prostitution by procurers constituted only 1.2 percent of Oboznenko's sample. Most St. Petersburg prostitutes did not enter the profession straight from the railroad station but had initially worked in other trades, as had their Western European sisters. Their entry was circumstantial, first and foremost a "response to local conditions of the local job market."[27]

Former domestic servants supplied the largest number of St. Petersburg prostitutes, over 40 percent. (For some of the reasons why, see Chapter 5.) The second largest number, 12.2 percent, claimed to have worked in the needle trades, which employed about 8 percent of the female workforce in 1890.[28] The needleworking trade was precarious and overcrowded; it involved seasonal unemployment lasting four to five months of the year, and the women who worked at it earned only about 64 percent of what men earned, barely enough for survival. Needleworkers in slow periods were as vulnerable as unemployed servants to the attentions of Medical-Police Committee agents. The third largest group of prostitutes, 6.4 percent, were former factory workers who themselves comprised about 6.7 percent of the female workforce of St. Petersburg in 1890.[29]

Factory workers were the only major group whose representation among registered prostitutes was lower than their proportion in the female laboring population as a whole. The reasons that factory women were less likely to bear and then abandon illegitimate children probably made them less likely to turn to prostitution, too. Moreover, the factory woman's work was steadier than that of the servant or the craftswoman, which meant that she was far less likely to attract the attention of the Medical-Police Committee agents. While unemployed servants and craftswomen are numerous among the women

---

26  Barbara Engel and Clifford Rosenthal, ed. *Five Sisters: Women against the Tsar* (New York, 1975), 147–8.
27  Walkowitz, *Prostitution and Victorian Society*, 14. See also Harsin, *Policing Prostitution*, 208–18. Although prostitution might be the world's oldest profession, its economic context could vary considerably, as could the motivations of women entering the trade. For comparison, see Sue Gronewald, "Beautiful Merchandise: Prostitution in China 1860–1936," *Women and History*, no. 1 (Spring 1982), and Pasuk Phongpaichit, *From Peasant Girls to Bangkok Masseuses* (Geneva, 1982).
28  Glickman, *Russian Factory Women*, 61.
29  *S.-Peterburg po perepisi 15 Dekabria 1890 goda*, pt. 1, fasc. 2, 26–54.

suspected of engaging in prostitution, not a single factory woman came under surveillance by police agents either in 1905 or in 1909.[30]

The rest of the women Oboznenko listed reported working in other trades that were typical for their sex. They had been day laborers, washerwomen, hat makers, corset makers, glove makers, stocking knitters, flower girls, and the like. Another fairly sizable group had been dependents of one sort or another: About 6 percent had lived with family members, about 2 percent with husbands, and 4 percent had been kept as mistresses (*soderzhanki*); 9 percent listed their former occupation as prostitute – 4 percent having worked in other cities, and 5 percent having plied the trade secretly before being registered.[31] Judging by employment histories alone, it is difficult to tell how the *meshchanki* and peasant women who became registered prostitutes differed from other women of their class, who had to eke out a precarious living in the urban job market.

In some respects, Fedorov's supposedly random sample of prostitutes conforms relatively closely to the patterns found in the aggregate studies cited above. The women came overwhelmingly from the lower classes: 46.8 percent from the peasantry and 34.2 percent from petty bourgeois or artisanal families. Their employment profile is similar, too. Close to 40 percent of the women were former servants; 27 percent had practiced some trade; 3 percent had worked in factories; 6.7 percent had lived with husbands or family members; 5 percent had been kept as mistresses; and 13.5 percent, a rather larger proportion than in Oboznenko's study, had previously worked as prostitutes.[32] But because Fedorov presents the women individually, their life cycles emerge more clearly, and as a result his data suggest some of the ways that the experiences of peasant women and the urban-born *meshchanki* might have differed. The most noticeable difference is in level of skill. The *meshchanka* was considerably more likely than the peasant woman or soldier's wife or daughter to have received training in a trade. This bears out Glickman's contention that "the greater the requisite skill [in a woman's trade] the greater the percentage of urban born."[33] At the same time, it

30  Based on a survey of documents in TsGIAL, fond 593, op. 1, delo 643 and 645.
31  Oboznenko, *Podnadzornaia*, 22–3.
32  All further references to Fedorov's tables are to his "Prostitutsiia," 42–9.
33  Glickman, *Russian Factory Women*, 66. About a quarter of the *meshchanki* and about half of the peasants had worked as servants before taking up prostitution; about a third of the *meshchanki* and a fifth of the peasants had practiced a craft. It may be worth noting that being urban-born did not necessarily mean that a woman derived from Moscow or St. Petersburg. Most *meshchanki* who lived in St. Petersburg had been born in one of the small towns of provincial Russia.

demonstrates how little security such training offered, because craftswomen were as disproportionately represented among prostitutes as domestics were.

Although they were less likely to have a skill, peasant women and soldiers' wives and daughters, like *meshchanki*, often found themselves making their own way in the world at a comparatively tender age. Only a portion of Fedorov's sample responded to the question "How long ago did you leave your parents?" Those who did, however, became independent, on the average, about age fifteen. In this respect, too, the women who became prostitutes were hardly distinguishable from their peers. Although the St. Petersburg census of 1900 registered as employed only a miniscule proportion (.4 percent) of the peasant girls and *meshchanki* under the age of eleven, it reported that close to a third (32 percent) of lower-class girls between eleven and fifteen earned their own keep.[34]

Urban censuses do not tell us what proportion of these working girls lived with family or had kin in the city.[35] But women who became prostitutes shared with their European counterparts a family background that was "unusually disrupted," in that an extremely high proportion of them had lost one or both parents.[36] According to the 1889 census of prostitutes, of 2,586 registered women in St. Petersburg province as a whole – about 200 more than in the city proper – only 75, or 3 percent reported they had both parents living; 69, or 3 percent, said they had a father alive; and 201, or 7.7 percent, said they had a mother. To put it differently, 86.3 percent claimed to be complete orphans, and over a quarter of the women (697) reported they had no family whatsoever.[37] Fedorov's smaller survey deviates from the pattern found in aggregate studies specifically in finding fewer with "disrupted" family backgrounds: Slightly less than half claimed to be complete orphans, while 15 percent reported both parents living. Under 2 percent had fathers alive; about 13 percent failed to answer the question.

In Russian rural society, where the extended family, rather than the

---

34  *S.-Peterburg po perepisi 15 Dekabria 1900 goda*, pt. 1, fasc. 2 (St. Petersburg, 1903), 121, 124–5. The census of 1900, the first to correlate age and occupational data, unfortunately does not correlate them with social background as well.

35  In his computations of the living arrangements of Russian workers, based on the census of 1897, N.A. Troinitskii omitted domestic servants. See *Chislennost' i sostav rabochikh v Rossii na osnovanii dannykh pervoi vseobshchei perepisi naseleniia Rossiiskoi imperii* (St. Petersburg, 1906).

36  Walkowitz, *Prostitution and Victorian Society*, 16. Parent-du Chatelet tells us only that a quarter of Parisian-born prostitutes were illegitimate, four times as many as those born elsewhere (cited in Harsin, *Policing Prostitution*, 115).

37  "Prostitutsiia v Rossiiskoi Imperii," in Troinitskii, ed., *Statistika*, 41–4.

nuclear, was most often the basic unit, it might be supposed that orphanhood would have less of an impact than it had, for example, in France, where the death of a father was "the single most decisive" factor in sending a daughter out to earn her keep.[38] The majority of Russian prostitutes did have some sort of family tie. Surveying 4,220 registered prostitutes in St. Petersburg, Oboznenko found that only 850 (around 20 percent) lacked immediate kin, and most of these women had been raised in foundling homes and shelters; while 2,662 (around 63 percent) had either a parent, a husband, or a sibling in the city or back in the village. A sizable minority of women who became prostitutes actively maintained their family ties, at least until the moment when they turned to prostitution. Of 600 prostitutes surveyed in 1910, close to 38 percent claimed to have helped their family with their wages as servants, seamstresses, factory workers, and the like.[39]

Judging by the atypically high proportion of Russian prostitutes who had neither father nor mother, however, having relatives was evidently not the same as having a parent. Elsewhere in Europe, women without parents were at greater risk of bearing illegitimate children.[40] The statistics on the family situation of registered prostitutes in Russia suggest a similar pattern: In impoverished households, the death of the father and, to a lesser extent, the mother could destroy the family economy and increase the vulnerability of the daughter.[41] It might also increase her freedom to follow her own inclinations. Women without fathers to protect and restrain them were more likely than women in family situations to come to the attention of the Medical-Police agents. In 1905 and 1909, the police investigated hundreds of women who had spent time in disreputable places, engaged in nonmarital sex, or done something else to violate official notions of propriety, but who turned out not to be "prostitutes." Although some of the women investigated by Medical-Police agents in 1905 or 1909 resided with kinfolk, not one lived with her father at the time.

38 Sarah Maza, *Servants and Masters in Eighteenth-Century France: The Uses of Loyalty* (Princeton, N.J., 1983), 43.
39 Oboznenko, *Podnadzornaia*, 30; L.P. Depp, "O dannykh anketa, proizvedennoi sredi prostitutok S.-Peterburga v marte 1910 g.," *Trudy Pervago vserossiiskago s''ezda po bor'be s torgom zhenshchinami i ero prichinami*, 2 vols. (St. Petersburg, 1911), 1: 138.
40 George Alter, *Family and the Female Life Course: The Women of Verviers, Belgium, 1849–1880* (Madison, Wis., 1988), 127; Rachel Fuchs and Leslie Moch, "Pregnant, Single, and Far from Home: Migrant Women in Nineteenth-Century Paris," *American Historical Review* 95, no. 4 (Oct. 1990): 1021; Caroline Brettell, *Men Who Migrate, Women Who Wait: Population and History in a Portuguese Parish* (Princeton, N.J., 1986), 252.
41 Harsin noted the same factors in the making of Parisian prostitutes. See *Policing Prostitution*, 208–12.

A girl without parents, and especially without a father to guard her chastity, may also have been more likely to engage in sex at a comparatively early age. In England, prostitutes typically first "went wrong" at the age of sixteen.[42] It is harder to identify a "typical" pattern in Russia. Having no particular reason to be accurate, and often having only an imprecise idea of their age in any case, they may well have provided a later age of first intercourse than the true one. For this reason, a comparison with the ages of women bearing illegitimate children in St. Petersburg is instructive. In 1895, only 29.8 percent of 3,463 women bearing their first illegitimate children were under twenty-one, while 45.7 percent more were between twenty-one and twenty-five, and the rest were older still.[43] Even if we assume the passage of several years between first intercourse and a conception leading to birth, the ages of these unmarried mothers suggest that if prostitutes were adding a few years to their age at first intercourse, as a group they nevertheless had become sexually active earlier than other lower-class women. According to Oboznenko's statistics, the vast majority of St. Petersburg prostitutes first had intercourse between the ages of fifteen and nineteen (see Table 6.2). Fedorov's sample suggests differences between the peasant girl and the *meshchanka*: By her own testimony, the peasant girl was more likely to have her first heterosexual experience early.

Peasant women were also far more likely than *meshchanki* to claim that their first sexual experience was coerced. When asked "Who deflowered you and how old was he?" 14 percent of the peasant women and 4 percent of the *meshchanki* were reported as answering "I was raped" (*nasil'no*). According to the census of 1889, 14.6 percent of registered prostitutes in the Russian empire as a whole said they had been raped at first intercourse.[44] Three of the peasant women who said they were raped at age ten or eleven were working as servants at the time. It is not difficult to imagine their vulnerability to sexual aggression. The merchant who raped one ten-year-old peasant girl kept her for the next three years. While it is impossible to ascertain whether they all told the truth, peasant women's stories of forcible sex are consonant with what we know about migrant peasant women's vulnerability, especially migrant peasant women who worked as servants. The smaller proportion of *meshchanki* claiming forcible initiation into sex reflects their

---

42 Walkowitz, *Prostitution and Victorian Society*, 17.
43 *Statisticheskii ezhegodnik S.-Peterburga. 1895* (St. Petersburg, 1898), 14.
44 "Prostitutsiia v Rossiiskoi Imperii," in Troinitskii, ed., *Statistika*, xxxii. Oboznenko reports 10.8 percent said they were raped and an additional 4.2 percent were drunk (*Podnadzornaia*, 31).

Table 6.2. *Age at first intercourse*

| Age | Peasants | | Meshchanki | | All Prostitutes | |
|---|---|---|---|---|---|---|
| | Number | Percent | Number | Percent | Number | Percent |
| Under 10 | | | | | 3 | 0.1 |
| 10 | 1 | 1.3 | | | 3 | 0.1 |
| 11 | 5 | 6.6 | 1 | 2.0 | 8 | 0.2 |
| 12 | 1 | 1.3 | | | 26 | 0.7 |
| 13 | 1 | 1.3 | | | 70 | 1.8 |
| 14 | 4 | 5.3 | 4 | 8.0 | 180 | 4.6 |
| 15 | 18 | 24.0 | 9 | 18.0 | 492 | 12.5 |
| 16 | 12 | 16.0 | 11 | 22.0 | 92 | 23.7 |
| 17 | 12 | 16.0 | 5 | 10.0 | 907 | 23.1 |
| 18 | 10 | 13.3 | 11 | 22.0 | 646 | 16.5 |
| 19 | 4 | 5.3 | 3 | 6.0 | 424 | 10.8 |
| 20 and over | 7 | 9.3 | 6 | 12.0 | 236 | 6.0 |

*Source*: P.E. Oboznenko, *Podnadzornaia prostitutsiia S.-Peterburga po dannym politseiskogo komiteta i Kalinkinskoi bol'nitsy* (St. Petersburg, 1896), 31; A.I. Fedorov, "Prostitutsiia v S.-Peterburge i vrachebno-politseiskii nadzor za neiu," *Vestnik obshchestvennoi gigieny* 13 (Jan.–Mar. 1892): 42–9.

different position and, especially, the fact that far fewer worked as servants. On the average, *meshchanki* began to engage in sex at a later age, when, presumably, they exercised greater control over their lives.

Whether forced or voluntary, the woman's first sexual experience did not coincide with her move into professional prostitution. Even the peasant woman who acknowledged trading her own virginity at age fifteen for a doll and fifty rubles worked as a servant for over a decade before she was registered as a prostitute in St. Petersburg. The story of Evdokiia Safonova is fairly typical. Safonova, a peasant from Dmitriev district, Moscow, had had sex for the first time at age twelve, thirteen, or fourteen (she was not really sure) with Ivan Lavrov, a worker at a textile mill in the town of Bogorodsk, who was a year older than she. Several years later, he married another woman, and Evdokiia entered a brothel in the city of Moscow.[45] Ages at registration suggest an average interval of several years between first sexual experience and professional prostitution (see Table 6.3). Fedorov's profiles confirm the pattern, although in this case, too, they deviate from the norm:

45 TsGIAgM, fond 203, op. 412, delo 26, 17.

Table 6.3. *Age at registration of prostitutes in St. Petersburg, 1890–1892*

| Age | Number | Percent of Total* |
|-----|--------|-------------------|
| 16 | 166 | 8 |
| 17 | 209 | 10 |
| 18 | 234 | 11 |
| 19 | 233 | 11 |
| 20 | 193 | 9 |
| 21 | 159 | 8 |
| 22 | 139 | 7 |
| 23 | 118 | 6 |
| 24 | 101 | 5 |
| 25 | 84 | 4 |
| 26 | 95 | 5 |
| 27 | 60 | 3 |
| 28 | 68 | 3 |
| 29 | 43 | 2 |
| 30–35 | 122 | 6 |

* Because the percentages have been rounded off to the nearest tenth, they do not add up to 100.
*Source*: P.E. Oboznenko, *Podnadzornaia prostitutsiia S.-Peterburga po dannym politseiskogo komiteta i Kalinkinskoi bol'nitsy* (St. Petersburg, 1896), 102.

Only about 26 percent of the women in his sample began to prostitute themselves at twenty or earlier, which means that they began somewhat later than the ages suggested by Oboznenko and others.

Why, then, did they take up the trade? Many surely succumbed to the same pressures that had led Printseva and Bykova to accept a "yellow ticket." In assessing the answers women gave to the question of why they had become registered prostitutes, it is essential to keep in mind the element of coercion and policing, as well as the problematic nature of the sources themselves. Policing transformed what might have been a supplementary source of income or a temporary expedient into a full-time profession and deprived a woman of control over her own life. And women had no good reason to explore their motivations for the benefit of upper-class interlocutors who were implicated in a regulation system the women abhorred. Despite the problems, women's responses provide a window, however murky, into aspects of their economic and personal lives. Published aggregate information on the motivations of prostitutes is both brief and formulaic: "it's easy earnings"; "I decided to"; "my wages were too low"; "I lost my job"; "friends enticed me"; "I started to drink"; and the like.[46] Fedorov's tables are somewhat more illuminating, because while they are also formulaic, they permit connections to be made between personal background and economic status and the move into prostitution. Of the peasants and *meshchanki* in his sample, 41.4 percent responded to the question "What led you to take up prostitution" with economic reasons: need, poverty, lack of work, or loss of their jobs.

But percentages cannot accurately convey the combination of economic vulnerability and emotional dependency that some of the entries suggest. One peasant woman, a former tailoress, linked the two explicitly. Having left her parents at the age of twelve, she became a prostitute at twenty because she had "lost her lover and her job" (*poteria liubvi i mesta*). Other stories are similar. A seventeen-year-old peasant girl, a shoemaker by trade whose mother worked as a cook, became a prostitute when the man with whom she had been living (perhaps the skilled worker [*masterovoi*] with whom she had first had intercourse two years earlier) returned to his village. Another peasant woman, who at twenty-one gave as her trade both chambermaid and "kept woman" (*soderzhanka*), wound up with a yellow ticket after being abandoned without support by the middle-aged stockbroker to whom she had given her virginity several years before. Likewise, a twenty-four-year-old *meshchanka*, who had left her mother at eighteen to live with a factory director, ended up on the street after he died. Another *meshchanka* had had her first sexual experience at sixteen with her husband and began to prostitute herself at age thirty-four, after she and he quarreled. It was not uncommon for runaway wives to engage in prostitution.[47] A woman who had come

46  See A.I. Fedorov, *Pozornyi promysel* (St. Petersburg, 1902), 6–7; Oboznenko, *Podnadzornaia*, 23–4.
47  For example, TsGIA SSSR, fond 796, op. 184, I stol, IV otd., ed. kh. 3580; op. 189, I stol, IV otd., ed. kh. 4740; op. 189, II stol, IV otd., ed. kh. 5341, 5498, 6021.

to depend on a man for all or part of her livelihood may have been more tempted to exchange sex for money. She certainly had fewer economic options than the woman who remained economically self-sufficient. Altogether, five women gave as their reason the loss of a lover, and three more said difficulties with a husband.

Still others seem not to have thought much about it. It is unlikely that many were as well off as one *meshchanka* who had lived quite comfortably with her parents. Her first sexual experience occurred with a skilled worker at age fifteen, but according to her, it was not this experience but "bad company" (*durnoe obshchestvo*) that led her to prostitution a year later. Suggesting the existence of a female subculture to which women turned for advice and information, seven other women provided similar explanations: "girlfriends enticed me"; "girlfriends advised me"; "girlfriends seduced me"; "girlfriends deceived me." Four more took to the streets because they drank. Five others responded simply "stupidity" or "thoughtlessness," although it is unclear whether they meant that this was the reason they became prostitutes or the reason they got caught and registered.[48] In either case, they were not fresh peasant girls, but women who had lived and worked in the city for several years.

On the basis of what they told investigators, only about half of the women can be classified in any straightforward way as victims, whether of need, of men, or of their own naïveté. In the lives of many, a kind of ambition, or at least the desire to "live better" or more easily, played a significant role. About one-sixth of registered prostitutes worked for brothels. Even in the cheap St. Petersburg establishments that catered to the lower class, at fifty kopeks a "shot," a prostitute could usually earn more than servants and many other laboring women: If she took on five customers a night, twenty-five nights per month, after paying the obligatory 75 percent to her madam for room, board, clothing, and protection, she would have fifteen rubles left. In 1890, 441 women, the majority of brothel prostitutes, worked in cheap houses in St. Petersburg. But the other 289 women earned more, and customers paid 106 of them five rubles for their services. If she worked the streets, as did five-sixths of registered prostitutes, the extremes of a woman's possible earnings were far greater: Some, although only a few, earned as much as seven hundred rubles a month; on the other hand, many more earned as much as forty to fifty rubles a month.[49] Only a highly skilled

48  These eight women misled by friends constitute close to 7 percent of Fedorov's sample; in Oboznenko's, they comprised 7.2 percent (*Podnadzornaia*, 23–4).

49  On the earnings of prostitutes, see Fedorov, "Prostitutsiia," 37–41.

male worker could earn as much. The life of a prostitute was not without its own real hardships and dangers, and it was certainly not to every woman's taste. Nevertheless, in terms of hours spent working and financial remuneration, it had advantages over other female occupations that were likely to be particularly obvious to a woman who had lost a job, was down on her luck, or wanted somehow to "live better." While few women were as well situated as the seventeen-year-old *meshchanka* who had lived comfortably with her mother before taking to the streets in search of "easy earnings," seventeen other women, when asked why they began to prostitute themselves, responded that they wanted to improve their lives. They said things like: "It pays better," or "I wanted to increase my income," or "It's more advantageous," or "It's an easy life."[50]

Some women implied that they simply preferred to become prostitutes, but it is difficult to assess many of those responses with certainty. Although it became more difficult for the police simply to round up women they suspected of prostitution, subject them to examination, confiscate their passports, and issue them yellow tickets after 1892, the police could still harass a woman in a number of ways, as we have seen. Therefore, when eighteen of the women responded "my own desire" (*sobstvennoe zhelanie*) or "my own inclination," to the question "what led you to prostitute yourself," they may only have been indicating, perhaps defiantly, that they were registering voluntarily and not under coercion. Other responses, while hardly more nuanced, leave little doubt that prostitution was the preference. A twenty-four-year-old orphaned peasant woman, a lacemaker by trade, who had had her first sexual experience at sixteen with a merchant's son of her own age, became a prostitute "because of the gay life" (*radi veseloi zhizni*). Two twenty-six-year-old peasant women, one a former servant and the other a prostitute for eleven years, responded similarly. And one *meshchanka*, a former nurse whose parents had died and who at twenty had been raped by her cousin, so she said, had become a prostitute because, in her own words, "It was gay. Everyone liked me."

Married women, too, sometimes preferred the life of a prostitute to the grim circumstances of the peasant woman's life. Take, for example, Avdotia, a peasant from Novoladoga district, St. Petersburg. The child of a widowed mother, from the age of thirteen Avdotia had worked as a servant in St. Petersburg. When she became eighteen, her mother had her passport with-

---

50 Eight percent of Oboznenko's respondents gave as their reason the desire to make more money, and 7.8 percent, laziness (*Podnadzornaia*, 23–4).

held, recalled her to the village, and married her off to a poor peasant. Avdotia stayed around for a few months, but she disliked her life, and when her new husband refused to grant her a passport of her own, she simply left the village without it. In St. Petersburg, she registered at a brothel, and with the madam's help and a bribe of four rubles to the porter, she obtained from the local city administration (*meshchanskaia uprava*) a passport falsely made out in the name of a *meshchanka*.[51] Another young wife ran away from her village in 1884, soon after her father-in-law began to "oppress" her. Without a passport, she could find no respectable work, she claimed, and so she began to work as a prostitute. When her husband brought her home by force to his village in Moscow, she refused to live with him. "I don't need you, when I have many," she asserted in the hearing of fellow villagers.[52] Serafima Iudina, a peasant from Tambov, left her husband in 1911, declaring that he no longer pleased her. She first found work as a servant in the provincial town of Tambov. Attracted by the lifestyle of two women who lived in the same apartment as she, and who "went with men for certain purposes," as the Synodal record delicately put it, Serafima soon followed their example.[53] That same year, Anastasia Terenteeva, twenty, a peasant from Novgorod, left her husband, Ivan, and voluntarily took a "yellow ticket." "Every day she has a new one" (*u nei kazhdyi den est' svezhen'kii*), the watchwoman, Anna Botina, alleged that Terenteeva had boasted.[54] To such women, prostitution offered an avenue of escape from confining village lives and in some cases, from the sexual monogamy that villagers demanded. In many ways, these women resemble the Englishwomen that Judith Walkowitz describes, whose broken family backgrounds released them from "the stranglehold" of standard female socialization to self-effacement, and who therefore more openly "resisted the conditions of subordination and dependency traditionally expected of them."[55]

There is considerable, if unsystematic, evidence that Russian prostitutes resisted authority too. Most registered prostitutes, for example, disliked the required examinations. They were conducted hastily and with no regard for the woman's feelings. And the very process was offensive. It was one thing to engage voluntarily in sex with a stranger, and quite another to be forced to have one's genitals coolly examined by a stranger. Why weren't their

51 *Sudebnyi vestnik*, 1869, no. 223, 2–3.
52 TsGIA SSSR, fond 796, op. 171, I stol, IV otd., ed. kh. 1776, 4–5.
53 Ibid., op. 199, I stol, IV otd., ed. kh. 961.
54 Ibid., op. 199, II stol, IV otd., ed. kh. 547; also op. 189, II stol, IV otd., ed. kh. 6021.
55 Walkowitz, *Prostitution and Victorian Society*, 20.

customers examined too, since men were the ones who gave women the disease in the first place, some prostitutes wondered. In the words of a letter signed by sixty-three prostitutes in 1909, "They're no better than us, participating in such a business."[56] A woman might find a physician that she liked and insist on visiting only him or her. But most tried to avoid the weekly required inspection whenever they could, regularly changing their address or briefly leaving the city.[57]

Prostitutes were rebellious in other ways, too. Women who were diagnosed with venereal disease were placed in the Kalinkinskaia hospital, where care was so poor and conditions so dreadful that some women fainted or grew hysterical when they learned they would be sent there.[58] Once in the hospital, the women became exceedingly unruly and difficult to control. "Disorders among women being treated for syphilis are frequent" complained the guardian of the Kalinkinskaia hospital in 1879. "The women often disrupt hospital routine and disobey openly the hospital authorities."[59] Complaints such as these eventuated in a new set of regulations, which enjoined women to obey medical authorities and to use "decent and inoffensive language," and which forbade women to speak loudly, to sing, to whistle, or even to lie on each other's beds.[60] Yet twenty years later, when Dr. B.I. Bentovin worked in the Kalinkinskaia hospital, women's unruly behavior had changed very little.[61]

Although in some ways Russian prostitutes conform rather closely to the model Walkowitz has provided of the rebellious or ambitious lower-class woman, Russian prostitutes were different from the English in at least one significant respect. Whether they were victims of economic need, or rebels against economic circumstances, Russian women almost never used the word "liberty" or expressed the desire for independence as a reason for taking up the trade. Nor did they aspire to be their own mistresses and to be in charge of their own lives, as some women apparently did in England.[62] This was the

---

56  *Trudy Pervago vserossiiskago s''ezda po bor'be s torgom zhenshchinami*, 2:511–12.
57  Fedorov, "Prostitutsiia," 54. Most of the prostitutes in the Medical-Police files were perpetually on the move, forcing the Medical-Police Committee to pepper the address office (*adresnyi stol*) with requests to track them down, which the office regularly did. See 593, op. 1, ed. kh. 547, 578, 584, 587, 592.
58  M. Kuznetsov, "Istoriko-statisticheskii ocherk," 55.
59  TsGIA SSSR, fond 760, op. 1, delo 899, 1–2. For resistance elsewhere, see the discussion in Bernstein, "Sonia's Daughters," 162–4.
60  TsGIA SSSR, fond 760, op. 1, delo 899, 23.
61  Bentovin, *Torguiushchaia telom*, 2–5.
62  Walkowitz, *Prostitution and Victorian Society*, 21. See Oboznenko, *Podnadzornaia*, 23–4, for Russian prostitutes' explanations in their own words.

case not only for brothel prostitutes, who enjoyed little or no freedom of action, but also for the far more numerous streetwalkers (*odinochki*), who plied their trade on their own. The reason for this is straightforward. In Britain, prostitution was hardly institutionalized at all, whereas in Russia, the regulation system served to ensure that a lower-class woman who sold her sexual favors to more than one man did not become her own mistress, even if she had thrown off the husband or lacked the father whom law had defined as her master.[63] Regulation may also have increased streetwalkers' dependence on pimps. Writing about prostitution in 1907, the physician V.I. Bentovin contended that every prostitute required a pimp to protect her when she walked the streets, to prevent her landlady from exploiting her, and to stop the police from harassing her.[64] The regulation system ensured women's continued subjection to male authorities.

The process of registration had an ambiguous effect upon a woman's relationship to other sectors of the lower class. Bentovin, among others, contended that registration made prostitutes an "outcast group" (*vybroshennyi obshchestvom za bort*), completely separate from the rest of society.[65] But in fact, lower-class attitudes were more complex. There is evidence to suggest that some sectors of the laboring poor regarded prostitution as simply another way of earning money. In the poorer sections of St. Petersburg, when women "sold their love," people were understanding and did not condemn them.[66] Neighbors recognized that a woman who went with a man for a meal in a tavern, a few yards of chintz for a blouse, or even for cash, was struggling like they were to survive. Boris Ivanov, who was raised in a working-class family in St. Petersburg, wrote of a woman of peasant background whom he described as having acquired a "rather large capital . . . through the force and charm of female beauty." But he refused to judge her: "Her personal life and her past are not my business. . . . Apart from feelings of gratitude and the memory of her as a good woman, I can say nothing."[67] Maxim Gorky put it this way: "In this hungry quarter of town, earning money [that] way was looked upon like any other kind of work."[68] Moreover, a sizable proportion of the lower-class prostitute's customers were themselves

---

63  Harsin, *Policing Prostitution*, 212–15 and 241–79, for an examination of the impact of registration in France.

64  Bentovin, *Torguiushchaia telom*, 194.      65  Ibid., 199.

66  E. Kalacheva, "Bezplatnyi narodnyi detskii sad," *Trudovaia pomoshch'*, May 1903, 218–19, and Sept. 1904, 253.

67  Boris Ivanov, *Zapiski proshlogo. Povest' iz vospominanii detstva i iunosti rabochego sotsialista* (Moscow, 1919), 20.

68  Maxim Gorky, *My Apprenticeship* (Baltimore, Md., 1974), 308.

members of the laboring classes. In his budget study of textile workers, Davidovich estimated that about half of the income that single male workers had left after they had met their ordinary expenses went to "so-called bachelor expenses." He could not be precise because for "understandable reasons" his researchers had refrained from inquiring about such a large item (*krupnaia stat'ia*) in the bachelor's budget, thereby manifesting a delicacy rarely displayed by interrogators of prostitutes.[69]

How workers felt about the prostitutes they patronized, however, is another question. On the one hand, many of the women who left prostitution went to live with working-class men who were surely former clients. On the other hand, there is evidence to indicate that more status-conscious members of the lower class disapproved of women who prostituted themselves. Many men ceased to attend and to bring their wives and children to evenings of dance for families (*semeino-tsantsoval'nye vechera*) arranged by a temperance society at the Putilov metal plant, when "those women," whom the workers had requested be kept away, nevertheless turned up.[70] Even women who were not registered prostitutes, but who went with men for pleasure or money, risked condemnation by them. The St. Petersburg Medical-Police archive is filled with letters anonymously denouncing women as secret prostitutes and supplying their addresses. Most of the letters were penned by lower-class men who had had sex with these women and believed that they had developed symptoms of venereal disease as a result. The authors insisted the women be subject to registration. As one such barely literate letter concluded, "You must investigate this, your honor. . . . Such women spread disease, and they should be given a ticket so that doctors will know who they are (*oni znali by doktorom*)."[71]

Some lower-class people evidently recognized that the registration system operated to control women, and they tried to manipulate the system for their own purposes. For example, the mother of a teenage boy penned an anonymous denunciation in 1904, requesting that Medical-police agents drive one Maria Novikova from the city, because by her behavior, Maria had "corrupted a boy of sixteen who supported his poor mother."[72] Maria Novikova, it turned out, was a nineteen-year-old peasant migrant from Vologda who shared a corner in a family apartment with her twenty-year-old sister. Both

69  M. Davidovich, *Peterburgskii tekstil'nyi rabochii v ego biudzhetakh* (St. Petersburg, 1912), 3.
70  *Peterburgskii listok*, 24 Nov. 1892 (quotation marks in the original).
71  TsGIAL, fond 593, op. 1, delo 645, 44; see also delo 643, 278, 293, 370, 402, 411, 454, 664;
    delo 645, 1, 23, 28, 42, 64, 77, 79.
72  Ibid., delo 643, 190.

young women had worked as servants; neither engaged in prostitution so far
as the agents could tell, and as we know, they rarely gave women the benefit
of the doubt. In 1905, another mother actually denounced her rambunctious
sixteen-year-old daughter, falsely, as a prostitute.[73] That same year, a peasant migrant from Myshkin, Iaroslavl', used the threat of registration to take
revenge on his estranged wife, who, he alleged, "led a debauched life with
any man who came her way." He wanted the police to issue his wife a yellow
ticket "so that she would be under surveillance, and have to appear for
examinations." The case was dropped after an investigation revealed that the
wife worked in a tea shop and was perfectly respectable, whereas the husband had treated her badly and failed to support her.[74] Occasionally, people
were prepared to use the yellow ticket as a threat – "I'll give you a yellow
ticket" – in time of personal conflict.[75] Lower-class people were well aware
of the significance of the yellow ticket. They knew that it marginalized and
isolated the women who received it, in addition to subjecting them to
humiliating procedures.

Indeed, the "yellow ticket" tended to increase the distance between a prostitute and the lower-class community. It made the woman's trade undeni-
able and meant that prostitution became the only way she could earn her
living. Respectable people became unwilling to rent her an apartment, so
that often she was forced to live in the more squalid sections of the city, such
as Haymarket Square.[76] Moreover, once she had been registered as a prostitute, it became more difficult for a woman to leave the profession and to fade
back into her former life. The degree of difficulty depended on where she
lived, since the statutes for the empire varied by locale. St. Petersburg's
requirements supplied considerable detail: A woman could rid herself of the
yellow ticket if she found other work, if she married, if she moved away from
the Medical-Police Committee's sphere of action, if she took refuge in a
shelter, if a relative requested it and promised to prevent her from prostitut-
ing herself again, or, finally, if a suitable person came forward to guarantee
her conduct. In short, if she wanted to remain in St. Petersburg, she had to
find someone else to take responsibility for her morals.[77] Even if a known
prostitute managed to find someone willing to hire her, to marry her, or to

73 The agents found no evidence that the charge was true. Ibid., 180–2.
74 Ibid., delo 643, 664–5.
75 V.N. Nikitin, *Mirovoi sud v Peterburge. Stseny v kammerakh sudei i podrobnyia razbiratel' stva*
    (St. Petersburg, 1867), 159, 197.
76 *Trudy Pervago vserossiiskago s"ezda po bor'be s torgom zhenshchinami*, 2:507.
77 *Vrachebno-politseiskii nadzor za gorodskoi prostitutsii* (St. Petersburg, 1910), 25–7.

take responsibility for her without taking advantage of her, the authorities did not immediately trust that she had left the trade, and the woman had to continue to appear for examinations over the course of several months, while the police continued to spy on her until they were certain that she had become "respectable."

It is not hard to imagine the negative impact of this process on a relative, a lover, or an employer. In some instances, and the cases of the peasant women Natalia Lukianova and Tatiana Mikhailova are two of them, the negative effect is discernible. In April 1900, three years after she had registered as a prostitute, Lukianova asked to be released from surveillance. She was no longer working as a prostitute, she claimed, but had found a position as a washerwoman and was living on her wages. Over the following months, the Committee attempted, unsuccessfully, to keep tabs on her as she moved from place to place, still without her own passport, because the Committee had not released her from registration and, in fact, refused to do so. In January 1904, she again requested to be freed from registration. This time, she was living with her younger sister, the wife of a railroad worker, and this time, the agent was able to keep an eye on her: Lukianova had ceased to be a prostitute, he reported, and was helping her sister with the housekeeping and the children.[78] Despite the favorable reports, on April 15 of the same year, Lukianova was summoned to appear before the Medical-Police Committee; by the following January, still a registered prostitute, she was no longer living with her sister. Only by leaving town did Lukianova finally succeed in escaping registration.

Tatiana Mikhailova experienced similar difficulties in escaping surveillance. In March 1900, three years after she had first registered as a prostitute, Mikhailova asked to be released from registration because she no longer earned her living as a prostitute and instead lived with a man and worked in a shoemaking shop on Apraksin Lane. Two agents began to watch Mikhailova. One reported that while she sometimes went off to work during the day, she had no definite occupation, and although she did live with a lover, "evidently she still engages in prostitution." The other verified her story completely, thereby demonstrating the arbitrariness that characterized the entire surveillance process.[79] Five weeks after her initial request, Mikhailova regained her passport and her freedom. The following November, however, she registered

78  TsGIAL, fond 593, op. 1, ed. kh. 578, 16.
79  In 1907, in about 10 percent of cases, the two agents assigned to watch women who requested release from professional prostitution wrote totally contradictory reports about their conduct.

once again.[80] Snoopy agents asking questions of neighbors or yardmen surely complicated the efforts of women like Lukianova or Mikhailova to live "reputable" lives and helped to sour some personal or professional relationships and to drive women back into the trade. Many of the women who were released from registration returned again to prostitution within a relatively brief period of time, as did Mikhailova and Printseva.

Judith Walkowitz has argued that in England, registration served to "professionalize" prostitution: Registered prostitutes tended to be older and to remain considerably longer in the profession than women who could freely take up and abandon the trade. The data is too slippery to write with precision about the age of Russian prostitutes, but judging by the length of time women remained registered, the system of regulation failed to "professionalize" them fully.[81] Not surprisingly, prostitutes in Russia remained prostitutes longer than the Englishwomen who were not subject to regulation. The majority of unregulated women stayed in the trade for a few days or weeks, at most for two years.[82] The 1889 census of prostitutes in the Russian empire indicated that 15.4 percent of registered Russian prostitutes had plied the trade less than one year; 15.6 percent for a year; 13.7 percent for two years; 11.3 percent for three; 9.1 percent for four, 7.7 percent for five, and the remainder for longer.[83] In St. Petersburg, Oboznenko found that 20 percent had been registered for less than a year; about 13 percent for over a year; about 15 percent for two years; about 12 percent for three; 9 percent for four, and the remaining 31 percent for five years or more.[84] On the other hand, this meant that only 31 percent of St. Petersburg's prostitutes stayed in the trade more than four years, by comparison with their Parisian sisters, 69 percent of whom remained under police control for more than four years.[85] According to Oboznenko, St. Petersburg prostitutes were divided into two "sharply distinct" groups. The first were the hard-core prostitutes who stayed registered for well over five years. The second were women who remained in the profession only briefly.[86]

The fact that a substantial proportion of women left registration fairly

80 TsGIAL, fond 593, op. 1, ed. kh. 578, 579.
81 Fedorov, for example, presents St. Petersburg prostitutes as older than the average in Russia in one article and younger than the average in another, published only nine years later. Fedorov, "Prostitutsiia," 57, and "Pozornyi promysel'," 7.
82 Walkowitz, *Prostitution and Victorian Society*, 263, n. 44.
83 "Prostitutsiia v Rossiiskoi Imperii," in Troinitskii, ed. *Statistika*, xxix; also see Depp, "O dannykh anketa."
84 Oboznenko, *Podnadzornaia*, 102.      85 Harsin, *Policing Prostitution*, 217.
86 Oboznenko, *Podnadzornaia*, 101.

quickly suggests that the obstacles that the system created were not solely responsible for the length of time some women remained registered or for the fact that others returned time and again to the trade. A woman who worked for a while as a prostitute might lose her taste for the unrelieved grimness and self-denial that characterized the "reputable" working-class woman's life and might find it hard to readapt. For example, after having spent four years in a brothel in Moscow, Evdokiia Safonova married the widowed Ivan Lavrov, the worker to whom she had lost her virginity years before. Soon after the wedding, she told him that she loved company and amusement and that she found it hard to get used to the monotonous life they led. While Ivan was off at work in the Bogorodskaia-Glukhovskaia Mill in the town of Bogorodsk, Evdokiia would entertain young people in their room and sometimes spend time alone with men. Occasionally, she disappeared for days on end. Once Ivan realized she had lived in a brothel – evidently, he learned this only after the wedding – he understood what was going on: "It makes sense that after such a debauched and dissipated life, the life she now lives would seem like a torment," he told a Synodal court.[87] A young worker who fell in love with a prostitute encountered comparable difficulty in convincing her to marry him. Having worked in the trade for several years, the woman found it impossible to abandon "the gay life" and to settle down.[88]

Women in the second category of prostitutes were far the more likely to leave the profession for good. These women, the majority, were temporary prostitutes who came under surveillance circumstantially; most managed to abandon the profession relatively quickly. Walkowitz contends that in England, the length of time women remained registered signified the isolation of prostitutes from lower-class life and a "growing inflexibility in social norms and a restriction in occupational identities and personal mobility."[89] By comparison with England and France, Russian society in the late nineteenth and early twentieth centuries was in enormous flux. It is possible that members of the Russian lower classes were more prone than members of the English or French working classes to resist attempts to regulate their sexuality. In

---

87 TsGIAgM, fond 203, op. 412, delo 26. Several years after initiating proceedings for a divorce, Ivan Lavrov halted them, having reconciled with his wife, who had proceeded to mend her ways.

88 *Peterburgskii listok*, 5 Jan. 1893. See also 15 June 1894.

89 Judith Walkowitz, "The Making of an Outcast Group: Prostitutes and Working Women in Nineteenth-Century Plymouth and Southampton," in *A Widening Sphere: Changing Roles of Victorian Women*, ed. Martha Vicinus (Bloomington, Ind., 1977), 90–1; see also Harsin, *Policing Prostitution*, 217.

any case, the Russian police were notoriously inefficient. Whatever the reason, it seems certain that most Russian women who no longer wished to work as prostitutes found a way to evade the system. By age thirty, 80 percent of registered prostitutes in St. Petersburg had left the trade for good.[90]

Their fates were varied, according to Oboznenko's study of 1,591 prostitutes who quit the trade between 1891 and 1893. Supposedly, so long as the police retained her passport, a woman was locked into prostitution, but the passport system was subject to considerable abuse. A woman might bribe someone to regain her passport, she might pay someone to forge one, or she might return to her village without a passport at all.[91] However they managed it, in the 1890s the great majority (almost two-thirds) of the women who had ceased to be registered prostitutes had simply "left the life," "left the city," or managed to elude the police ("unable to locate"). Those women who had set aside a few rubles in order to establish households of their own or were prepared to marry peasant widowers with children (the least desirable of mates) might take refuge in the village. Of the women who left, seventy-seven, or 4.7 percent got married. Many more found lovers or protectors in the city, an indication that some men, at least, did not view a woman's registration as sufficiently shameful to bar serious commitment to her. Anastasia Katushkina was one such woman. A nineteen-year-old migrant from Tver' without mother or father, Katushkina was literate enough to sign her own name when she appeared voluntarily before the Medical-Police Committee in June 1904. Two and a half months later, she asked to be released, having begun to live with a Colonel Lanskoi, who was supporting her. Typically, the Committee's agents gathered information in a fashion that must surely have destroyed Katushkina's anonymity and probably contributed to her eviction from the apartment she rented. Everyone around her, including Lanskoi himself and the owner of the outerwear shop where she found work in November, must have known about her previous profession. Nevertheless, Katushkina finally succeeding in regaining her passport in January 1905, and there is no evidence that she returned to prostitution.[92]

The proportion who chose to depend on one lover rather than many seems to have grown. In 1890 and 1891, about 12 percent of women left prostitution because someone had agreed to take responsibility for them according

90  Fedorov, "Prostitutsiia," 57 and *Pozornyi promysel*, 7.
91  Evidence of forged passports can be found in *Sudebnyi vestnik*, no. 224 (1869): 28; no. 8 (1870): 2–3, and *Peterburgskii listok*, 22 Jan. 1892. The trade in forged passports seems to have been lively.
92  TsGIAL, fond 593, op. 1, delo 615; see also 613, 626, 611.

to the Statistical Yearbooks; Oboznenko gives a lower figure, 7.1 percent. Another 2.7 percent had "found a position." By 1907, over half of the 262 women released from professional prostitution had found lovers. (About 20 percent of these, like Katushkina, had found a job as well.) About 20 percent of these women became involved with men of higher status than themselves; the rest formed liaisons with men of a peasant or *meshchanstvo* background that was comparable to their own – men who earned their living as factory workers, bakers, coachmen, tailors, typesetters, craftsmen, and the like. It seems unlikely that such men would adopt the patronizing manner that Alexander Kuprin describes in *Iama* (*the Pit*).[93] In the cohort leaving prostitution in 1907, only a very few had taken advantage of their experience to make their way up the ladder into the ranks of procuresses and madams as they grew older, although ten of the ex-prostitutes did keep apartments and let rooms to younger women who worked as prostitutes, and they may have been procuring clandestinely. Fourteen more cooked, cleaned, or washed dishes in the brothels where once they had plied their trade. About 10 percent more earned their living in trades that were typical for their sex: They took in sewing, engaged in domestic service, or worked in factories or as washerwomen. Relations, including mothers (six), fathers (one), sisters, brothers, aunts, and uncles, gave shelter to twelve more, belying Bentovin's contention that registration severed entirely a woman's ties to her family.[94] Five took off for their native villages. Some who simply left (*vybyli*, the record reads) probably disappeared into the criminal underworld.[95] Wherever they went, judging by the small proportion of registered prostitutes over age thirty in the various censuses, only a tiny minority were likely to end up "sadly, as elderly, painted streetwalkers, doing their business in alleys in the small hours of the morning for a handful of kopeks."[96] The lot even of these may have been no worse than that of other aged women whom the village rejected and no one would hire.

### Conclusion

This survey of prostitutes in St. Petersburg sheds light on two separate but related themes in the history of Russia's urbanization. First, it indicates the circumstances that put women on the margins of urban life, and secondly, it

---

93 Alexander Kuprin, *The Pit* (London, 1930).
94 Bentovin, *Torguiushchaia telom*, 199.      95 TsGIAL, fond 593, op. 1, delo 644.
96 Richard Stites, "Prostitute and Society in Pre-Revolutionary Russia," *Jahrbücher für Geschichte Osteuropas*, 31, no. 3 (1983): 354.

shows what happened when women in the city violated the narrow official standards of sexual propriety. In Russia, peasant women who became prostitutes tended to be among the more marginal members of the village community. Most came from "incomplete" families that had lost at least one adult breadwinner, and sometimes both, and had ceased to be economically viable. Unable to find a place for themselves in their native village, daughters, like sons, went off in search of work. But prostitution in Russia, as in many other places, cannot be understood solely in terms of the need that drove a woman from her village or the urban job market that denied her subsistence. While economic need was a major factor, personal circumstances also played a role. Women from "incomplete" families were more likely to migrate alone. Most of them lacked fathers to protect and restrain them in a society where the patriarchal family and not the state served as the primary source of welfare and of social control. As a result, they tended to be more independent, as well as more vulnerable, than women who remained in the village or women who migrated with their parents. When times got hard, they could rely only on their own meager resources. Unprotected, women became more vulnerable to rape or to sexual harassment; unrestrained, they also became freer to dispose of their sexual favors as they chose, even in the absence of firm guarantees for their own future, and to seek an easier or more pleasant life for themselves.

It was the freedom from patriarchal authority that seemed to trouble officials most. This was one of the reasons they sought to regulate prostitution in the first place and why they accepted illicit unions as reasons to release women from prostitution, although there is no evidence that officials approved of such unions. Indeed, reading documents in the Medical-Police archive, one gets the sense that police agents were more prone to release a woman who had found a steady lover than a woman who had only found a job; and the fate of former prostitutes in 1907 suggests that this sense is probably correct. A man, any man, was a better guarantor of a woman's behavior than a woman was of her own. While the system of regulation did not manage to subject every unruly woman to someone else's authority, by penalizing and publicizing women's socially deviant behavior, regulation certainly succeeded in restricting women's options and increasing their dependence on men.

# 7. Making a home in the city

By the early twentieth century, a more settled, more "proletarianized" workforce had evolved in Russia's major cities and in St. Petersburg in particular. There remains considerable debate among historians as to the number of such workers and their proportion of the labor force, but all agree about the characteristics of the proletarianized worker: He had greatly attenuated or severed his ties to the village, and he had come to depend upon his wages. He perceived himself as a member of the working class rather than as a peasant. Ties with fellow workers, instead of kinship or village ties, defined his social world. While few historians say so outright, the proletarian is gendered: When they use the word "he" they almost never mean "she." With the exception of Rose Glickman's ground-breaking study of the Russian factory woman, women are either omitted from this discourse or enter it as consorts of men.[1] For example, according to Sergei Bernshtein-Kogan, the fully proletarianized worker found it much harder to marry for economic reasons, but when he did he was usually in a position to support his family on his wage and "very rarely . . . [left] his wife in the village."[2] The new generation of literate women who took up factory work on the eve of World War I provided "more suitable mates for young literate skilled workers," writes Leopold Haimson.[3]

As the above quotations imply, the formation of urban families represents an important stage in the evolution of this urban working class. Having the wife in the city and not the village contributed to the severance of village ties and dramatically increased what a worker required in terms of wages and amenities. The urban family made it possible to forge new associations

1 Rose Glickman, *Russian Factory Women: Workplace and Society, 1880–1914* (Berkeley, Calif., 1984).
2 S.M. Bernshtein-Kogan, *Chislennost', sostav i polozhenie peterburgskikh rabochikh* (St. Petersburg, 1910), 55.
3 Leopold Haimson, "Changements demographiques et greves ouvrieres à Saint-Peterbourg, 1905–1914," *Annales ESC*, no. 4 (July–Aug. 1985): 798.

outside the workplace as well as within it and facilitated the formation of a genuinely working-class culture.[4]

This emergent working-class culture came to involve notions of an appropriate family order, with the male worker at its center. Male workers' growing sense of dignity led them to expect more from their personal lives: Unlike migrants who were prepared to endure long separations from a wife and children in the village, such workers expected to live together with them. And by contrast with the village order, where women played an active and vital productive role in sustaining the peasant family economy, and where children contributed according to their age and ability, in the emergent working-class order, men bore most of the economic responsibility for their wives and children. In the words of a report to the metalworkers' union (1909): "To the extent that the worker develops and becomes independent of his father's family, his demands increase, especially if he settles down as a married man. . . . For those who cross that threshold, difficult material circumstances often make family life precarious. When the wife and child are forced to exhaust themselves seeking additional earnings away from home, family life often becomes pure fiction."[5] A "real" family required a woman's time and energy. As others have noted, the more developed the worker, the more likely he was to have such expectations – to feel entitled to "the protection of his family hearth and the possibility of providing for the normal development and care of his children."[6] This chapter will explore how notions of a proper family order emerged from the encounter between the culture of peasant migrants and the material conditions they found in Russia's capital cities.

Before we begin to examine the evolution of this new family order, however, let us note the extent to which the discussion thus far has marginalized women. It bears repeating that the story labor historians usually tell is about men's consciousness and the development of a working class conceived as generically male. It is based on sources that privilege wage labor and struggles that originated at the point of production. Told from that standpoint, the narrative reveals almost nothing about women's experiences or what "normal" family life might have meant to them. It is remarkably difficult to shift the focus to women and to bring them back into the picture. As Rose Glickman has demonstrated so well, just about everyone, ranging from male

4 See, for example, the arguments in Haimson, "Changements," 801.
5 *Soiuz rabochikh po metallu. Materialy ob ekonomicheskom polozhenii i professial'nom organizatsii peterburgskikh rabochikh po metallu* (St. Petersburg, 1909), 89.
6 Quoted in Iu. I. Kirianov, *Zhiznennyi uroven' rabochikh Rossii* (Moscow, 1979), 267.

workers to *intelligenty* of various stripes, either ignored the woman worker or failed to recognize her legitimate concerns.[7] So much the harder is it to track down the married woman and to explore the life she lived outside the comparatively well-illuminated workplace.

To establish her social identity is hardest of all. Social historians ordinarily use social status and/or occupation to identify people: Men are workers, or artisans, or shopkeepers, or teachers, and so forth. In addition, Russian historians often try to determine if lower-class people are workers, or worker-peasants, or peasants – that is, where people stand on the continuum between village and factory or city.[8] Rarely do these historians concern themselves with personal identities. To paraphrase Barbara Omolade, they conceptualize history as being shaped by what men did during the day, but not what they did at night.[9] Because historians do not attend to the fact that their subjects were also sons and fathers, husbands and lovers, they often skew the history they write.[10] Personal identities were at least as important a component of the self-perception and life choices of women. Whether a woman was young and marriageable, a spinster, a widow, a wife, or a mother affected her participation in the workforce and in public life and how she conceived of her roles.

The problem of social identity becomes particularly complex when we try to define the working-class wife. Designating a man as working-class is tricky enough, because so many male wage workers had one foot in the village, maintaining an allotment and often a wife and family there. But the criteria are at least as difficult to establish for the married woman. In 1902, close to 40 percent of migrant women in Moscow were married. Between 1900 and 1910, the proportion of married women among migrants in St. Petersburg rose from 44 percent to 49 percent.[11] But how many of these married women can be considered working-class? If a woman did not work full-time for wages but was married to a waged laborer, did she see herself as a member of the working class and did ties with fellow workers define her social world? What if the family rented space to boarders and the wife stayed

---

7 Glickman, *Russian Factory Women*, chaps. 7 and 8.

8 Taking issue with this notion, Rose Glickman appropriately entitled an unpublished paper on women workers, " 'Backward Workers' in Skirts?" Presented at the Conference on the Social History of Russian Labor, University of California, Berkeley, Mar. 26, 1982.

9 Barbara Omolade, "Hearts of Darkness," in *Power of Desire: The Politics of Sexuality*, ed. Ann Snitow, Christine Stansell, and Sharon Thompson (New York, 1983), 364.

10 Here one might simply compare the growing significance of the history of the family in studies of Western Europe and the comparative neglect of the field by Russianists.

11 R.E. Johnson, "Mothers and Daughters in Urban Russia: A Research Note," *Canadian Slavonic Papers*, 30, no. 3 (Sept. 1988): 369, 378.

home and served them, as a considerable proportion of the wives of male
workers did? To what extent did she share her husband's experiences and
perceptions? Was the experience and worldview of a wife who stayed at
home and served boarders similar to her neighbor's, the wife of a shoemaker,
who left her two children every day to toil in a textile mill? What had the two
in common with the woman who lived downstairs, a textile worker who had
left her husband and children in the village? What had they in common with
a domestic servant or washerwoman who, although married to a factory
worker, lived apart from her husband? Was being married to a worker
sufficient to imbue women with a common "social, political, as well as economic identity as members of a *working class*" (emphasis in the original)?[12]
What was the impact of notions of an appropriate family order on women's
identity and choices? In examining these questions, this chapter will look at
Russia's working class from a different angle. Shifting the focus away from
the workplace and onto women and the family offers another perspective on
the complexities of working-class identities and the adaptation of peasants to
life in the city. But first a word about terminology: As the preceeding
discussion suggests, the terms *working class* and *working-class wife* remain
problematic in the Russian context; nevertheless, for lack of alternatives I
will employ them to designate individuals who either engaged in waged
labor themselves (including domestic servants) or who were married to
someone who did.

## Living and working in the city

At least until the early twentieth century, the working-class couple who
shared a roof was a relative rarity in Russia's major cities. The census of
1897 reported that in the city of Moscow a miniscule 3.7 percent of male
workers were heads of households residing with their families. Working-
class family life was only marginally more common in St. Petersburg, where
5.2 percent of male workers lived as heads of their households. Even among
relatively well-paid metalworkers, the proportion of men living with their
wives and/or children was under 16 percent. A "gradual trend toward an
urban-based family life" became noticeable early in the twentieth century
and accelerated after the Stolypin reforms of 1906–7, although how much it
accelerated remains a point of contention.[13]

12 Haimson, "Changements," 801.
13 Johnson, "Mothers and Daughters," 13; N.A. Troinitskii, ed. *Chislennost' i sostav rabochikh
   v Rossii na osnovanii dannykh pervoi vseobshchei perepisi naseleniia Rossiiskoi Imperii 1897 g.*,
   (St. Petersburg, 1906), 46–7; 66–7.

Some of the circumstances that made working-class family life so problematic in the city also promoted high rates of illegitimacy: the enormous expense of urban life and the difficulty men experienced in severing ties to the village. But several other factors played a role as well, and they suggest some peculiarities of Russia's urbanization. One of these was men's exceedingly low wages relative to the cost of living in the city, which made it virtually impossible for most husbands to support a wife there. As a result, a woman's first experience of wage earning often followed marriage, especially if she married in the village and followed her husband to the city, as wives commonly did. The physician Natan Vigdorchik put it this way: "Marriage in the workers' milieu not only fails to free a woman from the need to seek wages; it is one of the factors that impels her toward wage-earning."[14] This helps to explain why a high proportion of women workers in Russia's major cities were married. In 1882, well over a third (38.1 percent) of women textile workers in the city of Moscow were married; fifteen years later, the proportion of married female textile workers had risen to 47 percent. In 1897, almost a third of the entire female workforce (excluding servants) of 50,572 in Moscow were married. The proportion of wives in St. Petersburg's workforce of 36,604 women was virtually the same.[15] By contrast, in England and France, married women who worked in factories made up "only a small proportion" of women operatives.[16] The pattern in Moscow and St. Petersburg more closely resembles the one that George Alter has identified in Verviers, Belgium, where female textile workers were among the most stable in the workforce. Even after they married, even after they bore one or two children (although not more), many women continued to work.[17]

In Moscow and St. Petersburg, however, unlike in Verviers and other European cities, when a married woman continued to work for wages, the locus of urban workplaces could make it difficult, if not impossible, for her to reside with her husband. It was hardest of all for the domestic servant.

---

14 N. Vigdorchik, "Detskaia smertnost' sredi peterburgskikh rabochikh," *Obshchestvennyi vrach*, no. 2 (Feb. 1914): 219.

15 *Perepis' Moskvy 1882 g.*, 3 vols. (Moscow, 1885), 2: 203. In St. Petersburg in 1897, 44 percent of women textile workers and 31 percent of all women workers were married. Figures for 1897 from Troinitskii, ed., *Chislennost' i sostav*, 46–7; 66–7. The Moscow census of 1902 showed a virtually identical proportion of married women among factory workers. *Glavneishie predvaritel'nye dannye perepisi goroda Moskvy 31 Ianvaria 1902 g.* 6 vols. (Moscow, 1902–7), 6: 54–5.

16 Louise Tilly and Joan Scott, *Women, Work, and Family* (New York, 1978), 124.

17 George Alter, *Family and the Female Life Course: The Women of Verviers, Belgium, 1849–1880* (Madison, Wis., 1988), 99–102.

The experience of the Mitrofanovs was typical. Peasants from Novgorod, Olga and Pavel left for St. Petersburg in 1901 because of the lack of opportunities to earn money in their village. Olga soon found a position as a servant in a small family in one part of the city, while Pavel was hired as a watchman in another part.[18] The vast majority of servants lived with their employers, who demanded their complete devotion, housed them in a hallway, a kitchen, or some crowded corner, and forbade them a personal life. Despite the lack of time or space for themselves, servants married, and married women like Olga Mitrofanova worked as domestic servants. In the early months of 1890, 21 of the 103 peasant servants who bore children at the St. Petersburg Maternity Home were married women; a fifth of the married women giving birth in those months were employed as domestic servants. According to the Moscow census of 1902, a surprising 29 percent of domestic servants over the age of fifteen were married.[19] Of 70 peasant servants dwelling at number 14/2 Nizhegorodskaia Street between 1908 and 1909, 9 (almost 13 percent) were married. Only one lived with her husband.

Yet even women workers whose free time and choice of domicile were their own found cohabitation with a spouse extraordinarily difficult. Consider the case of the Efimovs. Domna Maksimova, a peasant from Riazan, had been working in a factory in Moscow for six years when in 1887, at age twenty-one, she married a worker, Mikhail, a peasant from Moscow. After the marriage as before, the couple lived apart, she employed at one factory, he at another, until the Easter holiday when they took off for his village to spend some time together.[20] The long hours of work, the location of urban factories, and the lack of affordable housing and accessible transport raised often insuperable barriers to cohabitation. Workdays could stretch as long as eighteen hours before 1897, when legislation limited them to eleven and a half. After 1897, employers frequently forced their workers to put in overtime, drastically reducing free time and making it virtually imperative that home be located near work. But the tobacco and textile factories that provided employment to many laboring women were often located across the city from the machine and metalworking plants that employed their husbands. If workers had to commute, they did it on foot, since until well into the twentieth century both Moscow and St. Petersburg lacked public transportation that was within the reach of the working-class budget. In Moscow,

18 Praskov'ia Tarnovskaia, *Zhenshchiny-ubiitsy* (St. Petersburg, 1902), 202.
19 TsGIAL, fond 145, op. 1, ed. kh. 112; *Glavneishie predvaritel'nye dannye*, 6: 54–5.
20 TsGIA SSSR, fond 1412, op. 221, delo 42, 7–8.

cheap trams began operating at hours convenient to the working class only in 1910. St. Petersburg acquired accessible tram service only after the revolution. A few of the most highly skilled and well paid of St. Petersburg's workers probably had the means to ride the streetcar to work regularly, but the majority of workers lacked both the time and the money to travel substantial distances to work. Despite the higher rents charged in factory districts, most workers probably lived within walking distance of their jobs.[21]

The company-owned dormitories that employers built to deal with the lack of affordable housing exacerbated as much as they solved the problem of cohabitation for working couples. In 1882, close to 90 percent of Moscow's factory workers lived in dormitories. The percentage gradually declined in the years that followed, but a large proportion of textile workers continued to reside in them at least until the early twentieth century. In 1897, about 10 percent of St. Petersburg's workers lived in company housing.[22] Some company housing lacked family quarters entirely; in others, it was limited and available only if both partners worked in the same factory. Even then, married couples might have to wait a year or so until a "family room" became available. During the waiting period, the woman would sleep in the women's quarters, her husband in the men's, and their "conjugal life" would consist of the occasional stolen night together beneath his cot in the worker's dormitory, with a drawn curtain to establish a bit of privacy. A wife's pregnancy might hasten things, as one woman worker found. She and her husband, a carpenter, had "taken their pleasure" on the shavings beneath his workbench in a Moscow factory before she became pregnant, and management at last assigned them a room.[23]

Occupational segregation, the cost of housing, and the lack of affordable and accessible transport created obstacles to cohabitation so formidable that at the end of the nineteenth century a substantial proportion of married couples did not share a roof, even when they worked in the same city. Here, the figures on working women living with family, cited in Chapter 5, are

21 James Bater, "Some Dimensions of Urbanization and the Response of Municipal Government: Moscow and St. Petersburg," *Russian History*, vol. 5, pt. 1 (1978): 58–9, and "The Journey to Work in St. Petersburg, 1860–1914," *Journal of Transport History*, 2, no. 4 (Sept. 1974): 222–3.

22 Joseph Bradley, *Muzhik and Muscovite: Urbanization in Late Imperial Russia* (Berkeley, Calif., 1985), 204; Kirianov, Zhiznennyi uroven', 230–1, 241.

23 I. Kor, ed. *Kak my zhili pri tsare i kak zhivem teper'* (Moscow, 1934), 8, also 21–2; S. Lapitskaia, *Byt rabochikh Trekhgornoi manufaktury* (Moscow, 1935), 55–6; D.L. Kasitskaia and E.P. Popova, "Polozhenie i byt rabochikh Prokhorskoi Trekhgornoi manufaktury" in *Istoriko-bytovye ekspeditsii, 1949–50*, ed. A. Pankratova (Moscow, 1953), 178.

worth reviewing from another angle. Although close to one-third of all women workers and almost half of women textile workers in Moscow were married, only 7 percent of all women workers (including women textile workers) lived with family, and an unknown and unknowable proportion of these women were daughters, sisters, and nieces, rather than wives. The proportion of women in a family situation was higher in St. Petersburg, where 14 percent of all women workers, and 12 percent of textile workers lived with members of their families, but the numbers still indicate that only a fraction of married women workers cohabited with their husbands.[24] Some of these women were married to men who had remained behind in the village, although it is impossible to know exactly how many. One survey of St. Petersburg textile workers, conducted in the early twentieth century, found that 7.7 percent of the married women had left their husbands in their villages.[25] The proportion of married women without husbands in the city may have been even higher in Moscow. In 1902, census takers examined a small sampling of 525 married women employed as factory workers and lower civil servants and found that 112 of them, that is, over a fifth, had left a husband in the village.[26] Still, these were the minority. It seems indisputable that the circumstances of their employment forced the majority of married women workers to live apart from their husbands in the city.

While many historians have noticed that working men lived alone and apart from the family, few have commented on married couples' separate residences in the city. Instead, most have assumed that every husband living alone had left his wife behind in the village.[27] How did workers regard this enforced separation? Workers themselves have left little explicit testimony about the matter, and other sources provide only indirect evidence. But what information there is confirms the observations made by intellectuals such as Sergei Bernshtein-Kogan: A male worker's growing sense of dignity gave rise to resentment against such involuntary separations. If he decided to marry at all, a man felt entitled to cohabit with his wife and to enjoy the benefits and services that customarily accompanied marriage.

24 In statistical compilations, married women are listed separately from those living with family, so it is impossible to know the proportion of married women who fell into the latter category.
25 S.K—n, "K voprosu o polozhenii peterburgskikh rabochikh," *Trud tekhnika*, no. 5 (1907): 218.
26 They left a total of 310 children as well, but, unfortunately, no one calculated the proportion of women who left both husband and children in the village. *Glavneishie predvaritel'nye dannye*, 6: 54.
27 Exceptions are Bradley, *Muzhik*, 226, and a footnote in Kirianov, *Zhiznennyi uroven'*, 241.

Such resistance to personal deprivation is most obvious in respect to village wives. Characteristically, newcomers from the village, short-term migrant males, seasonal workers, and those without skills had little choice but to tolerate separation when the wife was needed in the village and it made economic sense for her to stay there. How could they bring their wives to the city? wondered a group of unskilled workers. "Today we're here, but God knows where we'll be tomorrow. So that's how we live, each by himself."[28] However, as men's expectations rose, they became more likely to try to change such an arrangement or to avoid it altogether. One worker put the matter explicitly when he confronted his father over whether the son's bride would stay in the village or accompany him to Moscow. "I didn't marry for the village, but for myself," he insisted.[29] One form of workers' self-assertion was to refuse outright to marry "for the village," either by remaining single or by choosing a bride in the city.

One important piece of evidence of such self-assertion is a change in the rates of marriage during the revolutionary upheavals of 1905. That year, workers engaged in unprecedented actions to improve their economic circumstances and to gain a political voice. In October, they organized a general strike that brought the autocracy to its knees and forced it to make its most important concession, a quasi-parliament, the state Duma, elected by indirect and unequal male suffrage. As working women and men rose up en masse to claim political and economic rights, a significant minority also acted as individuals to assert control of their personal lives by choosing mates for themselves instead of for "the village." It is surely no coincidence that the number of marriages in some working-class districts of St. Petersburg increased noticeably in 1905, and much more modestly, in Moscow in 1906. In St. Petersburg, marriage rates had averaged about 73 per 1,000 inhabitants since the turn of the century in the second section of Vasilevskii Island, but 111 couples per 1,000 wed in 1905. In the third section, the growth was more modest but still considerable: from an average of 68 per 1,000 to 93 per 1,000. In 1905, about 1,900 "extra" marriages occurred in Vasilevskii Island 2, and roughly 1,130 "extra" in Vasilevskii Island 3, judging by the number of people living in those sections in 1900. Smaller increases occurred in Alexander Nevskii 1, and Vyborg 1 and 2 (see Table 5.2). A man's marry-

28 P. Timofeev, "What the Factory Worker Lives By," in *The Russian Worker: Life and Labor under the Tsarist Regime*, ed. V. Bonnell (Berkeley, Calif., 1983), 79.
29 O.N. Chaadaeva, ed., *Rabotnitsa na sotsialisticheskoi stroike: Sbornik avtobiografii* (Moscow, 1932), 129.

ing a woman he had met in the city constituted a kind of declaration of independence from the village. If the wife remained in the city, which she typically did, the village household was deprived of her labor and the vital role she played in the urban-rural nexus. The heady atmosphere of 1905 seems to have inspired a considerable number of working-class men and women to claim lives for themselves in St. Peterburg.

If wife and husband also managed to share a roof in the city, their lives were improved in a number of ways. This was particularly true for men, who were sometimes prepared to make considerable sacrifices to ensure that they lived with working wives. V.S. Volkov left a good position at a pharmacy in Moscow "because there wasn't enough money to live with my wife." Instead, both he and his wife found work as weavers at the Nikol' skaia mill in Tver'. In the early twentieth century, metalworkers who lived near the textile mills where their wives worked had to rise before 5:00 A.M. in order to make it to their own factory gates by 7:00 when work began.[30] A couple gained the pleasure of each other's company and a companion in their bed. Living together also reduced the overall cost of housing. In addition, husbands acquired the range of domestic services that a peasant man was accustomed to receive from a wife. In return for the "subjective rewards" of cohabitation, to borrow Rose Glickman's language – a husband's protection and the considerable benefits of his wage – working-class wives assumed virtually the entire burden of housework, even when they were fully employed themselves.[31]

Women kept house in the city under extraordinarily difficult circumstances and in the absence of the most basic amenities. To be sure, both living space and possessions were exceedingly modest and simple to care for. In dormitories or apartments, couples rarely had even a room to themselves. Furniture was basic – a bed, a table with stools or benches along the sides, perhaps a chest and a box for storage, and an icon case in the corner. But to obtain water for cooking and washing was both complicated and time consuming. As late as the 1890s, 85 percent of the apartments in the working-class section of Vyborg district lacked running water. Other quarters of the city were even more poorly supplied, and some of the industrial suburbs had no running

---

30 A.N. Pankratova, et al., ed., *Rabochee dvizhenie v Rossii v XIX veke. Sbornik dokumentov*, 4 vols. (Moscow-Leningrad, 1950–63), 3, ch. 1, 222; A.L. Blek, "Usloviia truda rabochikh na peterburgskikh zavodakh po dannym 1901 goda,' *Arkhiv istorii truda v Rossii*, kn. 2 (Petrograd, 1921), 78.
31 Glickman, *Russian Factory Women*, 123.

Fig. 8. Two young working-class couples at home in their shared basement room in St. Petersburg, early twentieth century. The bed of one couple is at the back, the other in the foreground. Their clothing and towels hang on the wall. Note the bare heads and urban dress of the women. (Courtesy of Tsentral'nyi Gosudarstvennyi Arkhiv Kinofonofotodokumentov.)

water at all. Residents obtained their water from a tap in the courtyard, from the local bathhouse, or from barrels brought into the neighborhood. When water had to be fetched, it was women who usually carried it along corridors and up stairs. Although municipal services expanded rapidly after 1890, they barely kept pace with the demand. In 1905 the majority of working-class quarters still lacked running water. Nine years later, on the eve of World War I, residents of at least a quarter of all the apartments in St. Petersburg and a third of those in Moscow had to leave their buildings to obtain their water. In working-class districts, the percentage of apartments without water was much higher.[32]

Lack of running water made it hard to keep people and clothing clean. In the 1890s, it cost five kopeks, then eight, to go to the baths near the Guzhon factory in Moscow. One large family of a worker who earned thirty to thirty-five rubles a month could afford to go only once every two weeks; six people shared the same towel, exchanging it for another only when the towel became thoroughly filthy.[33] Few families had the money to send laundry out to a laundress or pay the landlady to do it, and so the wife ended up doing the washing too. Rarely would landladies permit washing in the apartment; water cost money and the landlady paid for it. Public baths had once permitted their premises to be used for washing, but by the 1890s, this was the case only in a few quarters of St. Petersburg, Vyborg among them. To use the public baths, the women had to drag the laundry, the soap, and a washing trough from the apartment to the baths and then home again. In districts that lacked indoor facilities for washing, working-class families wore dirty clothes and slept on dirty bedding until the weather grew warm enough for the women to do their laundry in the city's canals, or, in the industrial suburbs, in pits behind the house.[34] In the damp, cold weather that prevails for eight to nine months of the year in St. Petersburg, and during the winter months in Moscow, women hung their washing to dry indoors, on cords strung across the very rooms in which they lived.

The lack of sanitary facilities complicated a wife's responsibilities even more. Where houses lacked garbage pits, as was the case in the Shlisselburg suburbs, people either tossed their refuse into the courtyard or kept it in the kitchen for days on end until someone came to collect it. In 1890, only about 12 percent of working-class apartments in St. Petersburg had water closets, and while the proportion grew to 41 percent over the next decade, it was the better-off workers in the center of the city whose apartments were most likely to have them. In 1900, residents of about a third of the apartments of Vasilevskii Island 2 and half of those in Vyborg 2 – both working-class areas

32 Kirianov, *Zhiznennyi uroven'*, 253; M.I. Pokrovskaia, "O zhilishchakh peterburgskikh rabochikh," *Vestnik obshchestvennoi gigieny, sudebnoi i prakticheskoi meditsiny* (Mar. 1898): 210–11; P.P. Aleksandrov, *Za Narvskoi zastavoi. Vospominaniia starogo rabochego*, (Leningrad, 1963), 6; Bradley, *Muzhik*, 197–8; *Statisticheskii ezhegodnik S.-Peterburga. 1903* (St. Petersburg, 1905), 16.

33 TsGAOR SSSR, fond 7952, op. 3, delo 273, 25.

34 *Peterburgskii listok*, 21 Oct. 1982; K.I. Sametskii, "Sanitarnyi ocherk prigorodov Peterburga, Shlissel'burgskago i Petergofskago uchastkov i prigorodnykh sel v 1894 g.," *Vestnik obshchestvennoi gigieny, sudebnoi i prakticheskoi meditsiny* (Sept. 1895): 242.

– lacked indoor toilets. The same uneven distribution of plumbing characterized Moscow. By 1912, almost all the apartments in the central districts had acquired indoor plumbing, but only 18 percent of the housing units in outlying, working-class districts like Serpukhov.[35] In the absence of indoor facilities, people used unheated outhouses, with primitive stools that were rarely cleaned. Located in the courtyard, and sometimes shared with residents of one, two, or even three or four other apartment houses, they often became extraordinarily filthy and smelly. Middle-class visitors to working-class housing sometimes found the stench almost unbearable and impossible to imagine if you had not visited the apartment yourself: " 'You can cut it with an axe,' as the saying goes."[36]

Whether migrant peasants shared this revulsion is hard to say. Some middle-class people were as likely to be shocked by the sanitary habits of the peasantry as others were by working-class housing. To be sure, villagers could dispose of their waste less conspicuously: Garbage could be fed to pigs and outhouses built further from human habitation. But in most peasant villages, educated observers found housekeeping standards to be deplorably lax: Cookware, crockery, and utensils sat unwashed on tables, left for cockroaches to "clean." Busy women might occasionally sweep the floors, but they almost never washed them, and fleas, bedbugs, and other insects were everywhere.[37] So a migrant wife and husband might not have minded so much the dirt and the stench, especially if they were relatively new to the city.

Still, even if she did not mind her surroundings, the working-class wife would have had trouble performing the most ordinary domestic chores – providing food, for example. Both the central districts and the outlying suburbs of St. Petersburg and Moscow were supplied by shops, open-air markets, and itinerant vendors, who purveyed their wares all over the city, both day and night. But a woman had to struggle to stretch a ruble even to buy the black bread, cabbage, and buckwheat groats that were the staples of the working-class diet. In the industrial suburbs, food was of poorer quality and far more expensive than in the heart of the city a few miles away, but even in the center, workers often spent proportionally more for food than more well-to-do urban dwellers. Lacking an icebox or a proper cupboard to

35 *Statisticheskii ezhegodnik S.-Peterburga. 1903*, 16; Bradley, *Muzhik*, 198.
36 Quote in Sametskii, "Sanitarnyi ocherk prigorodov Peterburga," 243.
37 P. Zorin, "Opisanie Bogorodskoi volosti v mediko-statisticheskom i sanitarnom otnosheniiakh," *Vestnik sudebnoi meditsiny*, no. 1 (1882): 62; Nina Berberova, *The Italics Are Mine* ( New York, 1969), 13.

store provisions, they had to buy them daily in small quantities and wound up spending more. Workers frequently bought on credit. Altogether, about half of the family budget went for food.[38] And when was a woman to find time to cook a meal? If she worked full-time away from home, a woman cooked cabbage soup or, much more rarely, potato soup perhaps three or four times a week. In shared apartments or factory dormitories, cooking was frequently a source of friction between the women. Each wife cooked for her own family, by contrast with the village, where one of the women of the household, usually the wife of the *bol'shak*, oversaw food preparation for the entire household and assigned a daughter-in-law to do the work. In urban apartments, all of the women crowded around the stove before mealtimes, pushing and shoving and trying to put their pots in the best place. The tensions were greatest before the midday meal, because husbands with only an hour off gave their wives a hard time if the food was not ready the moment they appeared.[39]

If she managed these and other tasks, a wife could raise her husband's level of comfort considerably. Despite the surrounding filth, the overcrowding, the lack of running water and other amenities, all observers of working-class life agreed that by comparison with single workers, family men lived well. Family quarters were relatively clean and neat. "In the apartments of families, you can see aspirations to comfort. You come across pictures, mirrors, soft furniture, good beds, and blankets."[40]

Virtually all of the tasks associated with housekeeping were the wife's responsibility. Sometimes, if the woman was employed full-time, her husband might occasionally lend a hand, perhaps picking up groceries at the market, or looking after the children, or helping to straighten up in the morning.[41] Nevertheless, there is little evidence to support M. Davidovich's contention that household burdens were "shared equally by husbands and wives."[42] Most workers were first-generation peasant migrants, who brought

38 M. Davidovich, *Peterburgskii tekstil'nyi rabochii v ego biudzhetakh* (St. Petersburg, 1912), 7; S.N. Prokopovich, *Biudzhety Peterburgskikh rabochikh* (St. Petersburg, 1909), 65.

39 M. Pokrovskaia, *Po podvalam, cherdakam i uglovym kvartiram Peterburga* (St. Petersburg, 1903), 73–4; F.P. Pavlov, "Ten Years of Experience," in Bonnell, ed., *The Russian Worker*, 129.

40 Quoted in Kirianov, *Zhiznennyi uroven'*, 257. See also A.N. Rubel, "Zhilishcha bednago naseleniia g. S.-Peterburga," *Vestnik obshchestvennoi gigieny, sudebnoi i prakticheskoi meditsiny* (Apr. 1899): 427.

41 V. Iu. Krupianskaia, "Evoliutsiia semeino-bytovogo uklada rabochikh," in *Rossiiskii proletariat. Oblik bor'ba gegemoniia*, ed. L.M. Ivanov (Moscow, 1970), 277, and M. Davidovich, "Khoziaistvennoe znachenie zhenshchiny v rabochei sem'e," *Poznanie Rossii*, kn. 3 (1909): 122.

42 Davidovich, "Khoziaistvennoe znachenie," 122.

Fig. 9. Two working-class women at work in a kitchen, St. Petersburg, 1909. (Courtesy of Gosudarstvennyi Muzei Istorii Leningrada.)

with them to the city the expectation that marriage entitled a man to his wife's labor. When A. Kommissarova's husband insisted she live in the city and not the village, for example, he said it was because, like his father, he needed someone to clean and wash for him.[43] The loss of his wife's services in the household prompted one fitter at a Moscow factory to lodge a complaint with his *volost'* administration in 1890. They had issued his wife a separate passport, which he wanted them to revoke because her departure

43 Chaadaeva, *Rabotnitsa*, 129.

Fig. 10. Three generations of a working-class family in their room in St. Petersburg, late nineteenth or early twentieth century. Both husband and wife were employed as weavers. Note the curtains, mirror, and tablecloth, evidence of aspirations to greater comfort. (Courtesy of Tsentral'nyi Gosudarstvennyi Arkhiv Kinofonofotodokumentov.)

had deprived him of services he clearly thought were his due. On account of her absence, he complained, he had suffered "various inconveniences, like having to spend too much on an apartment, on grub, and the like."[44]

The burden of housekeeping in the city and the expectation that women would do most if not all of it meant that when a woman worked for wages, she had to rise earlier than her husband to get some of the housework done in time to leave for work; at the midday break, if she lived nearby she would race home, prepare the food, serve it, clear up, and then race back to the factory and work until closing time. There were more chores to do when the woman returned home after work. A woman worker with a family had not

44 TsGIAgM, fond 66, op. 1, ed. kh. 17483, 3.

a second of free time and rarely enough sleep.[45] A few plants actually made allowances for women's domestic obligations. In the 1890s, married women workers at the Bogdanov tobacco factory in St. Petersburg arrived at work at 7:30 A.M., worked until 10:00 or 11:00, then went home to prepare a midday meal for husband and children; they returned to work several hours later and worked until closing time. Flexible hours reduced women's wages, however: The Bogdanov workers did piecework, earning perhaps twenty-five to thirty kopeks a day in the 1890s, about forty to fifty kopeks in 1913.[46]

Pregnancy and childbirth added to a woman's burdens and, at the same time, made her earnings all the more necessary. Hiring a midwife was beyond the means of the working-class population of the city, and even to give birth in a municipal maternity home cost more money than many workers could afford, so they had to convince the authorities to waive the fee.[47] The birth and christening of a child cost workers between four and a half and sixteen and a half rubles. If the wife stopped working, the additional drain on the budget could send the family into debt. Pressing economic need meant that the vast majority of pregnant factory women worked right up until the onset of labor, even after the passage of legislation in 1912 that granted them two-weeks leave before childbirth. One study, conducted in 1912, found that close to 72 percent of pregnant women stayed on the job until the last moment.[48] Among the clientele of the Drop of Milk, a society that dispensed sterilized milk to the working poor, the pattern was much the same: In 1913, eleven of seventeen women factory workers toiled until the very last days of their pregnancy, and eight of them were back at work within a month.[49]

What was a woman to do after her baby arrived? Since few factories allowed time off for nursing, if a woman returned to work she had to give her baby milk from a bottle. Milk was one of the most expensive items in the

45 Krupianskaia, "Evoliutsiia semeino-bytovogo," 278; E.M. Dementeev, "Zhenskii fabrichnyi trud v Rossii," *Promyshlennost' i zdorov'e*, kn. 2 (1902): 16. If the husband had to commute to work and lost a lot of time in traveling, he was even less likely to help out with the chores, however heavy the weight of domestic obligations and however busy his wife.
46 I.E. Eremeev, ed., *Gorod S.-Peterburg s tochki zreniia meditsinskoi politsii* (St. Petersburg, 1897), 497. See also Lapitskaia, *Byt rabochikh*, 49, and E.A. Kabo, *Ocherki rabochego byta: opyt monograficheskogo issledovaniia domashnego rabochego byta* (Moscow, 1928), 204–5.
47 TsGIAL, fond 1648, op. 1, delo 148, 246, 317. Nine rubles seems very high, but that is the amount these documents give.
48 N. Vigdorchik, "Detskaia smertnost'," 219.
49 Being married nevertheless made a difference. Two of the unwed factory mothers were back at work within three and seven days, respectively, whereas the married women took no less than ten days apiece. See TsGIAL, fond 251, op. 1, kh. 7.

working-class diet, priced at one ruble sixty kopeks a pail in St. Petersburg, and one ruble fifteen kopeks in Moscow. Babies were expensive: Not counting child care, the family spent around forty rubles a year on a child between the ages of one and two.[50] This put the mother in a contradictory situation. On the one hand, the expense of an infant increased the need for the mother's earnings; on the other, who would look after the child if the mother went out to work? By contrast with their village sisters, urban workers rarely had resident kin who could help them. Almost any sort of child care was costly, and even a couple of rubles a month was more than most families could afford. If mothers worked, children were left to nurses of twelve, thirteen, or fourteen years of age, to landladies, to aged women, to each other or to themselves, locked in rooms, locked out of apartments, left to wander the streets until adults returned from work. When the same factory employed them, parents might work separate shifts. A male worker at the Prokhorov factory in Moscow remembered how he would take their baby to the factory gates and wait for his wife when the shifts changed. "My wife would come out, take the baby and go home with him, and I'd go to work. We'd do that every day, whatever the weather."[51]

Even so, children reduced a working woman's earnings. For one thing, artificially fed babies became sick more frequently than infants whose mothers were at home. Women bought milk from vendors on the street, who sometimes adulterated the milk with water and were not especially scrupulous about storing it. Even if mothers knew that the milk had to be boiled and sterilized before it was fed to the infant, they had the opportunity to boil it only once a day, in the morning before they went off to work. The milk would then be stored in a bowl. By the time an infant drank the milk, often it had gone bad, especially in hot weather, so infants developed stomach disorders.[52] It was the mother who cared for a sickly child all night and then came late to work and was fined the following morning. One woman weaver reckoned that she lost three to four days a month, about one month a year, in connection with bearing, christening, caring for, and burying her children.[53]

These circumstances help to explain why a substantial number of working-class infants perished in the first year of life. Although infant mortality

50 Davidovich, *Peterburgskii tekstil'nyi rabochii*, 5; K—n, "K voprosu," 218.
51 Lapitskaia, *Byt rabochikh*, 67.
52 M. Pokrovskaia, "Moia dumskaia praktika (ocherk iz byta rabochago naseleniia v Peterburge," *Mir bozhii*, no. 3, 1898, 22.
53 Davidovich, *Peterburgskii tekstil'nyi rabochii*, 25. See also P.F. Kudelli, *Rabotnitsa v 1905 g. v. S.-Peterburge* (Leningrad, 1926), 5.

Fig. 11. Street scene, including a woman weaver and her son, St. Petersburg, late nineteenth or early twentieth century. (Courtesy of Tsentral'nyi Gosudarstvennyi Arkhiv Kinofonofotodokumentov.)

declined in both Moscow and St. Petersburg in the decades following the emancipation of the serfs, it nevertheless remained high. In Moscow, the overall rate dropped from a high of 360 per 1,000 births in 1868–72, to about 300 per 1,000 in 1909. In St. Petersburg in 1909, about 250 of every 1,000 infants died before the age of one. However, studies that focus on the urban working–class show much higher rates – as high as 400 for every 1,000 births among a cohort of working-class families in St. Petersburg in 1912.[54] These infant mortality rates were even higher than the rates in most of the provinces of Russia from which peasant migrants derived and more than twice as high as rates in many major European cities.[55]

It is no wonder then that the village beckoned when a woman became pregnant, especially when a husband and working wife lived apart. If the

54 Vigdorchik, "Detskaia smertnost'," 231–2.
55 Vigdorchik provides rates for other European cities and several Russian provinces, 236. See also the discussion in Chapter 2.

family retained ties to a village household, the woman might leave her job and return to the countryside to give birth, and sometimes to raise her infant until it reached the age of two or three, when the child was stronger and needed less care.[56] According to the physician Maria Pokrovskaia, the prevalence of this practice helps to explain why urban working-class families had so few dependents: Only one child lived in the city, while the rest were in the village, cared for by their mother or by kin.[57] The one study of working-class life that investigated childrearing patterns suggested that a sizable minority of married textile workers preferred to raise children in the village. There were 1,931 married women among the St. Petersburg textile workers surveyed by V. Leontiev between 1900 and 1902; of these, about 15 percent left their children in the village.[58]

The precariousness of the urban family economy, the vulnerability of infant life, and the difficulties each newborn represented must surely have made many working-class mothers long to limit the number of their children. According to physicians, Russian working-class women increasingly resorted to abortion, even though it was illegal. Physicians believed that the abortion rate had grown steadily since the 1890s and that it skyrocketed after the revolution of 1905.[59] While they certainly exaggerated the frequency of abortion, especially within the working class, there is evidence that working-class women did regard abortion as a form of birth control. Members of the working class were actually queried about their birth control practices as part of a study of infant mortality among married St. Petersburg workers. Conducted in 1911 at the initiative of the Marxist physician Dr. Natan Vigdorchik, the study had the support and assistance of representatives of the labor unions but was conducted at a time of reaction and political persecution. The investigators obtained satisfactory responses from only 765 of the 5,000 workers they had targeted, due to the closing of one of the unions and the persecution of some of the workers who had agreed to distribute questionnaires. Among other questions, respondents were asked whether they employed any artificial measures to prevent pregnancy. Only 28 respondents

56 Blek, "Usloviia truda rabochikh," 80; Dementeev, "Zhenskii fabrichnyi trud," 11–12.
57 M. Pokrovskaia, "Peterburgskie rabochie i ikh ekonomicheskoe polozhenie," *Vestnik Evropy*, no. 3 (Mar.–Apr. 1899): 333.
58 These figures omit all the women who might have returned along with them: 27.3 percent of married men had children in the village. Cited in S.N. Semanov, *Peterburgskie rabochie nakanune pervoi russkoi revoliutsii* (Moscow–Leningrad, 1966), 51.
59 Laura Engelstein, "Abortion and the Civic Order: The Legal and Medical Debates," in *Russia's Women: Accommodation, Resistance, Transformation*, ed. Barbara Clements, Barbara Engel, and Christine Worobec (Berkeley, Calif., 1991), 185–207.

replied, perhaps because they felt that their sexual practices were nobody's business but their own, quite likely because most birth control methods, and abortion in particular, were illegal. Fifteen of those who responded said merely, yes, they tried to limit pregnancy. The few who provided more specifics referred to abortion as often as they did to contraception. Women drank chamomile or "drops," or subjected themselves to hot baths. This led Vigdorchik to conclude that these respondents had misunderstood the question. More likely, their answers reflect an attitude similar to the one that Angus McLaren has identified among English working-class women of an earlier period. In the circumstances of working-class life, the Englishwomen found abortion to be the most convenient means of birth control and, unlike coitus interruptus, a method that was under the woman's control. In the decades after the Revolution of 1917, when abortion became legal and was the only available method of birth control, working-class wives and mothers would widely employ it to limit the number of their children, until abortion again became illegal in the mid 1930s.[60] The more cultured the couple, the more likely they were to try to limit the number of their children, investigators found, suggesting yet again the connection between a growing sense of working-class dignity and heightened expectations of personal life. The responses to the questionnaire led Vigdorchik to conclude that "in the working-class milieu, the demand to limit fertility is obviously becoming pressing."[61] But while demand might be pressing, it was rarely satisfied. Even in this sample of relatively skilled and well-paid workers – half of the men were metalworkers – the majority of women were unable or unwilling to limit the number of their pregnancies. The 367 women respondents became pregnant, on the average, almost every two years.

Women's lack of control over their fertility made it all the more difficult to combine wifehood and motherhood with waged labor. Their double burden led many women to leave the waged labor force, at least temporarily, if it was at all feasible financially. Here, the husband's earning capacity could be decisive. Vigdorchik's survey found that a woman's participation in the wage-labor force was directly linked to the wages her husband earned. More than half of the wives (398 women) did not work for wages outside their households: When the husband earned over fifty rubles a month (six hundred rubles per year), a mere 6.6 percent of the wives went out to work; if

---

60 Angus McLaren, "Women's Work and Regulation of Family Size," *History Workshop* 4 (Autumn 1977), 70–81; Wendy Goldman, "Women, Abortion, and the State, 1917–1936," in Clements, Engel, and Worobec, eds., *Russia's Women*, 243–66.
61 Vigdorchik, "Detskaia smertnost'," 248; also 250–1.

the men earned between thirty-one and fifty rubles, 70 percent of the wives stayed home; even when men earned under twenty rubles a month, a pitiable sum, over 40 percent of their wives did not work full-time for wages.[62] Among relatively poorly paid textile workers, where a second worker was essential to survival in the city, the second worker was not necessarily the wife. According to one survey, wives in about 10 percent of textile workers' families remained at home.[63]

It is hard to know how typical such surveys are. Their respondents were workers who were more highly urbanized and educated than the vast majority of St. Petersburg's labor force, especially after the Stolypin reforms of 1906–7, which brought a flood of young and unskilled laborers into Russia's cities.[64] But other evidence suggests that if anything, they overstated the proportion of workers' wives who were themselves employed full-time. One source of evidence is the registration lists for the Society of the Drop of Milk. Aimed at reducing infant mortality, the Society was founded in 1901 and modeled on existing organizations in Western Europe. It dispensed sterilized milk daily to lower-class infants; and twice a month, its physicians provided medical examinations for the babies and advice to their mothers.[65] Unlike purely philanthropic organizations, which aided the utterly destitute, the Society served a clientele consisting of the working poor and, occasionally, the lower middle class. The society was located in the first quarter of the Narva district. The majority of mothers came from neighboring working-class sections of either the Narva district or the Alexander-Nevskii, where the proportion of dependents to wage earners was the second highest in the city. Crowded together in tenements along Ligovskaia Street, the Obvodnyi Canal, and Zabalkanskii Prospect, some residents of these districts earned their livings as craftsmen or artisans, but most were skilled and unskilled workers.[66] The clientele of the Society, comprised overwhelmingly of waged laborers, reflects this social milieu.

Despite men's meager earnings, it was rare for both husband and wife to go out to work when the husband was employed. This is not to deny the existence of dual-earning couples such as the Meshcherenkos or the

62 Ibid., 217–18.

63 Davidovich, "Khoziaistvennoe znachenie," 122. Prokopovich's survey of St. Petersburg's working class simply assumes that the wife does not earn money.

64 Robert McKean, *St. Petersburg between the Revolutions: June 1907–February 1917* (New Haven, Conn., 1990), is particularly good on the character of the post-Stolypin workforce.

65 V.O. Gubert, " 'Kaplia moloka' v Rossii, kak sredstvo bor'by s ranneiu detskoiu smertnost'iu," *Obshchestvennoe i chastnoe prizrenie v Rossii* (St. Petersburg, 1907), 243–7.

66 Eremeev, ed., *Gorod S.-Peterburg*, 520–64.

Alekseenkos. Both men were metalworkers, earning a ruble and a half a day, and forty rubles a month, respectively. Mrs. Meshcherenko (her name is not listed) had two children and earned twenty-two rubles a month as a factory worker; Mrs. Alekseenko, the mother of four and also a factory worker, brought home eighty-five kopeks a day.[67] But such couples were unusual among the clientele of the Society: In 1913, no more then 28 of the 107 wives (26 percent) whose husbands brought home wages labored full-time away from home. Even this number might be too large. Several months after bearing a child, 5 of the 28 working mothers had not yet returned to their jobs. Thirteen of the women workers were employed in factories; the others were laundresses (10), tradeswomen (2), seamstresses (2), and one was an un-skilled laborer. Her husband's wages was the most significant factor sending the wife out to work: Only three of the husbands of working women earned thirty-five rubles a month or more, and eighteen earned twenty rubles a month or less working as shop assistants, bookbinders, tradesmen, or, by far the most common, unskilled laborers. When they went out to work, a third of the women left three or more children behind, presumably in the care of older siblings or an older woman.[68]

On the other hand, a husband's miserable earnings did not invariably send his wife out to work full-time. Over two-thirds (fifty-eight) of the eighty-three husbands of women at home earned twenty-five rubles or less a month, and thirty-two of these earned less than twenty rubles. Only four earned the fifty rubles a month or more that Sergei Prokopovich estimated was necessary to support a family in St. Petersburg in 1909. Some of these women had probably never worked for wages and had come already burdened with children to join their husbands in the city. But other women quit their jobs to stay home, to care for children and to keep house, although a woman's "house" was most commonly a corner of a room. Maria Vasilieva is typical. Vasilieva worked in a factory earning twenty rubles a month until she quit two days before giving birth to her fourth child, probably because the cost of child care for four children would have absorbed virtually her entire wage. Her husband, an unskilled laborer, brought home eighty kopeks a day.[69] Another woman, a literate, twenty-two-year-old tailor married to a twenty-three-year-old soldier, had earned twelve rubles a month before quitting her

---

67 TsGIAL, fond 251, op. 1, ed. kh. 5, 326, 526. The lists rarely name the workplace of the clientele.
68 There is no apparent correlation between the number of children and their mother's decision to stay at home.
69 TsGIAL, fond 251, op. 1, ed. kh. 5, 344–7.

job six months before the birth of her first child. Because women had to
bring their babies to the dispensary, taking time off and losing wages if they
were employed, the Drop of Milk sample may be skewed toward mothers
who stayed at home.

The evidence of the few house administration books that have survived
from buildings with substantial numbers of working-class inhabitants suggests a similar pattern, however, and for childless wives as well as women
with children. Among the thirty working-class couples residing at 14/2
Nizhegorodskaia Street in 1908–9, for example, a mere three of the wives
went out to work, two as servants and one as a laundress. The vast majority
of the "dependent" women were young (under thirty), and all but three of
them had no children. Most were married to unskilled laborers. In 1912,
twenty-six working-class couples lived at 18 Zabalkanskii Prospect, located
in the fourth section of the Moscow quarter. A third of the husbands were
employed as unskilled laborers. Although most men earned very little, twenty-
two of their wives (seven with children) were recorded as dependents. All
of the wives who earned wages were unskilled laborers. Next door, at 20
Zabalkanskii Prospect, there were forty working-class couples in residence
in 1913. Twenty-one of the men were unskilled laborers, the rest worked
as stonemasons, waiters, fitters, typesetters, carpenters, shoemakers, watch-
men, and the like. Although only nine of the couples had children, all the
wives were recorded as dependent with the exception of the wife of a carpenter from Galich, Kostroma, who was employed full-time as a servant.[70]
Lack of opportunity does not explain the wives' dependent status. These
buildings were inhabited by substantial numbers of unskilled women workers
(workplace undesignated) and a few skilled ones, but the women workers
were single, widowed, or living apart from their husbands.

Lack of opportunity is equally implausible as an explanation for the
pattern we find at 16 Bol'shoi Sampsonievskii Prospect in 1915. The building was situated in the second section of the Vyborg quarter, where several
textile factories were located, and it was one of the most heavily working-
class neighborhoods in St. Petersburg.[71] Ten of the thirty working-class

---

70 TsGIAL, fond 1026, op. 1, delo 173 and 200. The number of working-class couples had
grown dramatically since 1910, when only fourteen such couples had been in residence. See
delo 198. I have included only workers of peasant origin.

71 Ibid., delo 442. Among the residents were Sergei and Olga Alliluev, the future in-laws of
Joseph Stalin, but the fourteen-year-old Natasha, his future wife, was not living with them.
Although the book supposedly covered the year 1915, in fact registrations began much
earlier in January 1914.

husbands were metalworkers, but an even larger number, thirteen, were unskilled laborers. Although many women workers (mostly unskilled) lived in the building too, only one of them was married and living with her husband. An unskilled worker, she was married to a peasant from Iaroslavl', also an unskilled worker. Only one of the wives listed as dependents had children living with her. While their categories cannot be correlated so as to show in comparable detail the patterns that house administration books reveal, census materials suggest a similar picture. In 1902, for example, the Moscow census indicated that 41 percent of married women supported themselves, as compared to 80 percent of other women.[72]

Economically dependent women represented a significant modification of the gender division of labor in the village, including villages near rural factories, where so long as they remained close to home, women were able to engage in productive activity and, at the same time, to attend to their households and rear children, often with the help of the extended family. If anything, women's productive activity took precedence over child care and housework in the village, an ordering of priorities that may have contributed to the unusually high rates of infant mortality among Russian peasants.[73] In the city, the extraordinary difficulty of combining full-time wage earning with motherhood and running even a tiny household led migrants to make a different choice and to give precedence to child care and housework, broadly construed. In the words of M. Davidovich, if it was at all feasible, the working-class family "tried to keep the mother of a family at home." Their efforts had little in common with middle-class ideas about a proper family life or aspirations to having an "angel in the home." These ideas were just developing in Russia; there is no evidence that they influenced the working class. The desire to have a wife at home, however, does suggest a growing working-class (male?) desire for comfort, however modest, and concern for the well-being and future of children. Studies showed that infant mortality rates were lower when the wife did not work for wages. There were other reasons to stay home as well. Observers were convinced that a woman at home compensated for the loss of her wages by creating a higher level of material well-being than a woman who went off to work.[74] Married women may have left the labor force in Russia with immense relief. There can be no question that many men longed to leave it. As P. Timofeev

72 Johnson, "Mothers and Daughters," 370.
73 David Ransel, "Infant-Care Cultures in the Russian Empire," in Clements, Engel, and Worobec, eds., *Russia's Women*, 116–9.
74 Davidovich, "Khoziaistvennoe znachenie," 122.

wrote of factory workers, "I have rarely met anyone who did not dream of changing his occupation. . . . [They] lived in the hope that they would someday scrape up enough money to leave the factory behind so as not to be bound by any bosses or factory whistles."[75] Some women workers clearly dreamed of changing their lives as well. Of the thirteen factory women who attended advanced classes at the Smolensk Sunday School at the turn of the century, five used them as an avenue of mobility out of the laboring class.[76] Natalia Agafonova had worked as a typesetter in Moscow before her marriage to a wheelwright in 1901, but she stopped working immediately after the wedding.[77] Alfred Kelly, discussing the German working class, put the matter succinctly: "Work usually equaled body and soul-destroying drudgery; it was something to be avoided. Most working-class men (and probably women too) felt that it was the height of good sense and decency to subject as few family members as possible to the hardships of work."[78]

To point this out is not to argue that married working-class women were invariably just wives and mothers, nor to take issue with Rose Glickman's contention that "a growing segment among women workers was as fully proletarian, as stable in the factory, as it was possible for a worker to be in tsarist Russia."[79] But it is to contend that married factory women constituted a minority of the women married to and living with working-class men. This was certainly the case in 1897, and there is no reason to believe that circumstances in Moscow and St. Petersburg became more hospitable to working-class family life afterward, in the years before World War I.

At the same time, census takers' or building administrators' reports of wives who had "no occupation" and supposedly "lived on the husband's

75 Timofeev, "What the Factory Worker Lives By," 101.
76 Glickman, *Russian Factory Women*, 140.
77 TsGIA SSSR, fond 1412, op. 212, delo 31, 7.
78 Alfred Kelly, ed., *The German Worker: Working-Class Autobiographies from the Age of Industrialization* (Berkeley, Calif., 1987), 25. Jane Humphries makes a similar point, from a different perspective, in "Class Struggles and the Persistence of the Working-Class Family," *Cambridge Journal of Economic History*, no. 1 (1977): 241–58.
79 Glickman, *Russian Factory Women*, 90. I do question whether in the cities of Moscow and St. Petersburg, the proportion of married women in the factory labor force increased from two-fifths to about one-half between 1880 and 1908, as Glickman asserts on page 104. The data she uses to support her contention are drawn from Moscow province as a whole, where more women were employed outside the city than within it. In 1897, almost 48 percent of the women working outside the city were married (as compared to 32.2 percent of urban women workers); whatever their marital status, 64 percent of women workers outside of the city of Moscow lived in a family situation, in striking contrast to their sisters in the city. As we saw in Chapter 4, in rural areas family and kin networks facilitated the employment of married women, even when they had children.

wages" are misleading. Most observers ignored the casual labor of "unemployed" wives, work that was irregular and poorly paid but flexible enough
to allow a woman to tend to her family's needs, a pattern of women's work
similar to the one that prevailed elsewhere in Europe.[80] We know virtually
nothing about such women's lives, by contrast with the lives of women
workers, which Rose Glickman has illuminated so well.

It was virtually impossible for families to survive on only the man's wages
in cities as expensive as Moscow or St. Petersburg, even when the family
lived crowded together in a corner of a room, as did thirty-five of the clients
of the Drop of Milk whose husbands were listed as sole breadwinners. In
order to help to make ends meet while remaining at home, the wife took in
washing or sewing, hired out as a cleaning woman from time to time, or took
in boarders to earn the extra income the family needed. The Onufriev family
is typical not only in the patterns of the wife's labor but also in that she had
come to the city after her marriage in the village, as did the majority of
working-class wives, I suspect.[81] In 1885, Pyotr Onufriev brought his wife,
Olga Nikitichna, and their four children from the village to live in one room
of a five-room apartment, a five-minute walk away from the Baltic Shipyards, where Onufriev was employed as a metalworker. Because his wages
could not support such a large family, Olga Nikitichna hired out by the day,
doing laundry and washing the floors of wealthy families.[82] When another,
equally large working-class family was unable to live on the thirty to thirty-
five rubles a month that the father earned at the Guzhon factory in Moscow,
the mother helped by doing laundry and washing floors for the factory
administrator. In return for two days a week of such work, she might bring
home between eighty kopeks and a ruble. But her wages were supplemented
by benefits in kind, particularly likely to appeal to the mother of a large
family. Her employers provided her meals and allowed her to take home the
leftovers from their table to give to her children.[83] The person who filled out
the registration forms for the Society of the Drop of Milk, or the husbands
who usually provided the information, ignored this casual labor just like
everyone else, or perhaps husbands tried to conceal it for fear of losing

---

80 See the discussion in Tilly and Scott, *Women, Work, and Family*, 129–45.
81 This suspicion is based upon no systematic survey, but on my impression from the data in
   house administration books and the continuing low rates of urban marriage compared to
   rates in the countryside. Drop of Milk records shed no light on this question.
82 E. Onufriev, *Za nevskoi zastavoi* (*Vospominaniia starogo bol'shevika*) (Moscow, 1968), 4–5.
83 TsGAOR SSSR, fond 7952, op. 3, delo 273, 27. See also P.G. Timofeev, *Chem zhivet
   zavodskoi rabochii* (St. Petersburg, 1906), 87.

benefits. The prevalance of such casual labor explains the apparent contradiction found in so many of the registration forms: The wife is not employed, they declare, and on the same page, they note that she worked until the very last days of her pregnancy and resumed working within a few days or weeks of giving birth.

The most common source of supplemental income was to take in boarders. A married couple would rent an apartment, taking one of the rooms or a corner of one of the rooms for themselves and subletting the rest by the room, by the corner, or even by the bed to single workers or to other families. This arrangement might enable a couple to afford a life together in the city. That was what the Dorofeevs hoped. A stonemason by trade, in 1893 Dorofeev worked at the Okhta powder plant in the suburbs, where he shared a room with the Semenov brothers. His wife lived with her cousin in the heart of St. Petersburg, spending the night with her husband from time to time while the couple searched for an apartment near his workplace that would be large enough to rent corners to workers. Anna Ivanova, a needleworker, quit her job at a workshop and began to work at home in 1908 after she married Aleksei Fillipov, a worker at the Bromlei factory in Moscow. In 1913, they moved into a three-room apartment in a small wooden house near the Donskoi Monastery. They rented one of the rooms to a lodger, Aleksei's mother and younger brother occupied another, and the couple took the third room for themselves.[84] Often, subletting helped to solve the problem of both supporting and caring for children. Families with more then two children were particularly likely to rent to boarders. The story of the Aleksandrovs illustrates the pattern. Pavel Aleksandrov, a landless peasant from Tver', came to St. Petersburg in 1896 and found work at the Putilov Metalworking plant; two years later, his wife, two daughters, and son left the village to join him. Aleksandrova did not go out to work. To earn more money, Pavel made items like trunks at home in his spare time. But children continued to arrive and his expenses to grow. In 1906, there were ten mouths to feed in his household. According to his son, he began to rent apartments of two and then three rooms, and to take in boarders with large families like his own, keeping the kitchen and the dark storeroom for his family's use.[85]

Such arrangements helped to cover the extraordinarily high cost of housing.

84 *Sudebnaia gazeta*, no. 13, 31 (Mar. 1891): 9–10; TsGAOR SSSR, fond 7952, op. 3, delo 96, 122.
85 Aleksandrov, *Za Narvskoi*, 20.

Boarders who paid nine to ten rubles a month for a room, or five and a half rubles for a corner could cover most of the rent. Renting a damp and dark apartment in the second section of Vyborg for nineteen rubles a month, the Baranovs charged their four boarders five and a half rubles apiece. Without this arrangement, the family could not have survived on the seventy kopeks a day that Baranov earned as an unskilled laborer at the Vil'kens plant.[86] Of the families with "unemployed" wives who received milk from the Society of the Drop of Milk in 1913, at least thirteen (16 percent) rented rooms or corners to boarders, judging by the rents people paid. Other than by taking in boarders, how else could a family afford rents ranging from twenty-six to forty-two rubles a month for an apartment, when the wife was unemployed and the husband earned, on the average, between twenty and twenty-five rubles a month?[87] Thus, some couples devised ways to wed and cohabit, despite the low wages of the husband.

In return for the rent the family received from boarders, the *khoziaika* (roughly, landlady) assumed a substantial workload. A *khoziaika* looked after the entire apartment, fetched the wood to heat it, brought in water if there was no indoor plumbing, kept the kitchen in order, and heated the cookstove. She also provided personal services for her boarders. Rising around 5:00 A.M., she boiled water for their tea. She cooked, cleaned, and for a few more kopeks did laundry for the bachelors, and if both adults worked for wages, she sometimes cleaned up after families as well. A *khoziaika* received about sixty kopeks a month from each of the adult boarders in return for cooking and cleaning. For an additional three to four rubles a month, she might look after their children too. At the end of the long day, a *khoziaika* was thoroughly worn out from racing from shop to shop, and cleaning up and looking after her own children. And if her family needed additional income, the *khoziaika* took in sewing and washing or hired out to wash floors on a daily basis.[88] It is hard to know how representative the Society of the Drop of Milk sample is, or how many working-class *khoziaiki* there were. Urban censuses underreported their numbers because proprietors of buildings often tried to conceal this source of income. Different studies of working-

---

86 TsGIA SSSR, fond 1409, op. 15, ed. kh. 170 (1902); see also ed. kh. 840.
87 I suspect that the proportion letting space was closer to 50 percent and that most of the thirty-two families that rented a room sublet a corner of that room to someone else. How else could an unskilled laborer with four children earning eighteen rubles a month afford nine rubles rent for a room? Or a worker with four children and a wage of twenty-five rubles afford to pay ten rubles in rent for a room?
88 Davidovich, "Khoziaistvennoe znachenie," 124; Krupianskaia, "Evoliutsiia semeino-bytovogo," 277.

class life yield different percentages. Very likely their numbers increased after 1905, along with the number of working-class families living together in the city.

Unless women were employed full-time, it is difficult to calculate their contributions to the family budget in terms of cash. Studies of working-class budgets, which rely on calculations of rubles and kopeks and tend to ignore contributions in kind, seriously underreport the economic significance of the "unemployed" wife's labor. As the student of working-class life M. Davidovich argued at length, it was a mistake to evaluate a wife's contributions only in terms of cash.[89] To cash earnings should be added rent money saved and the fact that renting to lodgers often ensured a family at least a room of their own. Moreover, whatever the wife did to supplement income, when she was at home the family's standard of living improved. Renting out rooms or taking in washing or sewing allowed a more flexible schedule than working full-time in a factory or shop, where work could last more than twelve hours, and enabled the woman to care for her household and children. Mothers could nurse their infants longer and care for them better, lowering infant mortality rates. Living quarters tended to be cleaner and better kept. And even when her staying home lowered the family income, family members tended to eat better and more nourishing meals, because the housewife had time to stretch a ruble and vary the diet and to prepare hot meals every day. When she came home from washing, doing laundry, and scrubbing floors for the factory administration, one working-class wife and mother prepared a hot meal of cabbage soup, with a second course of boiled potatoes and peas, or buckwheat kasha. She made clothing for herself and underwear for the entire family. Another, in addition to hiring out by the day, made clothing for her four children, washed and mended for her family, and prepared hot food every day. "Mother's life was hardest of all," her son remembered.[90]

Despite the economic significance of the wife's labor in the home, caring for boarders or engaging in casual labor tended to reinforce traditional authority patterns in the household, and to limit a woman's contacts with the larger world. Most working-class men assumed the prerogatives of their peasant fathers and brothers, running the affairs of their own household and managing financial and other transactions with outsiders. "My father was the master of the house," remembered the son of a worker at the Guzhon

---

89 Davidovich, "Khoziaistvennoe znachenie," 128–9.
90 TsGAOR SSSR, fond 7952, op. 3, delo 273, 27; Onufriev, *Za nevskoi zastavoi*, 4. Onufriev was one of very few male working-class authors to pay attention to his mother, and the only one that I read who actually named her.

factory, himself a worker. "He had all the authority and we all obeyed him until we were grown."[91] Although it was the mother who brought her infant to the Society of the Drop of Milk every morning, most commonly, the father became spokesman for the family, taking charge of responding to questions for the registration lists.[92]

In most cases, it was the husband who decided to rent to boarders too. Husbands took the rent from them and assumed ultimate responsibility for their well-being.[93] When Praskovia Timofeeva, mother of one child, left the apartment without heating water for their lodgers, her husband, Fyodor, a fitter, sat on her neck and beat her until a neighbor dragged him away.[94] Men were more likely than their wives to succumb to the temptation to make a little more money by squeezing in a few more beds and taking on a few more boarders. The feminist physician Maria Pokrovskaia was convinced that if it were up to the wife, she would prefer to live in a tiny room and to have no boarders at all. Boarders generated conflicts and sometimes more work than a woman with children could accomplish by herself. *Khoziaiki* were notoriously pale and exhausted. Serving an artel of men was hardest of all, and women did it only when the husband insisted.[95]

Whether or not a woman worked full-time away from home, her horizons were often more limited than her husband's. She was far less likely than he to be able to read. A woman migrant from the village might live for decades in the city and remain unable to decipher a street sign, or read an advertisement, or scratch her name on a piece of paper. This was true of virtually every one of the hundreds of migrant peasant women who appealed to the Philanthropic Fund of the Empress Maria for assistance between 1890 and 1914. For example, Elizaveta Zhukova, forty-nine, was a migrant from Iaroslavl' and the wife of a shoemaker. She stayed at home, looked after her husband and their two children, and served several boarders. In 1899, thirty-three years after first settling in St. Petersburg, she still could not read. Fekla Barinova, thirty-eight and married to a worker at the Arsenal, took in wash and looked after her two small children. In 1905, after sixteen years of living in St. Petersburg, she, too, was illiterate. Literate men were apparently

91 TsGAOR SSSR, fond 7952, op. 3, delo 273, 25.
92 This contrasts with philanthropic organizations, to which women ordinarily appealed for assistance even when husbands were alive and in residence (although invariably ailing). In this case, families may have tried to take advantage of notions of women's helplessness.
93 In his study of working-class budgets, Prokopovich attributes the income from renting to the male head of household (*rabochii-kvartiroderzhatel'*), 64.
94 *Sudebnyi vestnik*, no. 61 (1875): 3–4.
95 Pokrovskaia, "Moia dumskaia praktika," 24–7.

unable or unwilling to share those skills with their wives. In 1904, Marfa Konovodova, a migrant from Tver', lost her husband, a skilled and literate worker at the Baltic Shipyards. Until his death, she had supplemented his wage of one ruble, forty kopeks a day by taking care of boarders in their three-room apartment in Vyborg 3. When he died she was still illiterate, although she had lived with him in the city for over a decade.[96] Literate women are much more numerous among couples receiving assistance from the Drop of Milk in 1911–13; even so, women's literacy remained a fraction of men's. In 1913, 88 percent of the husbands said they could read, as compared to 44 percent of the wives. Whether women worked in a factory or took in laundry or stayed at home made little difference: Literacy rates of women who worked full-time for wages were virtually identical to the rates for women who did not. Although some literate husbands and sons probably read aloud to women as the women went about their household tasks, women's inability to read limited their capacity to respond on their own to the cultural and political opportunities offered by urban life.

Women's social contacts were likely to be limited as well. We know remarkably little about women's workplace culture, which historians of other times and places have found to be an important element in women's organization and resistance.[97] Outside the workplace, however, women's opportunities for contact were highly circumscribed, because the length of their working day and the burden of their domestic labors left them no time to socialize outside the workplace, especially if they worked full-time. Women did not gather in the tavern or the pub as men so often did, not only because they had no time for it, but also because women who frequented such places were considered to be prostitutes.[98] As a result, women, and especially women who did not work for wages, interacted chiefly with neighbors and with kin. In Russia, as we have seen, family networks and regional or *zemliak* ties helped to cushion the shock of urban life for migrant men and women and to provide a measure of support in hard times. These systems operated in the lives of married couples as well. For example, of the thirty Russian working-class couples residing at 14/2 Nizhegorodskaia Street, five had a kinsman or woman in the very same building; two more shared an apartment

---

96 TsGIA SSSR, fond 1409, op. 15, ed. kh. 173, 820, 1122.
97 See Sandra Morgan, "Beyond the Double Day: Work and Family in Working-Class Women's Lives," *Feminist Studies*, 16, no. 1 (Spring 1990): 53–67.
98 Catriona Kelly, " 'Better Halves'? Representations of Women in Russian Urban Popular Entertainments, 1870–1900," in *Women and Society in Russia and the Soviet Union*, ed. Linda Edmondson (New York, 1992), 12–13.

with *zemliaki*. Kinship ties sometimes helped to structure the lives of women who appealed to philanthropic associations, although such women, among the most desperate of the urban poor, were probably least likely to have close kin in the city. In 1905, for example, Evdokiia Egoreva appealed to the Empress Maria's fund only because her sons were treating her badly. A migrant from Tambov, Egoreva had been in St. Petersburg for twenty-seven years and lived with her two grown sons, both turners at the Baltic Shipyards, in a two-room apartment with a kitchen. Their complex household arrangements suggest how kin connections might adapt themselves to the circumstances of urban life. In the apartment lived the lover of Egoreva's twenty-seven-year-old son. A niece of forty who had separated from her husband lived there, too, together with her illegitimate four-month-old and her son of twenty-two, also a shipyard worker.[99] Other sources also suggest the important role that kinship often played in the lives of the laboring poor. After he stopped living with his parents at the age of seventeen, angry because they dressed him so poorly that he was ashamed to appear on the streets, a young worker at the Guzhon factory in Moscow moved in with his uncle. As soon as Aleksei Filippov, a worker at the Bromlei factory in Moscow, rented a three-room apartment in 1913, he settled his mother and younger brother in one of the rooms.[100] Kin could usually be expected to lend a hand when relatives were in need, although the longer peasants lived in the city, the less likely they became to respond to appeals for assistance.[101] Nevertheless, without even being asked, godparents and relatives who were marginally better off might give children articles of clothing such as hats, shoes, and jackets.[102]

Urban family life itself was rarely situated in a privileged private space: The quarters that most couples shared provided virtually no privacy. In dormitories or apartments, couples rarely had even a room to themselves. Although the revolution of 1905 improved working-class wages and the living standards of an elite of workers, for the majority of recent migrants, living conditions remained at least as crowded after 1905 as before. The

99  TsGIA SSSR, fond 1409, op. 15, ed. kh. 820. See also ed. kh. 63 (1902); 4 (1904); 595 (1904); 154 (1908); 143 (1911); 4 (1913); 1592 (1913); 919 (1913).

100 TsGAOR SSSR, fond 7952, op. 3, delo 273, 25–6; delo 66, 122.

101 For examples, see TsGIA SSSR, fond 1409, op. 15, ed. kh. 1104, 1910. For the decline of mutual aid in the city, see the discussion in S.N. Prokopovich, "Biudzhety Peterburgskikh rabochikh," *Zapiski Russkago tekhnicheskago obshchestva*, 43, no. 3 (1909): 101–2.

102 Davidovich, *Peterburgskii tekstil'nyi rabochii*, 68; E.P. Kalacheva, "Bezplatnyi narodnyi detskii sad i sel'sko-khoziaistvennyi priiut," *Trudovaia pomoshch*, no. 5 (May 1903): 214–15; Kabo, *Ocherki rabochego byta*, 136–7.

influx of migrants after 1906–7 simply overwhelmed scarce facilities and drove up rents more quickly than wages. According to historian Iurii Kirianov, almost 52 percent of textile workers' families in Moscow and St. Petersburg occupied less than a room in 1908, and 45 percent occupied less than a room as late as 1914. Recent work by Robert McKean has suggested that even these figures are overly rosy and that the housing situation of the majority of workers deteriorated after 1905.[103] The records of the Drop of Milk support his point. In 1912–13, the overwhelming majority of the families to whom the Society dispensed milk could afford to rent only a corner, or at most half of a room, for five to six and a half rubles a month, unless they rented an apartment or a room and took in lodgers, as approximately a quarter of the families did. Under such circumstances, it was impossible to get away from everyone else. "You can't even spit without everyone noticing it," as one working-class woman put it.[104] All of life, "down to its most intimate details," took place before everyone's eyes.[105] Living cheek by jowl with boarders – if not in the same room, then almost invariably in a neighboring one – meant perennial quarrels and conflicts, but it also made it easier to know what someone else needed and to provide it.

Women's neighborly contacts provided important sources of support. They extended across differences of occupation and linked women together whether or not they left the household to earn wages. The poor practiced a customary kind of philanthropy, sharing the little they had with those who had even less. When they received meat, bread, and other goods from kin in the village, women might contribute some of it to a destitute neighbor. The poor woman who had extra scraps of bread or leftover cabbage soup was likely to share them with the needier family downstairs. Servants who worked for the well-to-do would collect cast-off clothing and scraps of food from the kitchen in order to distribute them to destitute families.[106] In the city as in the village, married women found sociability and gained support from kin and community. This support helped women to fulfill their responsibilities as wives and mothers and to provide for their children. The connections surely helped women to coordinate their actions later, when they engaged in bread riots during the wartime years. However, the transiency of lower-class

103 McKean, *St. Petersburg*, 39–41.
104 F.P. Pavlov, "Ten Years of Experience (Excerpts from Reminiscences, Impressions, and Observations of Factory Life)," in Bonnell, ed., *The Russian Worker*, 126.
105 M. and O., "Tsifry i fakty iz perepisi Sankt-Peterburga v 1900 g.," *Russkaia mysl'* 23, no 2 (Feb. 1902): 77.
106 Davidovich, *Peterburgskii tekstil'nyi rabochii*, 68; Kalacheva, "Bezplatyi narodnyi," 214.

life may have deprived some women of even this neighborly support. With few material goods to their names, many working-class families moved around a lot in the city, forever in search of more favorable circumstances. Close to half of the migrant peasant couples living at 14/2 Nizhegorodskaia Street remained in the building less than six months before moving on. Sergei Zhirnov, a metalworker in Moscow, remembered that his parents moved from one basement apartment to another ten times between 1898 and 1914, seeking the best accommodations they could get for their seven to ten rubles a month rent.[107] Transiency left families more isolated and vulnerable and probably more dependent on the wages of the husband.

The isolation mattered much less to men, who were more likely to seek sociability with co-workers than with neighbors. The tavern allowed men to meet with their mates and to escape from overcrowded apartments, wailing infants, and dulling routine. Drinking together helped to forge bonds between men. Alcohol, usually vodka, was an essential element in many workplace rituals, and it accompanied virtually every working-class social occasion. Few men abstained entirely, and married workers were even more likely to indulge than single ones: According to one count, 84.4 percent of all single workers and 91.5 percent of married ones spent part of their income on drink and tobacco. To be sure, by comparison with workers elsewhere, Russians did not drink that much – about half as much as Germans, on identical salaries, and slightly less than the English workers of Lancashire. And married workers spent a lower percentage of their income on drink than single men did. Nevertheless, the amount married men spent annually on drink and tobacco grew as their incomes did, both in terms of the number of rubles and as a proportion of the family food budget, at least until income reached the high of eight hundred rubles per year.[108]

While a man's drinking might forge bonds with other men, it could

---

107 TsGAOR SSSR, 7952, op. 3, delo 95, 11.
108 Prokopovich, "Biudzhety," *Zapiski*, no. 3, 93; N.K. Druzhinin, *Usloviia byta rabochikh v dorevoliutsionnoi Rossii* (Moscow, 1958), 52; Davidovich, *Peterburgskii tekstil'nyi rabochii*, 69; Michael Anderson, *Family Structure in Nineteenth-Century Lancashire* (Cambridge, 1981), 70. Textile workers with an income of up to three hundred rubles per year spent on the average five rubles, or 5.4 percent of the food budget, on alcohol and tobacco, while textile workers earning between three hundred and eight hundred rubles spent thirty-eight rubles on the average, or 10.5 percent of the family food budget. Prokopovich's study of a more highly qualified group of workers gives a different result: In his sample, alcohol absorbed only 3 percent of the food budget of workers earning three hundred to four hundred rubles a year, and 3.4 percent of the budgets of those earning up to eight hundred rubles. S.N. Prokopovich, "Biudzhety Peterburgskikh rabochikh," *Zapiski Russkago tekhnicheskago obshchestva*, 43, no. 2 (Feb. 1909): 65; no. 3, 93.

corrode his ties to his family. No one has successfully calculated the proportion of working-class men who seriously abused alcohol. But anyone who
reads working-class memoirs, both published and archival, cannot help but
be struck by how often alcoholic fathers or comrades figure in the narrative,
and the enormous toll that men's drinking took on other members of their
families.[109] E.S. Goriacheva, a textile worker, remembered that her father
was a willing worker and a kindly and hospitable man, but excessively fond
of the bottle. His drinking bouts would last a week, ending only when he had
expended not only his own wages but her mother's as well, so that the family
had nothing to eat until the mother borrowed money from someone against
her next week's wages. Vasilii Zhirnov had lived in Moscow almost since
childhood, earning his livelihood as an unskilled laborer, then apprenticing
as a metalworker, and finally working as a shoemaker; his wife was a fringe
maker who worked at home. Together, they earned between thirty and forty
rubles a month, but because Vasilii spent most of his income on drink, the
family subsisted primarily on bread and water. In the words of his son,
Sergei Vasilievich, "The times when father wasn't drunk my mother considered a holiday, because there were no brawls, no one was driven from the
apartment, and the family's diet improved."[110] A man's drinking was particularly hard on the family when the woman earned no income of her own.
A. Serov, a worker at the Bromlei factory in Moscow, lodged with a co-
worker, also a metalworker, in 1898. The wife of his comrade stayed at home
with her three children and looked after the apartment and their four boarders. Every evening, exhausted from her long day, she would wait nervously
for her husband to return. As soon as he knocked, she raced to open the
door. If he returned in a "normal" state, that is, only slightly tipsy, she
would smile, Serov recalled. But even when her husband came home drunk,
she would say not a word, merely taking off his shoes and putting him to
bed. Only the following morning would she plead with him to cease taking
bread from the mouths of their children. The masculine society of the tavern
tempted him at least as much as the alcohol itself. Her efforts to convince

---

109 For example, Semyon Karpukhin's father, a stove maker in a series of Moscow factories,
   drank a lot. He would often come home drunk and make such a fuss that his wife, a textile
   worker, was forced to take refuge at a neighbor's to avoid his fists. See TsGAOR SSSR,
   fond 7952, op. 3, delo 273, 30; and also 26–7, a different memoir. While drunken fathers
   may have become a convention of postrevolutionary narrative, nevertheless the details that
   memoirs provide are sufficiently different to indicate that the convention was based on
   experience.
110 *Istoriko-kraevedcheskii sbornik*, vyp. 2 (Moscow, 1959), 216–17; TsGAOR SSSR, fond 7952,
   op. 3, delo 95, 11–32.

him to drink more cheaply at home always came to nothing after an evening or two of domesticity.[111]

Fears for their families prompted some women to contest passionately men's appropriation of money for drink. Accounts of working-class life commonly depict wives waiting outside factory gates on payday, determined to get a share of the husbands' wages. In the words of one metalworker: "Every payday, wives waited for husbands and 'expropriated' their wages. This involved considerable struggle, and sometimes the couple wound up in a brawl, with male comrades standing on the sidelines, cheering on the 'oppressed' husband."[112] Whether or not one agrees that the struggles between men and women were "class warfare," as this worker-memoirist facetiously observed, his images of disheveled, sometimes pregnant women, desperately tackling their considerably larger and stronger husbands for a share of the family income are a reminder of how much a married woman with children might be dependent on her husband's wage.

The images of struggle also confirm that the working-class family in Russia, as elsewhere in Europe, could be a site of conflict as well as of co-operation and that this conflict often arose over the allocation of family resources. Women's sense of responsibility for the family, and especially for their children, might conflict with men's loyalty to comrades and their perception that they had a right to dispose of what they earned.[113] Life in the city could foster "different centers in the emotional exchanges" between migrant men and women, women's centered on the family and men's on work.[114] Moving away from the village did not alter most peasant women's fundamental loyalty to household and family, although the move no doubt made their responsibility harder to fulfill. Even when a wife and mother left home to work full-time, the well-being of her children was usually uppermost on her mind, and "labor" and "love" were inextricably linked.

This helps to explain women and men's sometimes different responses to

111 Ibid., delo 96, 165.
112 A. Buzinov, *Za nevskoi zastavoi: Zapiski rabochego Alekseia Buzinova* (Moscow-Leningrad, 1930), 25–6. On wives outside the factory gates, see also Davidovich, *Peterburgskii tekstil'nyi rabochii* (1919), 63; A.M. Buiko, *Put' rabochego: Zapiski starogo bol'shevika* (Moscow, 1934), 15; Eremeev, ed., *Gorod S.-Peterburg*, 632.
113 For comparable assumptions in England, see Ellen Ross, " 'Fierce Questions and Taunts': Married Life in Working-Class London, 1870–1914," *Feminist Studies* 8, no. 3 (Fall 1982): 575–602.
114 Hans Medick and David Sabean, "Introduction," in *Interest and Emotion: Essays on the Study of Family and Kinship*, ed. H. Medick and D. Sabean (Cambridge, England, 1984), 15.

political involvement, which in the repressive climate of tsarist Russia might doom a person to many years of prison and exile. The risks made working-class wives suspicious and fearful; women's anxieties evoked activist men's condemnation. According to Semyon Kanatchikov, once a worker became "conscious," his personal tragedy began. "If the worker was an older family man, conflicts would immediately arise within his family, primarily with his wife, who was usually backward and uncultured. She could not understand his spiritual needs, did not share his ideals, feared and hated his friends, and grumbled and railed at him for spending money uselessly on books and for other cultural and revolutionary goals; most of all, she feared losing her breadwinner."[115] Vera Karelina, a woman of working-class background herself, was more understanding of the working-class wife's concerns. "Women are desperately anxious about the family," Karelina wrote, "and if the husband is arrested, not only he but the whole family will perish."[116]

Different family roles and occupational identities might occasionally divide working-class women. In 1905, at least one activist working woman openly resented the claims that a working-class wife might make on a husband's income and loyalty. Anna Boldyreva, a Bolshevik representative from the Maxwell textile mill, accused male metalworkers of standing back from the struggle and blamed it on their wives. "You accustom your wives to eat and sleep well, and it's therefore frightening for you to be without wages."[117] Like Kanatchikov, Boldyreva embraced a different value system than the one that village women left behind, or the one that shaped working-class domestic arrangements in which the wife remained at home. Both of them were Bolsheviks; after the revolution of 1917 they and many others continued to regard most lower-class women as backward and their power in the family as a threat to the revolution.[118]

In fact, however, working-class women exercised little power in the urban family, by comparison with women's position in the village. The rich and complex rituals in which village women played such a significant role became in the city superstitious whisperings and frequent attendance at church.

115 Reginald Zelnik, ed. *A Radical Worker in Tsarist Russia: The Autobiography of Semën Ivanovich Kanatchikov* (Stanford, Calif., 1986), 102.
116 V. Karelina, "Vospominaniia o podpol'nykh rabochikh kruzhkakh brusnevskoi organizatsii," in *V nachale puti. Vospominaniia Peterburgskikh rabochikh 1872–1897*, ed. E.A. Korol'chuk (Leningrad, 1975), 283–4.
117 Cited in Gerald Surh, *1905 in St. Petersburg: Labor, Society, and Revolution* (Stanford, Calif., 1989), 372–3.
118 Lynn Mally, *Culture of the Future: The Proletkult Movement in Revolutionary Russia* (Berkeley, Calif., 1990), chap. 6.

And in the city, women could not anticipate gaining power as they aged. The young themselves often rejected the older woman's role in arranging marriages, preferring to choose a partner for themselves. Moreover, urban families were usually nuclear, not extended, so that the older woman lost her authority over her daughters-in-law.

Reflecting, perhaps, their powerless position, working-class women did not loom large in their children's awareness. Although this is a topic that merits more systematic attention than I have given it, most of the memoirs I have read seem curiously silent about the role of the mother in the city, whether or not the woman went out to work. These mothers are most often either shadowy figures or victims of their husband's violence, in contrast with the feisty mothers who emerge from the accounts of the English working class.[119] Judging by memoirs, few seem to have valued women's endless struggle to keep their dwellings clean, the family's clothes mended, and food on the table. Life wore women down and offered little in return. The constant struggle to cover expenses, the deaths of infants, the screams of hungry children left working-class wives old before their time. In the words of E. Kabo, who surveyed working-class life in Moscow in the period immediately following the revolution, "Life seems to have passed them by, providing infrequent and minimal pleasures and an abundance of deprivation and care." Their experiences left the women irritable and bitter and fearful of change.[120]

It is hard to say whether these women's lives were any more difficult in material ways than the lives of working-class women elsewhere in Europe. However, to the working-class wife, the developing Russian proletarian culture offered no satisfactory substitute for the family values of peasant Russia, although it certainly retained male peasants' contempt for women, if in a somewhat different form than in the village. The new culture was centered around the workplace and comradeship forged at the point of production. The political organizers who helped to shape the new culture tended to conceive of the worker as generically male, although to do them justice, they recognized some needs of workers who were women and mothers, often agitating for maternity leave and child care, as well as other changes that

---

119 Ellen Ross, "Labour and Love: Rediscovering London's Working-Class Mothers, 1870–1918," in *Labour and Love: Women's Experience of Home and Family, 1850–1940*, ed. Jane Lewis (Oxford, 1986), 84–90.

120 Kabo, *Ocherki rabochego byta*, 223; see also E.P. Kalacheva, "Narodnyi detskii sad v S.-Peterburge," *Trudovaia pomoshch*, no. 7 (May 1898): 92–3.

would greatly have eased the lives of women factory workers with children, and that we still lack in the contemporary United States. The best representatives of working-class culture, the "conscious" workers, were frequently uneasy about the family and women's attachment to it, viewing both women and the family as hostile forces, antithetical to the workers' collective as they conceived of it. For reasons explored in this chapter, their perception may often have been correct.

Denying the significance of the family and women's role did not make them go away, however; it simply kept them hidden from view. The denial permitted a master narrative of Russia's urbanization and proletarianization based almost exclusively on the experience of men, acknowledging women only as workers and then only marginally. Substantial numbers of married migrant women were not factory workers or garment workers, however, but cleaning women, washerwomen, servants, casual laborers, *khoziaiki*, and the like. An examination of their experiences of urbanization and proletarianization yields a quite different and far more ambiguous picture than a study focused on the workplace. The extraordinary difficulty of combining wifehood, motherhood, and a full-time occupation placed a crushing burden on the shoulders of the married woman worker. Rather than bear it, some married women remained outside the full-time labor force, others left it as soon as they could. Judging by the materials cited in this chapter, only a minority of such women were married to skilled and highly paid men; many more were the wives of unskilled laborers, who could barely eke out a living. The number of such couples no doubt increased after the Stolypin reforms, which forced or encouraged the poorest peasant couples to pull up stakes and move to the city. Whatever their economic situation, their living patterns in the city suggest similar aspirations to shared domestic life and better care for their children.

It was women who held primary responsibility for fulfilling these aspirations, as their absence from the full-time labor force and their efforts to establish comforts in the most inhospitable surroundings attest. This affected their outlook. The move to the city might broaden a man's horizons and extend them into politics; most women's remained focused on family concerns. Married women's shared interest in the family and the welfare of their children might enable them to join together to take action around consumer-related issues, as women did most notably in February 1917, in the bread riot that led to the overthrow of the tsar. But there is no evidence that women organized systematically around the issues that concerned them as women, as did English working-class women, for example, in the Woman's

Cooperative Guild.[121] In the political and union organizations that arose in Russia, married working-class women seem to have played only the most minimal of roles.

If women often proved "conservative," it seems no wonder: The change that many women migrants experienced may have raised their expectations of family life and their hopes for their children's future. But it neither empowered them nor made their lives easier in any appreciable way. The situation might be different for single women, and it was certainly different for the next generation, for these women's children. If they grew up in the city, young women and men could take advantage of the educational and cultural opportunities that had passed their mothers by. After the Bolshevik revolution of 1917, survivors of the civil war enjoyed vastly enhanced social and political opportunities.

Although you would rarely know it from the histories of these years, they had their mothers' struggles and sacrifices partly to thank.

121 Catherine Webb, *The Woman with the Basket: The History of the Woman's Cooperative Guild 1883–1927* (Manchester, 1927).

# Conclusion

Judging by the picture presented in these pages, how the historian assesses the impact of social and economic change on peasant women of the Central Industrial Region depends a lot on where she looks and on what criteria she uses. The growth of a capitalist wage economy and its urban setting offered an attractive alternative to the village for some spinsters, young widows, and, perhaps most of all, discontented wives. These, the most marginal women in the village, could earn a living in the city, while its relative anonymity enabled them to forge a new life for themselves. They might elude the prying eyes of their community and enjoy the consensual sexual relations that village morals denied them, or, in the case of a spinster and a widow, they might even find a husband, although this was certainly much rarer. The city also offered all women migrants a more varied range of experiences than the village did. It is hard to say how large a proportion of women migrants consciously favored the city. On the basis of the Moscow census of 1902, Robert Johnson has calculated that young women were more likely to settle in that city for short periods and older ones to make a more permanent move.[1] If his calculations are correct, they suggest that for every woman who left for the city because she wanted to go there and then chose to stay, many more might have preferred to remain at home.

This serves as a reminder of the positive dimensions of a patriarchal order, at least in its ideal form: It protected and looked after women, even as it constrained and sometimes oppressed them. In that sense, nineteenth-century observers were right to see in the migration of young marriageable and married women evidence of the breakdown of the peasant family economy. Although some women migrated to take advantage of the growing urban demand for their labor, most women left the village as a result of the grinding poverty at home that loosened patriarchal constraints on their

---

1 Robert Johnson, "Mothers and Daughters in Urban Russia: A Research Note," *Canadian Slavonic Papers* 30, no. 3 (Sept. 1988): 368.

mobility. Thus, as the number of women migrants steadily increased, young single women were far more likely to leave the impoverished villages of Tver' than they were to depart from the comparatively well-off areas of Iaroslavl' and outmigratory Kostroma.

Moreover, in most cases the urban job market offered migrant women few reasons to remain in the city. The supply of unskilled, usually illiterate women outstripped the demand for their labor, and most of the positions available paid poorly. To be sure, some young and single migrant women, factory workers and craftswomen in particular, enjoyed the opportunities that urban life provided. Their tastes became more developed, and their horizons broadened as they took advantage of their relative freedom to shape their own lives. However, only a minority of migrant women (albeit a grow-ing minority) worked in factories, and few peasant migrants were employed as craftswomen. Right up until the outbreak of World War I, the majority of laboring women were in the semidependent position of domestic servant, if they had steady work at all. In 1900, there were 57,848 women employed in industry in St. Petersburg and 92,000 women employed in domestic service; as late as 1910, there were twice as many domestic servants as factory workers in Moscow.[2] These numbers undoubtedly understate the situation, because the makeshift arrangements of an unknown number of migrant women eluded the census takers altogether. In return for their days of toil, most women workers earned barely enough to survive. When such women remained in the city, it was often because they had no other choice.

It may well be that the poverty that sent so many migrant women from the village and the conditions they encountered in the city made the transi-tion from village to city more cruel and difficult for them than it was for women in, say, England or France, where entire families migrated together, and together weathered the shock of urban life. Material circumstances certainly made it hard for a migrant woman to find a husband in the village and they made it harder still to court successfully in the city. A women migrant had nothing to offer a suitor but her miserable earning power or, in the case of the frugal servant, the tiny nest egg she had scraped together – not much of a temptation to a man with an allotment in the village and under pressure to marry a woman there. This led some women to abandon the hope for family life that their socialization had led them to expect and to

2 Rose Glickman, *Russian Factory Women: Workplace and Society, 1880–1914* (Berkeley, Calif., 1984), 60; David Ransel, *Mothers of Misery: Child Abandonment in Russia* (Princeton, N.J., 1988), 164.

remain celibate; others settled for less, engaging in transient encounters or settling into a consensual union. High illegitimacy rates in both Moscow and St. Petersburg indicate that a substantial minority of migrant women either were seduced with the promise of marriage and then abandoned, or settled for less than marriage.

It is hard to avoid the conclusion that Russia's urbanization and industrialization favored men more commonly than women. Many more men than women gained skills and found industrial employment; whatever work men did, they earned higher wages. Urban life provided men with access to public spaces like taverns and pubs that offered comradeship and conviviality. Many of the public spaces that men occupied were off-limits or dangerous for women. When a woman went out walking without a man, she risked harassment by men; and if she went out walking at night, or stopped for a drink in a tavern or hotel bar, she risked attracting the attention of agents of the Medical-Police Committee too. Lower-class men who misbehaved in public were labeled hooligans; the women became known as prostitutes and were subject to regulation.[3] Living away from the village enabled men to experiment with their sexuality without suffering social consequences.[4] Men's very freedom to experiment, however, left women all the more vulnerable, given the absence of effective birth control, women's lack of economic clout, and the complex circumstances that made it so hard for men to marry in the city even when they wanted to. From that perspective, the Stolypin reforms of 1906–7 improved some migrant women's lives by increasing their chances of finding a husband in the city.

However, the overall effect of the reforms on women is more ambiguous. The reforms brought to the cities enormous numbers of unskilled laborers of both sexes; and unskilled men became more likely to bring their wives and children along with them than they had been in the earlier period. The Stolypin reforms forced marginal families out of the village and made it more difficult to send small children to be raised there. This would help to explain the growth in the number of urban dependents that Leopold Haimson has noted. The greater number of working-class families may have contributed to the formation in their neighborhoods of "more coherent working-class societies and cultures," as Haimson has surmised.[5] It enabled children

---

3 Joan Neuberger, "Stories of the Street: Hooliganism in the St. Petersburg Popular Press," *Slavic Review* 48, no. 2 (Summer 1989): 185.

4 Men risked contracting a venereal disease, of course, as did women.

5 Leopold Haimson, "Changements demographiques et greves ouvrieres à Saint-Peterbourg, 1905–1914," *Annales ESC*, no. 4 (July–Aug. 1985): 801.

to attend school and to acquire a higher level of skill than their parents. The widows discussed in Chapter 3, who tried to educate and train their children, were far from unique: Reading appeals to philanthropic organizations, I was repeatedly struck by the efforts of even the most destitute mothers and fathers to provide for their children's future. However, having children in the city usually doomed their parents to a life of the most grinding poverty, or so the Drop of Milk records suggest.

It was particularly hard on the mothers. Without resident kin to provide child care, mothers had difficulty working for wages full-time. The growing sense of entitlement of some working-class men to a decent family life made their wives' full-time work less likely still. In addition to small children, the demands of urban housekeeping might keep a woman at "home," however tiny that "home" might be. This meant that the move from village to city sometimes disrupted the economic interdependence of men and women. Although women who did not work full-time almost invariably took in sewing, washed floors, hired out by the day, or served as *khoziaiki*, they were in some ways more dependent economically on their husbands than village women were. Back home, women kept chickens and cows; they toiled in the kitchen garden and could feed and clothe themselves and their children with the fruits of their own labor. In the city, to feed themselves and their children, they depended on their husbands' wages. Records of philanthropic organizations overflow with pleas for help from desperate widows and abandoned wives with children, deprived of their breadwinners (*kormilitsa*).[6] Given this potential for dependency in the city, it should not be surprising that some married women preferred to return to the village, especially when they had small children.

Thus, we are left with an ambiguous, even contradictory picture. Even as the city attracted some women away from the village, the limited opportunities for women and the hardships of urban life left other women longing for home and the shelter of a village roof. Perhaps ironically, women who were most unambiguously empowered by the wage economy were those who did not participate in it directly, but remained behind in the village while their husbands earned wages in the city. Elsewhere, both in villages near factories and in the city, the wage economy tended most of all to democratize patriarchy: Without freeing women from the power of men, it weakened that power and distributed it more broadly, enabling many younger men to shake

6 I am thinking in particular of materials in TsGIA SSSR, fond 1409, op. 15. In most cases, these women's descriptions of their impoverished state were confirmed by visitors' reports.

off their fathers or village elders' authority and to shape their own lives, their personal lives included. By comparison, just about every opportunity that the city offered women brought considerable risk. This neither stilled some peasant women's longing for the "free life of the city" nor stopped others from enjoying their independent wages and the opportunity to forge a life that pleased them. However, for every woman who pined for freedom and enjoyed it when she found it, how many more would have clung to the security, predictability, and familiar satisfactions of village life, if only they could?

# A note on sources

I was fortunate to conclude research for this book in the early months of 1991, when the (then) Soviet archival regime had significantly eased, making it possible to consult finding aids (*opisi*) and to gain access to new archival documents, some of which had been off limits earlier. Many of the sources I used proved invaluable for my understanding of the lives of lower-class Russian women in the period surveyed in the book. What follows is a discussion of the sources I found most useful. It is intended to assist others who want to explore similar or related topics.

### Tsentral'nyi Gosudarstvennyi Istoricheskii Arkhiv SSSR (currently Rossiiskii Gosudarstvennyi Istoricheskii Arkhiv)

*fond 796, Kantseliariia Sinoda*

opisi 150–99, I and II stol, IV otdelenie. Brakorazvodnye dela.

These holdings contain divorce cases from all over Russia in the period 1870–1914. *Opisi* list each case individually and usually provide the social estate of the plaintiff and often his or her province of origin. The *dela* are uneven in quality: Some of them are brief and superficial summaries of the divorce proceedings. Others, however, provide not only complete statements by plaintiff and defendant but also the testimonies of witnesses, usually friends and/or neighbors of the couple. The holdings are not complete. In some years, almost all *dela* have been lost (*vybyli*). Peasants comprised the majority of plaintiffs in the later years. But other social estates, especially the nobility and the *chinovnichestvo*, are also well represented.

*fond 1409, Sobstvennaia e. i. v. Kantseliariia po uchrezhdeniiam imp. Marii*

opis' 15. This collection contains the dossiers of the clientele of the charities of the Empress Maria. The women derived mainly from the lower classes and were, in most cases, migrants from the countryside to St. Petersburg. They were the wives of disabled workers or workers who had succumbed to drink, widows with children unable to make a living in the city, and single mothers burdened by too many children. Their backgrounds are briefly described in case histories. Some of the dossiers contain reports by investigators of the domestic circumstances of the clients.

244

*Fond 1412, Kantseliariia po priniatiiu proshenii, na "vysochaishee" imia prinosimykh*

opisi 212–41. This collection contains petitions of wives who sought either a divorce or, much more commonly, permission to live apart from their husbands. The *opisi* are organized alphabetically, by case, and provide the social estate of the petitioner. The petitions themselves tend to be formulaic, but often the authorities investigated the truth of the petitioner's claim and, in those cases, *dela* contain revealing correspondence and sometimes the testimony of witnesses concerning the personal and social circumstances of the estranged couple. Other social estates besides the peasantry are represented among the petitioners.

## Tsentral'nyi Gosudarstvennyi Istoricheskii Arkhiv Leningrada

*fond 251, opis' 1. Obshchestvo "Kapl' Moloka"*

dela 2–7 hold the registration lists of the Society of the Drop of Milk for the years 1911–13. The lists provide the names, addresses, and ages of the clientele; the occupation and wages of the husband and, if she was employed for wages, the wife in the case of married couples; and the occupation and wages of single mothers and sometimes of the father of an illegitimate child. They state how many children the woman had already borne, their ages, and whether or not they were still living. The lists also record whether clients were literate, where they lived (a corner, a room, half a room, etc.), and the amount they paid in rent. In many cases, passport information is also provided, making it possible to ascertain a parent's district and province of origin and the term of his or her passport. The registration lists for 1913 offer even more detail, including the age the woman bore her first child, whether and when she stopped working before the birth of her current infant, and whether and when she resumed work afterward.

*fond 593, opis' 1. Peterburgskii vrachebno-politseiskii komitet*

dela 643 and 645 contain the records of hundreds of women alleged to be prostitutes, most of whom escaped registration. Included are the denunciations that often brought the women under suspicion and the reports of the police agents about their occupations and behavior.

delo 644. Doklady ob osvobozhdenii zhenshchin ot vrachebnykh osmotrov.

This holding provides information about the women who were released from registration in 1907, including the name and age of the woman, her occupation, and the estate and occupation of her protector, if she had one. It also contains the reports of the agents who surveyed her behavior in the interim between her request for release and its satisfaction.

Other *dela* in the archive of the St. Petersburg Medical-Police Committee are the dossiers of the hundreds of women who became registered prostitutes in the years 1859–1910. Some of the *dela* provide abundant details about the backgrounds, occupations, ages, and lifestyles of the registered women.

*fond 1026, opis' 1. Domovye kontory goroda Peterburga-Petrograda.*

This collection holds the house administration books of more than five hundred residences in the city of St. Petersburg for the years 1849–1922. In the nineteenth century, they were essentially lists of residents. They recorded only the name and occupation or calling of the resident and the duration of his or her passport. But in the early twentieth century, house administrations also began to record a resident's place of origin and the term of his or her passport; when she or he arrived and from where; his or her age, religion, family status and the composition of her or his family (resident children are listed by name and age), and sometimes his or her place of work; the date of her or his departure and the new address. Each book covers only a brief period, about two years. Most of the buildings whose records have survived were situated in upper-class neighborhoods and housed the well-to-do and their servants. The residents of the buildings I examined (dela 173, 198, 200, 347 [14/2 Nizhegorodskaia Street], and 442) were more diverse and consisted of the laboring poor, artisans, tradesmen, bureaucrats, and professionals.

A very helpful introduction to these and other holdings in TsGIAL is T.M. Aleksandrova, "Vidy massovykh arkhivnykh istochnikov dlia issledovaniia semeinogo byta naseleniia Peterburga XVIII–nachala XX v.," in *Etnograficheskie issledovaniia severo-zapada SSSR: Traditsii i kul'tura sel'skogo naseleniia. Etnografiia Peterburga* (Leningrad, 1977). 155–74.

### Tenishev Archive, Gos. Muzei etnografii narodov SSSR, fond 7, opis' 1.

At the end of the nineteenth century, the Ethnographic Bureau of Prince V.N. Tenishev employed hundreds of local correspondents to amass data about the ethnography of peasants of "Central Russia." Correspondents from twenty-four provinces responded to over four hundred questions concerning popular life and culture. Included were queries concerning family life, childrearing, the relations between the sexes, the role and status of women, and sexual practices, and they yielded responses that are particularly valuable for historians of women and the family. *Dela* are listed according to province and topic. A sense of the range of the archive's holding can be obtained from N. Nachinkin, "Materialy 'etnograficheskogo biuro' V.N. Tenisheva v nauchnom archive gosudarstvennogo muzeia etnografii narodov SSSR," *Sovetskaia Etnografiia*, n. 1 (1955): 159–63.

### Tsentral'nyi Gosudarstvennyi Istoricheskii Arkhiv g. Moskvy

*fond 66, opis' 1. Moskovskoe gubernskoe po krest'ianskim delam prisutstvie (1861–1889)*

The Moscow Provincial Committee on Peasant Affairs received thousands of petitions from peasant women and men, complaining of difficulties in obtaining their passports and requesting that their passports be issued or renewed despite the refusal of village or *volost'* authorities. Each *dela* contains a petition and the administrative response to it, and sometimes they include details about the circumstances of the plaintiff. The gender of the petitioner is identified in the *opis'*; women constituted perhaps 5 percent of complainants. After 1889, the committee was replaced by the Moskovskoe gubernskoe prisutstvie. Similar materials can be found in fond 62, opis' 1.

### *fond 184, Moskovskaia gubernskaia zemskaia uprava*

opis' 2, delo 873 Khovrinskii priiut. Contains information on the backgrounds and sometimes the fates of children considered candidates for this provincial children's shelter in the years 1896–7. Case histories suggest the strategies employed by destitute women to earn a living and raise their children.

### *fond 203, Kantseliariia Sinoda*

opis' 412. Brakorazvodnye dela. In this holding are divorce cases from Moscow province that were resolved on the local level and therefore not forwarded to the chancellory in St. Petersburg. The cases are more varied than the divorce cases I found in the central archive: Some plaintiffs were unfamiliar with procedures, requesting a divorce, for example, on the grounds of incompatibility; others reconciled with their spouses and agreed to drop their cases. Plaintiffs derived from the peasantry as well as other estates.

### Tsentral'nyi Gosudarstvennyi Arkhiv Oktiabr'skoi Revoliutsii SSSR

### *fond 7952, Gosudarstvennoe izdatel'stvo "Istoriia fabrik i zavodov"*

opis' 3. Dokumental'nye materialy po istorii fabrik i zavodov g. Moskvy i Moskovskoi oblasti. In these archives, devoted to the history of factories and plants, can be found hundreds of worker memoirs in manuscript and typescript. Factory life occupies only a portion of worker recollections: They are a rich source of detail on social origins, circumstances of migration, working history, living conditions in the city, leisure activities, and working-class culture. Each dela (ed. kh.) contains many memoirs. They are by no means formulaic: Details were occasionally controversial enough that someone crossed them out in pencil, although they can still be read. The overwhelming majority of the memoirists were men. I used materials in ed. kh. 95, 96, and 273.

# Index

Abashkina, M. (textile worker), 137, 217–8
abortion, 137, 146, 217–18
adultery, 20, 24, 55–8, 59
Africa, 64
Arkhangel province, 176
Asia, 64

Belgium, 202
Bentovin, B. I. (physician), 188, 189
Berlin, 127
birth control, 111–12, 146–7, 217–18, 241
birthrate, 47, 109, 112
Boldyreva, Anna (textile worker and Bolshevik activist), 79, 235
bol'shak, 13, 19–20
bol'shukha, 15
brideprice, 118
Buzinov, Aleksei (metalworker), 138, 139

Central Agricultural Region, 11
Central Industrial Region, 4, 11
    economic conditions in, 72
    marriage in, 11
    migration from, 3, 37
    rural factories in, 102
    and Stolypin reforms, 62
    women's role in, 127
childbirth, 47, 49, 214
child care, 227
    and agricultural labor, 46, 49
    and wage-earning mothers, 107, 111, 214–15, 217
Chukhloma district, see Kostroma province
contraception, see birth control
cottage industry, 2, 102–3, 107–8
    decline of, 66–7, 107
    earnings in, 107–8

and factory production, 66, 107
in Iaroslavl' 42–3
in Kostroma, 108, 111
in Tver', 42–3
courtship
    in the city, 139, 156
    and domestic servants, 144–6
    and illegitimate births, 147
    in industrial regions, 117
    nightcourting, 8
    in villages, 8, 41, 44
    women's power in, 9–10
craftswomen, 72–3, 75, 240
    and prostitution, 177–9
    unemployment of, 142, 169, 177–8
    as unwed mothers, 134, 147, 159

divorce, 17, 19, 26–7
domestic servants
    age of, 146
    and courtship, 144–6
    and dowry, 144
    duration of labor, 142
    in England, 141
    in France, 141
    and infant abandonment, 148–9
    and kinship ties, 135
    literacy of, 141
    living conditions of, 141, 144–5
    and marriage, 144, 145–6, 202–3
    in Moscow, 140, 141, 146
    and motherhood, 149
    philanthropy of, 231
    and pregnancy, 147–8
    proportion of female workforce, 140, 240
    and prostitution, 177
    in St. Petersburg, 140, 146

248

savings of, 142–4, 146
and sexual abuse, 181–2
and spinsterhood, 85, 146
unemployment of, 134, 169, 177–8
as unwed mothers, 134, 146
wages of, 142
working conditions of, 73, 140–2, 144,
  148, 203
dowry, 18, 77–8, 118, 144

England
  abortion in, 218
  male workers in, 232
  prostitution in, 187, 188–9
  women's migration in, 240
  women workers in, 109, 202, 236, 237
Estland (Estonia), 175, 176

Fedorov, Aleksandr (physician), 173–4
foundling homes, 112, 118, 136, 180
France
  prostitution in, 194
  women's migration in, 64, 180, 240
  women workers in, 109, 202

Germany, 109, 223, 232

Haymarket Square, 132, 191
Holy Synod, 18, 22

Iaroslavl' province
  cottage industry in, 42–3
  economic conditions of, 69, 72, 74
  female migrants from, 72–3, 74–5, 82,
    89
  infant mortality in, 48–9
  literacy in, 50–1
  marriage in, 11, 38–40
  male migrants from, 69–70
  migration from, 38, 68
  peasant women's work in, 36, 42–3, 46
  prostitutes from, 176
  spinsters in, 84
  widows in, 53, 85
  wifebeating in, 52
  women's status in, 53, 54n
illegitimacy
  in industrial regions, 119
  rates of, 119, 126–8, 136, 158, 160
  rural, 9, 136

illegitimate children
  fate of, 118–19
  mothers of, 88, 126, 134, 146–7,
    159–64, 181
  peasant attitudes to, 17, 20
industrialization
  and rural factories, 102, 103
  in Russia, 2–3, 102
  in the West, 2, 3, 103
  and women's work, 66
  and women workers, 149
infant mortality
  in factory regions, 112–13
  in Iaroslavl', 48
  in Kostroma, 48
  and maternal welfare, 49–50
  in Moscow, 215–16
  rate of, 48, 63, 215–16, 222
  reasons for, 215–16, 222
  in St. Petersburg, 215–16
  and women workers, 112–13
  see also child care
Ivanovo-Voznesensk, see Vladimir province

Kalinkinskaia hospital, 188
Kaluga province, 38, 68, 176
Kanatchikov, Semyon (metalworker,
  Bolshevik), 139
Karelina, Vera (worker and organizer), 235
Katenina, L. (physician), 111, 121
Khitrov market, 132
*khoziaiki, see* landladies
Kineshma district, see Kostroma province
Kokhma, see Vladimir province
Kostroma province
  birthrate in, 47
  childbirth in, 46–7
  courtship in, 41, 44, 117
  economic conditions in, 35–6
  factory workers of, 103–6, 108–111,
    114, 115–16
  female migrants from, 43–4
  infant mortality in, 48–9
  literacy in, 50–1, 121–2
  male migrants from, 36–7, 52
  marriage in, 37–9, 116, 122
  prostitutes from, 176
  reading habits in, 122
  sexual relations in, 46–7
  widows in, 43, 52–3